WITH MUSKET & TOMAHAWK
Volume II

With Musket and Tomahawk

—VOLUME II—

The Mohawk Valley Campaign in the Wilderness War of 1777

MICHAEL O. LOGUSZ

CASEMATE

Philadelphia & Oxford

Published in the United States of America and Great Britain in 2015 by
CASEMATE PUBLISHERS
908 Darby Road, Havertown, PA 19083
and
10 Hythe Bridge Street, Oxford OX1 2EW

Copyright 2012 © Michael O. Logusz

ISBN 978-1-61200-225-5
Digital Edition: ISBN 978-1-61200-083-1

Cataloging-in-publication data is available from the Library of Congress
and the British Library.

10 9 8 7 6 5 4 3 2

Printed and bound in the United States of America.

For a complete list of Casemate titles please contact:

CASEMATE PUBLISHERS (US)
Telephone (610) 853-9131, Fax (610) 853-9146
E-mail: casemate@casematepublishing.com

CASEMATE PUBLISHERS (UK)
Telephone (01865) 241249, Fax (01865) 794449
E-mail: casemate-uk@casematepublishing.co.uk

Contents

Acknowledgments

In Oswego, New York, stands the Fort Ontario State Park. Its origins actually date back many decades before the eruption of the Revolutionary War and the events of 1777. Fort Ontario is also one of several forts which stood, at one time or another, in and around Oswego, and at present is the only one remaining. It was in Oswego where my project was initially greeted with great enthusiasm and encouragement.

Fort Ontario's director, Paul Lear, directs this site which also has a library. Though not formally open to the public, it may be utilized for research. This library holds many old and recent books, journals, and manuscripts pertaining to not only the Revolutionary War but also to many other historical events associated with Oswego. Mr. Lear not only kindly permitted me to utilize this library but he also answered my questions as best as he could.

Another key player in Fort Ontario is Richard LaCrosse, Jr. Author of a fabulous book *The Frontier Rifleman: His Arms, Clothing and Equipment During the Era of the American Revolution, 1760–1800*, Mr. LaCrosse is an expert both on riflemen and their weapons, tactics, equipment and uniforms. He has written numerous articles pertaining to the historical events of that era and he frequently lectures the public on what occurred during this historical American era.

Reverend George A. Reed, an ordained minister who also reenacts the role of a Civil War Colonel in the Union Army's Chaplain's Corps, is also a very strong his-torian. He has written extensively on Oswego's history, from its beginning to the present. His work, *Fort Ontario*, found in Fort Ontario's archives, is a classic. Someday, I would like to see it published into a book. Reverend Reed read my chapter on General Barry St. Leger and, through his input, enabled me to produce a stronger chapter on what occurred at Oswego during the Revolutionary War in 1777.

The late professor Ruth Nesbitt, Oswego's renowned historian, also read my chapter on St. Leger as well as several other chapters, including the one on the women who resided in the wilderness prior to and during the monumental events of 1777. Her invaluable input also cleared up some matters for me and enabled me to have a clearer understanding of what occurred in the western theater during the Wilderness War of 1777. On several occasions, I also telephoned her to ask a specific question about some historical event. Always, she had an answer. Doctor Nesbitt's efforts were tremendously appreciated, and future historians will benefit from her activities.

My deepest appreciation is extended to Gail Goebricher, who not only assisted me immensely with my first book but also with this one. Ms. Goebricher carefully edited and typed on her computer some of the major chapters. Her input and ideas enabled me to produce a stronger work. Without her, my mission would have been much more difficult. Gail, once again, Thank you so very much.

In Rome, New York, where the famous Fort Stanwix stands, curators and historians William Sawyer and Craig Davis tremendously assisted me with the events which occurred during the siege of Fort Stanwix during the monumental month of August, 1777. One of the thorny issues which plagues historians to this day is whether the American flag was actually first flown in combat at Fort Stanwix in 1777 and what, exactly, was the fort's overall personnel strength at the time of its encirclement. Via our discussions and various source materials suggested by them, I was able to reach this conclusion: clearly, the American flag was actually first flown in combat during the Wilderness War of 1777. But, whether it was flown further to the east on a battlefield at an intersection adjacent to the settlement of Hubbardton in Vermont, or on a wilderness hilltop position in the vicinity of Fort Anne to the southeast of Lake George, is, and always will be, disputed. Regardless, as to where our nation's flag first flown during combat and in the face of an enemy force, without a doubt it first flew in Fort Stanwix. As for the troop and support strength found in Fort Stanwix during its siege, after several discussions with Mr. Sawyer and studying the various references and source materials he suggested, I have concluded that a strength of close to or about 850 would be a correct figure. To these fine gentlemen and Fort Stanwix's staff, I extend my thanks.

Fort Ticonderoga's chief historian, Christopher Fox, was also of tremendous help. Through several phone conversations, we discussed the events of 1777 and the critical decisions made in the main Northern Army headquarters located in Albany, New York, by Northern Army commander General Philip John Schuyler. A solid tactician and logistician, General Schuyler was the one who stopped the entire British thrust both from Canada via Oswego into the Mohawk Valley and their secondary thrust from the vicinity of Oquaga (near present day Binghamton, New York), through the Schoharie Valley and Susquehanna River region. Both thrusts were to link up with British Army General John Burgoyne's army pushing southward from Canada toward the vicinity of Albany. Once halted and repelled, these events heralded the true beginning of the end of the entire British campaign of 1777. Sir, thank you so much for your help.

In the Wilderness War of 1777, people of African descent played a vital role in not only helping the Northern Army achieve a victory in that year but, just as importantly, in establishing the new American nation. Needing a strong authority to ensure that what I presented about their contributions was factual, I consulted with William Watkins, who is a leading expert on the issue of slavery in New York State. Prior to retiring from the New York State Parks and Recreation Service, Mr. Watkins managed several historical sites in eastern New York. As he acknowledged, the issue of slavery, which finally collapsed in New York State in the early part of the 19th century, was a difficult and trying period for the state which actually started well over a century before New York State was officially born in 1777. Mr. Watkins also kindly sent me a work he once had published, titled "Slavery in Herkimer County: African-Americans Were Here from the Beginning." This journal is filled with fascinating information and because of his efforts, I am able to present to my readers a stronger work pertaining to the role people of African descent played in the turbulent year of 1777.

In the Highlands region of New York State to the north of New York City at West Point lies our nation's United States Military Academy (USMA). Within this academy exists a library filled with many old and most recent books, documents, military accounts, paintings, and other artifacts. Indeed, it is a treasure trove of history. Here, I also had the pleasure to meet Alan C. Aimone, the Senior Archivist and Special Collections Librarian at USMA. Prior to meeting him, I had already written a considerable amount on the British attack into the Highlands in October 1777. (In the upcoming months my intent is to turn this chapter into a book titled *With Musket & Tomahawk. The West Point-Hudson Valley Campaign in the Wilderness War of 1777.*) But as importantly, we also discussed how the events which occurred in and around New York City, West Point and other nearby regions in the end impacted negatively on both the main thrusts coming in directly southward from Canada, southeastward from Oswego, and northeastward from Oquaga. With his kind assistance, I was able to better understand what truly happened at West Point prior to and during the critical year of 1777. After departing West Point I kept in contact with Mr. Aimone, rewrote the chapter, and submitted it to him. Not only did he carefully read it but he also made a number of fruitful corrections and suggestions. When returning the chapter to me, he included a sizable bibliography of books and journals. In fact, Mr. Aimone has provided me with such a wealth of reference source materials that if ever in the future I decide to write an entire book on West Point's first years, I will now be able to do so. Sir, to you and the USMA library staff, my deepest thanks and gratitude.

Once again, down in New York City, Mr. William "Bill" Nasi proved to be an asset. A first-rate historian and very informed on what life in New York City was like during the British occupation, Mr. Nasi gave me the facts. And it was no picnic! In fact, he was so informative that I sometimes think that Mr. Nasi actually lived in the city in 1777. To him, I say again, "Thanks, Bill, very much."

In Washington, DC is located the Charles Sumner School Museum. An African-American Institute, its floors are filled with numerous artifacts, articles, documents, photographs, and letters relating to African-American history. Harriet Lesser is the curator and director of this exhibit. Among the items on display is a huge map depicting where men and women of African heritage served and fought on the North American continent. Battles, along with dates, are cited. Of importance to note is that in virtually every battle of the Revolutionary War, men and women of African heritage supported, fought and, in some cases, died for the newly established American nation. Here, in this museum, I was able to obtain the additional names and deeds of brave African-American volunteers who served in the Northern Army in 1776–77 and left their impact. I extend my thanks and appreciation to Ms. Lesser and her staff.

In Brewerton, New York, between Fulton and Syracuse, exists the Brewerton Fort (in actuality, a blockhouse). But in 1777, the army of General Barry St. Leger actually camped at this sight as it proceeded eastward to Fort Stanwix. Inside its small library a number of interesting books and Revolutionary War items exist such as an old, two-barreled over-and-under flintlock rifle like the kind that the famous rifleman Timothy Murphy utilized so effectively in the Wilderness War of 1777. To its staff, I present my gratitude.

In the village libraries of Fair Haven and Hannibal, New York, some old books, but especially those which cite the early histories of Cayuga and Oswego Counties and written in the early 1800's, reveal a good amount of information on the Revolutionary War period. The old books dealing with the land grants are especially interesting to study because they not only reveal the names of the individuals who inherited land but, to an extent, their activities during the American Revolutionary War. Various other books, which I also needed, were found and ordered by the staff of the Fair Haven library. To these individuals, I owe my gratitude as well.

The various New York State Historic Site Tour Guide Pamphlets, published by the New York State Office of Parks, Recreation and Historic Preservation, were of immense help. The information and simple maps enclosed in them proved very valuable, especially in depicting battle events. To the publishers of these pamphlets, I express my thanks.

Ms. Darby O'Brien, a director at the Utica Public Library in Utica, New York, and the museum board, gave me permission to use the famous painting depicting General Herkimer and his militia fighters in combat during the Battle of Oriskany. Painted by Frederick C. Yohn and exhibited at the Utica museum, the painting is a powerful tribute to what occurred on that monumental day. I express my sincere gratitude and thanks to her, the Utica Trustees, and its library.

George Sheldon, my dear friend in Fair Haven, New York, is an avid sportsman who hunts and shoots with a muzzle-loading rifle. During my writings, on more then one occasion I needed to know something about this weapon. With the patience of a first-rate instructor and realizing that I needed to fully grasp the lethality of this weapon, George even took me out to a range on a couple of occasions where we fired his rifle. George is so proficient with it that he can actually reload it while on the run. Environmentally minded, he is currently employed with O'Brien & Gere, a major company which undertakes the clean-up of various pollution sites. "George, thank you and keep up the good work! Future generations will benefit from your efforts."

Again, my gratitude to the renowned American painter, Don Troiani, for the use of another of his paintings depicting a battle fought during the Wilderness War of 1777. Titled *The Oneidas at the Battle of Oriskany—August 6, 1777* this work truly portrays the harshness of the battle and the role the brave Oneida warriors undertook that bloody day as they fought side-by-side with the Patriots for the American cause and the newly established American nation.

And my appreciation is extended once again to the brilliant artist David Wright for several of his evocative works that capture the look, and feel, of America's early wilderness frontier.

And to Michael G. Trent, CW5, U.S. Army, with whom I served during "Operation Iraqi Freedom." A teacher for many years, Mr. Trent carefully reviewed and edited my original work. His efforts and advice led to a stronger work. Sir, thanks so much.

To the memory of my father, Taras, who loved to live in nature and taught us to do so and to the memory of my late uncle, Lubomyr Lou Kurylko. As I walk the ground of our old homestead in Sterling, in northwestern New York State, through which so many European, Northern Army soldiers, militiamen, Indians, loyalists, and mercenaries traversed upon back and forth in the year of 1777, I can actually feel the presence of these two fine gentlemen. It was also here, years ago, where my uncle and I cleared a parcel of land for the many trees soon planted by my father, mother, and sister. Today, they stand tall and are a tribute to what a close and loving family can accomplish in the world of nature.

Last, but not least, this book is dedicated to all those who have served in our nation's armed forces—both in peace and war, and to those serving now.

C'est la Guerre!

Introduction

In America's history, 1777 was a monumental year. The year following the Declaration of Independence saw a vicious struggle fought throughout the entire frontier wilderness of New York and its adjoining colonies, by men on both sides wielding the tomahawk, musket, rifle, knife, bayonet, spear, war club, and bow and arrow. The fighting of 1777 would affect every single man, woman, and child living in and around the raging inferno, which rightfully may be recorded as the terrible Wilderness War of 1777.

In military history, the Battle of Saratoga, fought in the vicinity of Albany, New York, is regarded as being one of the top twenty decisive battles in world history. On 17 October 1777, after months of combat, British Army General John "Gentleman Johnny" Burgoyne surrendered with some 6,000 troops—the remnants of his army—to the Patriots' Northern Army. Though the American Revolutionary War would continue for six more years, Saratoga was truly the beginning of the end of Britain's rule on the North American continent.

Unlike many of history's decisive clashes, fought in one particular location, the Saratoga campaign really consisted of numerous thrusts, battles, raids, and skirmishes, fought over tens of thousands of square miles from Oswego on the eastern shoreline of Lake Ontario across the New England states, and from the present United States–Canada border south to New York City. This war was not just fought with every imaginable weapon of that era, but was furthered by the use of numerous spies, agents, saboteurs, and urban guerrillas. Also, a massive campaign of propaganda was undertaken by both sides to win support either for or against the newly established American nation. Oswego, Fort Stanwix, Fort Edward, the Mohawk and Schoharie Valleys, Oquaga, Saratoga, the Hudson Highlands, and West Point were just a handful of the places that in 1777 witnessed their share of the conflict known to the world as the Saratoga campaign. In the end, the events that occurred throughout this vast and mostly wilderness territory halted and destroyed the entire British northern offensive of 1777.

My previous work, *With Musket & Tomahawk: The Saratoga Campaign and the Wilderness War of 1777,* focused on the events happening from Canada southward into the Saratoga (Albany, New York) region. While reference was made to some of the events which circled around Burgoyne's main thrust in both the western (Mohawk) and southern (Catskill and Highland) regions, these could not be discussed in depth due to the constraints of space. Therefore, to reveal the other activities in this theater in 1777, comes a second work: *With Musket & Tomahawk: The Mohawk Valley Campaign in the Wilderness War of 1777.*

The campaigning in the Mohawk Valley region to the east of Lake Ontario had originated in the minds of British military planners at least two years previously, in 1775. In his military thesis, "Thoughts for Conducting the War From the Side of Canada," General Burgoyne had envisioned a secondary, but formidable, striking force that would originate in Canada, assemble in an old port and trading town known as Oswego, and proceed to overrun the Mohawk Valley, destroying any pro-American Patriot forces, gathering up the supposedly numerous pro-British Loyalists, and securing a vital food base for the British Crown. Once this was accomplished, this western force was to continue to march east toward Albany, where it would link up with Burgoyne's force advancing southward from Canada and the military force advancing northward from New York City. In conjunction with these three main thrusts, a fourth thrust, originating in the Oquaga area to the east of present-day Binghamton, New York, was to advance northeastward though the Schoharie Valley toward Albany to conduct a link-up with the force advancing inland from Oswego. Once united, the combined forces were to rendezvous with the main thrusts appearing from Canada and New York City.

The planners of the 1777 campaign did not envisage it would be difficult, or drawn-out. This was not an unreasonable assumption given that the key advantages seemed to lie with Great Britain. Most of the major cities, along with entire coastal regions and centers of communication were held by the British, not to mention their grip on the St Lawrence River and the Great Lakes. Led by commanders with previous experience of campaigning in North America, the British armies were composed of professional soldiers with years of fighting behind them, reinforced with many loyal American sympathizers as well as Indian warriors. Their plan of campaign called for the British to operate on inner lines, forcing their enemy to move around them.

In contrast, the Patriots' Northern Army—the force in which the defenders of the newly established nation volunteered to serve—was just a shell. Lacking men, materiel, and firepower, the loosely organized and scattered forces barely had a supply or support system. Some Patriot forts were still under construction, while those completed were undermanned. While the British possessed a strong unity of command, the Northern Army's command was slack. Internal squabbles among the Patriots further threatened their unity of action.

The Northern Army was truly an exotic fighting force. From within and around the wilderness regions of the northeast, many stepped forward to serve in this force created by America's Continental Congress in late 1776. The mission of the Northern Army was to contest and counter the British in Canada and to protect and control both the New England region and the newly forming New York State. The army was composed of Regular Army Continental regiments and battalions, various militia units, scouts, and irregular (guerrilla) fighters; the army also benefitted from the actions of numerous agents, spies, couriers, and propagandists. The Northern Army consisted of volunteers ranging from teenagers to men of 60 years of age; within its ranks, whites, blacks, Indians, and immigrants fought side by side. In 1777, the Northern Army proved that whites and minorities could coexist and serve equally in an army. Racism was not entrenched and tolerance was the norm. So diverse was this fighting force that no fewer than thirty languages and dialects were spoken within its ranks. Ultimately, this diversity played a major role in enabling the newly formed Northern Army to overcome an adversary whose army possessed a proud tradition stemming hundreds of years.

In 1777, the western and central region of upper New York was, by and large, one massive, continuous wilderness. Some roads existed, but they were few and far between, and mostly seasonal. Rain or a thaw could result in entire sections flooding. Although central and western

Europe also had forests, these mainly cultivated woodlands were a world away from the wild and primeval forests found on the North American continent. While sparsely populated by humans, numerous animals, flowers, bushes, and trees—many of the latter over fifteen feet in thickness—abounded in this wilderness.

Those who had settled in the region, from the central and eastern fringes of the Mohawk Valley, had carved out a way of life for themselves in the wilderness. Proud men and women, they longed to live free of any rule. By the time the Revolutionary War had erupted in 1775, people of different European ethnicities, races, and religions resided in the region. Thriving farming communities were intermixed with centers of commerce so that trade and lumber, food products, pelts, grain, home-spun goods, metallic items, and other products made their way to Albany via the Mohawk River, and from Albany to New York City and the ports of the world.

Many of those living in the region had little or no understanding of the American Declaration of Independence or their newly created state constitutions and related political matters. Many, if not most, did not even care to know. For them, the newly established American government—with its consequent taxation, regulations, rules, and laws—was meaningless. Yet, sadly, few could avoid the conflict. Forced to take sides, they became involved in a struggle that ultimately would decide their fate. Their stories, along with that of the combatants on both sides—the human aspect of warfare—are crucial to the history of the Wilderness War, and so I will examine what it was like to live in 1777, to fight, and ultimately to sacrifice everything for one's cause.

Sitting on his saddle against a large beech tree, his badly wounded leg bandaged, Brigadier General Nicholas Herkimer calmly directed his militiamen as they fought the forces dispatched by British General Barry St. Leger to intercept, engage, and destroy Herkimer's attempt to raise the siege of Fort Stanwix, an outpost held by American soldiers deep in the wilderness region. Shortly after this epic battle on 6 August, Herkimer succumbed to his wounds. An American of German ancestry, Herkimer's ancestors had arrived years earlier from Germany to settle in the beautiful Mohawk Valley. Their hopes of living in peace had been shattered as they first became embroiled in revolutionary politics espousing independence, and after 1775, in the massive and vicious wilderness war raging around them.

After the Revolutionary War, Herkimer's deeds and ordeals were known not only to the residents of the Mohawk Valley but to those elsewhere in the new nation because, fortunately, there were those who carefully recorded the events of that bloody day. Among them was Colonel Samuel Campbell, a Continental Army officer who served on Herkimer's staff. From the 1830s, Revolutionary War scholars such as James Phinney Baxter, William Campbell, Benson Lossing, and William Leete Stone began to gather up accounts by veterans of the Revolutionary War and by civilians who witnessed a specific event or participated in the conflict. Some accounts were oral, while other written records were provided by family members or from some military sites. These accounts truly capture the hardships, horrors and agony endured and witnessed by brave soldiers, militiamen, and civilians on both sides in 1777.

Some of the accounts might be difficult to believe, or seem incidental to the campaign, but I wanted to capture the full human spectrum. One can only imagine the fears, loneliness, and uncertainty felt by the young Private William Colbrath of the 3rd New York Continental Regiment, when besieged for several weeks in Fort Stanwix. Like undoubtedly so many others, Colbrath set off joyfully to what he thought would be an adventure. Amid the world of endless trees, dark nights, and nightmarish days, he learned differently.

The year 1777 was monumentous because the victory achieved at Saratoga was a decisive world event—but there were other reasons as well. Officially, in this same year, New York State was born; Governor George Clinton, a general in the Northern Army, was elected as New York's first governor in a free election. Issues pertaining to the emancipation of black people and the termination of slavery arose, and the role of women in a free society was addressed. The tragic consequences for the British and their Loyalist (Tory) allies as a result of their defeat in the wilderness began to unfold, and various national and international issues arose. The destruction of the Iroquois Confederacy and the magnificent wilderness began, and hunger and harshness was experienced by tens of thousands of people—especially during the winter of 1777–78. These were just some of the political, economic, social, and physical ramifications that resulted from the Wilderness War of 1777.

Perhaps all of these events can best be summed up by the actions of two brave and loyal Oneida Indians, Honyery, and his wife, Two

Kettles Together. As they fought for the Patriots side by side at Oriskany and later at Saratoga, they truly exemplified the spirit of those who strove to live free. Until the very end, these two demonstrated a true spirit of honor and loyalty. Stories, like the one to be presented about Honyery and Two Kettles Together, is why I decided to continue my pursuit of fully presenting the epic events of the Wilderness War of 1777.

St. Leger's Preparations in Canada

In his military thesis, "Thoughts for Conducting the War From the Side of Canada," General John Burgoyne envisioned a major subsidiary offensive to supplement his main thrust due south along the Hudson River to sever New England from the rest of the rebellious colonies. Similarly originating in Canada, it would set out from Oswego on the eastern shore of Lake Ontario and terminate its advance in Albany.[1] After advocating this secondary offensive in his thesis, Burgoyne abandoned the plan, writing to Clinton on 7 November 1776 that he had given up the idea because there was "a lack of provisions" for it. However, in early 1777, Burgoyne reconsidered his November decision and concluded that a secondary offensive from Oswego toward Albany via the Mohawk Valley would benefit him tremendously.

Burgoyne's desire to have a striking force coming in from the west toward Albany was based on a number of factors. Militarily, the force would create an excellent diversion. It would force the Northern Army to move badly needed troops, arms, supplies, and equipment from the vicinity of Albany into the western and central sector of the wilderness region, further weakening the Northern Army. Although the western striking force would not equal the size and strength of Burgoyne's forces, or those of Howe which were expected to move north from New York City, any military strength advancing inland from Oswego[2] to Albany via the Mohawk Valley would pose a serious threat to Patriots and their families residing in their path. Politically, a western striking force would ensure the British firm control of the Iroquois Confederacy[3] as well as any other Indian tribes found adjacent or near the Great

Lakes. Many of these native warriors could also be enlisted as allies. Economically, controlling the Mohawk River Valley as well as the Hudson River Valley, would deny the Patriots vital food bases and transportation routes[4] between New York, New Jersey, Pennsylvania, and the entire region of New England. General George Washington was also feeding his Continental Army from these food bases.[5]

A British victory in 1777 would gain world attention, allow them to retain control over the American colonists in the northeast, and demonstrate that the newly formed Continental Congress was weak, incapable, and lacked authority. A victory for Britain in 1777 would diminish support for the revolutionary cause especially among the Americans themselves.

Since the force launched from Lake Ontario would have to act independently from the main British thrust, it was vital that it be commanded by an officer who possessed both skill and dynamism. General Burgoyne requested Lieutenant Colonel Barrimore Matthew "Barry" St. Leger, a combat leader he personally knew, trusted, and respected.

Born in Ireland around 1739 of Huguenot descent, St. Leger was a career army officer who Burgoyne had come to know well, and who was thus requested by him to spearhead the 1777 attack from the west.[6] As St. Leger would be undertaking a vital mission and would be commanding a significantly larger force than one normally commanded by a lieutenant colonel, Burgoyne requested that St. Leger be temporarily elevated to the rank of brigadier general, with the full powers and authority of the rank. Burgoyne's request was approved by Canada's Governor-General Guy Carleton, the Secretary for the American Colonies, Lord George Germain, and even by King George III.

Brigadier General St. Leger was a highly dedicated soldier. He was also loyal, brave, resourceful, and mission-minded. During the French and Indian War, he had served in North America, and was a veteran of several battles, including that on the Plains of Abraham outside the city of Quebec. However, his knowledge of the wilderness was limited, and he had not previously commanded Indian forces. Determined to progress in rank and stature, however, and seeing an opportunity for advancement, St. Leger immediately accepted the assignment.

Indeed, it was a very dangerous task. To operate deep within a wilderness with a command limited in numbers is a hazard in itself. Besides problems caused by weather, lack of roads, and environmental dangers, St. Leger would be operating hundreds of miles from his main base in Montreal. He would encounter both regular and militia Patriot forces, reinforced with Indian warriors, and time—always a critical factor in any military operation—was something that could not be wasted. Weather-wise, heavy rains followed by the first snows have been known to commence in late September or early October in central and northern New York. But it could be done—St. Leger was confident of success.

In the later part of June 1777, General St. Leger's force rowed from Montreal down the St. Lawrence River to a village named Lachine, which lay directly southwest of Montreal, on the same island.[7] The Ottawa River drains into the St. Lawrence below Lachine. Because of its location, Lachine was the first main assembly area for the force. St. Leger received his first supplies here, including a large chest filled with gold and silver coins that he was to take all the way to Albany, where it would be used to pay the soldiers, Loyalists, and Indians.

Prior to St. Leger's departure from Montreal, civilian ship-builders and carpenters had been engaged in finishing a number of bateaux on Carleton Island, which lies in the St. Lawrence River where it leaves Lake Ontario.[8] Supervising the construction of these flat-bottomed craft were two very competent British naval officers—Lieutenants John Schanck and William Twiss—who would later be known for developing new innovations to upgrade naval ships. Also at Carleton Island, specially designed bateaux—referred to as the "King's boats"—were constructed. Each vessel could transport approximately 40 soldiers with their equipment and supplies. On some of the heavier bateaux, cannons were even mounted. Chained into position, the cannons could be fired—if the need arose—while the bateau was moving. The island was heavily forested, ensuring that there was not only enough wood available for the construction of the bateaux but also for the construction of barrack buildings to house St. Leger's troops.

Notes

1   John Luzader, *The Saratoga Campaign of 1777* (Washington, DC: National Park Service Publications, 1975), p. 9. See also p. 31. Robert Leckie, *The Wars of America* (Updated Edition) (New York: Harper Collins Publishers, 1992, p. 169; Oscar Theodore Barck, Jr., "The Three-Cornered Campaign" in *Colonial America* (New York: The MacMillan Company, 1958), p. 625, and map on p. 624. According to Reverend George A. Reed in *Fort Ontario* (Fort Ontario Archives, unpublished text), p. 51, in December 1776, General

Burgoyne, when presenting his plan to isolate the New England colonies, proposed that Howe advance northward to Albany (capital of New York State) and "a third expedition from Fort Ontario was to descend the Mohawk to meet [Burgoyne and Howe] in Albany." In Richard Ketchum, *Saratoga, Turning Point of America's Revolutionary War* (New York: Henry Holt and Company, Inc., 1997), p. 84, a force would advance from Oswego to Albany to join Burgoyne's Canada Army and Howe in Albany. (Hereafter cited as *Saratoga, Turning Point*). See also "St. Leger's Attack on Fort Stanwix in 1777 Proved Fiasco" in *Oswego Palladium Times,* Tuesday, November 20, 1945, p. 4. (Hereafter referred to as *St. Leger's Attack.*) For Burgoyne's changing views on the Oswego offensive see William B. Willcox, *Portrait of a General. Sir Henry Clinton in the War of Independence* (New York: Alfred A. Knopf, Inc., 1981), pp. 145–147. According to Crisfield Johnson, *History of Oswego County, New York, 1739–1877* (New York: 1878), p. 39, "a large army under General Burgoyne marched into northern New York, which was to be supported by another strong force, entering by way of Oswego and sweeping down the Mohawk Valley." (Hereafter cited to as *History of Oswego County.*)

2   Old British records, dating back from the 1740s, cite a "trading towne" as already existing. In the 17th century, French planners proposed to construct a settlement in Oswego based on the fur trade, and a small post was constructed in 1655. Between 1722 and 1727, fur traders established a seasonal trading post on the western mouth of the Oswego River, which became the foundation for a settlement. In 1727, England's Royal Governor Burnet ordered the construction of a two-story "stone house of strength" adjacent to the trading post. Between 1741 and 1743 this was surrounded by an outer U-shaped stone wall with two attached one-story buildings. This "castle" was named Fort Oswego. By 1743, this settlement and Oswego's fur trade came to be measured in millions of Spanish pieces of eight. (See "Furs and Forts" in *The Forts of Oswego*) (Oswego: Fort Ontario Archives).

In 1754, the French and Indian War erupted. Because of Oswego's critical position, William Shirley, the British Royal Governor of Massachusetts and the Assistant Commander-in-Chief of all of England's forces on the North American continent, ordered the construction of a new fort, Fort Ontario; a smaller work, Fort George; outer earthworks around the existing Fort Oswego; and the construction and launching of a British fleet from Oswego. This would be the Royal Navy's first Great Lakes squadron. (See "New Forts and a Fleet" in *The Forts of Oswego*). Oswego was now a port town, a boat-building site, and fur-trading post, as well as a base of operations for the British Empire, and home to a British army garrison and a small naval fleet. Oswego suffered many raids in early 1756, and in August 1756 the Marquis de Montcalm arrived with a massive force comprising thousands of French regulars augmented with Canadian mercenaries and numerous Indians.

A map of Oswego as it appeared prior to the 1756 attack by Montcalm shows the town with at least 60 buildings, some with two stories. Montcalm's attack resulted not only in the entire destruction of Oswego's three forts—Forts Ontario, Oswego, and George—but the entire town. (A copy of the original map is found in Oswego's Fort Ontario archives, *Gentleman's Magazine* (1757, London)). (See "Montcalm takes Oswego" in *The Forts of Oswego.*)

Among the notables who resided in pre-Revolutionary Oswego was Francis Lewis, who would sign of the Declaration of Independence as a representative of New York. His business was destroyed by Montcalm's army and he was captured. Montcalm permitted the Indians fighting alongside the French to torture about thirty of the captives, and Lewis was one of those selected. He was, however a linguist, and managed to converse with his Indian captors, who consequently spared him torture. After his experiences in 1756, Lewis became a strong advocate of those seeking to end Europe's dominance in the New World.

Montcalm left Oswego destroyed and deserted. Perhaps feeling remorse, he ordered that a huge cross be erected upon a hill to honor the dead. Other than the cross, nothing else stood for several years. On 17 August 1759, British General Thomas Gage began to construct a new Fort Ontario. (See "A New Fort Ontario" in *The Forts of Oswego.*) Forts Oswego and George were never rebuilt. In 1760, Fort Ontario served as an assembly area for Major General Jeffrey Amherst, the British Commander in Chief. No less than 10,000 British troops, augmented with many Indians and colonial troops, received their final training in Oswego.

During the Revolutionary War, Fort Ontario served as a staging area for Loyalists and British troops. In 1778, Patriot forces took Oswego after St Leger's defeat, but shortly afterwards, British troops reoccupied the site and built a new fort. The fort remained as a British possession until 1796, and following their withdrawal, Fort Ontario was reoccupied by a permanent U.S. Army garrison which remained there until 1948. In the first two decades in the aftermath of the Revolutionary War, few inhabitants resettled into the area. But by 1840, Oswego was once again a thriving and sizable town. For additional information on Oswego see Allan W. Eckert, *The Wilderness Empire* (Boston: Little, Brown and Company, 1969); Reverend George Reed, *Fort Ontario*; Wallace F. Workmaster, *The Forts of Oswego: A Study in the Art of Defense* (Fort Ontario Archives, Oswego, NY); Mr. George T. Clark, *Oswego: An Historical Address* (Fort Ontario Archives, Oswego, NY).

3 Reverend George A. Reed, "Revolution" in *Fort Ontario*.

4 As early as 1741, Lieutenant Governor Clarke, an appointed British official, wrote to the House Lords of Trade about "the fertility of the lands now generally known to be very good and far exceeding any other in the Province." Along with wheat, referred to as "The King crop of the Valley," peas, rye,

flax, and other crops were raised as well. In Albany, on an average day, it was not uncommon to see 31 or more sloops at the docks. Each sloop transported 400–500 barrels of flour to New York City and made at least 11–12 round trips a year. For the importance of the agricultural trade in the Mohawk Valley see Charles Gehring, *Agriculture and the Revolution in the Mohawk Valley* (New York: Fort Klock), pp. 1–4.

5   According to Charles Gehring, grist mills abounded. With melting snows in the spring, these mills operated at peak efficiency. Therefore, it was critical "to destroy the [Mohawk] Valley's capacity to supply wheat to the northern Army and the New England states."

6   According to *Revolutionary War Dates Referring to Oswego*, p. 3, as early as 28 February 1777 Burgoyne, in a memorandum to Lord George Germain about the proposed expedition from the northwest, also requested a commanding officer: "I would wish Lieutenant Colonel [Barry] St. Leger."

7   Lachine is not to be confused with Lachenaie, which is located directly north of Montreal across the St. Lawrence River.

8   In French, the island was referred to as Isle au Chevreulis. Its Indian name was Kahihououage and it was also known as Deer or Buck Island. The island is a part of the Thousand Island chain. It was also referred as Carleton Island during Sir Guy Carleton's rule as Governor-General of Canada from 1775–1778. After Sir Frederick Haldimand replaced Carleton, he officially named the island after him in 1779. See Adrian G. Ten Cate, *Pictorial History of the Thousand Islands* (Canada: Besancourt Publishers, 1982), pp. 25, 265, also the map section.

General Herkimer Meets with Chief Joseph Brant

As General St. Leger made preparations in Lachine and Lieutenants Schanck and Twiss were constructing bateaux on Carleton Island, farther to the southeast at Unadilla, in the heart of the Mohawk Valley, General Nicholas Herkimer was having a confrontation with a Mohawk leader whose Indian name was Thayendanegea, but whose English name was Joseph Brant.[1] General Herkimer tremendously admired the American Indians, among whom were some of his closest friends—in fact some sources say that Herkimer and Brant were actually neighbours and friends before the Revolutionary War—but Herkimer now despised Brant.

Since the late spring of 1776, Brant had been on the warpath. On 10 June 1777, Colonel John Harper, a militia commander, had written to General Herkimer requesting an ammunition supply in the event Brant should attack the area of Schoharie.[3] Already a number of Unadilla's residents had been attacked, while others, fearing for their lives, had fled to German Flats.[4] In June, Brant had requested food "for his famished people" from the Johnstone Settlement, making it clear that if they did not provide sustenance, "the Indians would take them by force." At the time, Brant informed the settlement's Reverend Johnstone that "he had made a covenant with the King [George III] and was not inclined to break it." Although the settlement did provide Brant with some food, Brant was "not satisfied [and], drove off a large number of cattle, sheep, and swine," assisted by about 80 warriors. "Not feeling safe in their remote settlement, the whites abandoned it and took refuge in Cherry Valley [though] some families in the neighborhood of

Unadilla fled to the German Flats, and others to Esopus and Newburgh, on the Hudson River."[5]

Therefore, in an attempt to stop Brant's raiding and win him over to the American side—or at least convince him to remain neutral—it was determined by General Schuyler, under whose jurisdiction the region fell, that Herkimer should meet with Brant. Herkimer therefore organized a meeting between himself and Brant at Unadilla.[6]

Accompanied by members of his militia force, Herkimer met with the Indian leader in an open field in Unadilla on 27 June. Escorting the Patriot commander were Colonel Ebenezer Cox,[7] Captain Henry Eckler, two lieutenants, and a force of nearly 380 well-armed militiamen.[8] Herkimer hoped to sway Brant with a show of force; however, because both Herkimer and Brant had previously agreed that no more than ten men[9] from either side were to be present during the discussion, Herkimer positioned the bulk of his force in a small field nearby. Though instructed to rest, the militiamen were placed on standby. Should the talks fail and Herkimer decide that he had no option left but to kill Brant, a keyword phase—"the matter is ended!"—would be announced loudly. Immediately, three assassins, each armed with a concealed pistol, would step forward to shoot Brant.[10] One of the designated shooters was a fiery young patriot named Wagner who, in turn, had selected two of Herkimer's nephews—Abraham and George Herkimer[11]—to assist in the killing.

As they approached one another, Herkimer noted that only four warriors accompanied Brant. All were bare-chested, and none were armed. About 130 warriors stood nearby, armed mostly with tomahawks. The two men greeted each other cordially and shook hands. After an initial exchange of words, Herkimer pointed out that Brant personally knew Colonel Cox and Captain Eckler, and several others of those accompanying him, and affirmed that they had come in the cause of peace.[12] Brant demanded to know, however, why Herkimer had arrived with 400 men, and the conversation threatened to become unfriendly, so Herkimer returned to the matter in hand, directly asking whether Brant would remain at peace.[13]

Brant said that his people would not, and elaborated how their fathers and grandfathers had always been in agreement with the British king. He went on to denounce the "Boston people," and criticize General Schuyler and Herkimer.[14] Herkimer replied by defending the new nation and its government, and warned that opposing it would not be wise.[15] Brant, now angry, replied that further discussion was pointless. Suddenly, Herkimer bellowed, "The matter is ended!" The signal for the assassins was given.

But the plot failed. For some unknown reason, only Wagner stepped forward. As he attempted to quickly pull out his concealed gun, he began to stumble; possibly, his gun got caught on a piece of clothing. Sensing danger, Brant quickly raised his right arm. In instant response, the terrifying cries of the 130 Indians nearby, shouting in unison with hundreds of others who suddenly appeared from different directions, pierced the air.[20] Heavily armed, they quickly encircled Herkimer's entire force, and for the first time some Loyalists were spotted among them as well. Herkimer and Brant signaled for their men to remain calm, and Herkimer ordered his failed assassin to drop his pistol. Turning to Brant he said again that he had not come to fight.[17] Herkimer, in fact, was not lying. He had not come to fight. He wanted to talk and win Brant over. True, if push came to shove and he had to kill, Brant was to be the only target and no one else. Herkimer did not want to battle either the Indians or Loyalists.

Brant replied that if Herkimer wanted war, they were ready. He meant business, but Herkimer succeeded in keeping everyone calm, and it was agreed that both groups would withdraw peacefully. Herkimer, however, made an error of judgment in requesting that Brant hand over the Loyalists. The request was refused, and immediately he realized the folly of his appeal. Unable to secure the Loyalists, Herkimer only exhibited further incompetency and failure.[18]

Parting from Brant, Herkimer knew that he had failed and nothing had been accomplished. Brant had outmaneuvered him and the patriot militia commander had come close to having his force wiped out. Herkimer knew that it would be useless to try to convince General Schuyler or anyone else that a measure of success had been achieved. Frustrated and seething with anger, Herkimer's hatred of Brant and the Loyalists only intensified as he marched off.

Notes

1   Born in 1742 in the Mohawk tribe in the British Royal Colony of New York, Thayendanegea (which in Mohawk means "bundle of sticks" and denotes strength) was renamed "Joseph Brant" by Sir William Johnson, the Superintendent of the Indian Department for the British Crown. His sister was

renamed as Molly Brant. (Lossing, *Field Book of the Revolution*, Vol. 1, p. 237, however, cites that Joseph was actually born in Ohio because Brant's parents had moved to Ohio. When his father passed away when Brant was about two, his mother returned to Canajahorie with him and his younger sister.) Joseph Brant attended the Moor's Indian Charity School in Lebanon, Connecticut, and was converted to the Episcopalian Church. His sister, Molly, married Sir William Johnson in an Iroquois marriage and had eight children. Robert Calhoon, *The Loyalists in Revolutionary America, 1760-1781* (New York: Harcourt Brace Jovanovich, Inc., 1973), p. 428, cites "Mary [Molly] Brant, Joseph [Brant's] sister, and at one time Sir William Johnson's housekeeper and mistress." According to Cannon, *Frontiers Aflame!*, p. 19, Molly Brant and Sir William Johnson were married in an Iroquois marriage and together, they had eight children. (Ibid.). According to Reverend George Reed and Mr. Richard LaCrosse a marriage, via an Iroquois ceremony, did take place between Sir William and Molly Brant. Therefore, within the Iroquois confederacy, their marriage was a legal one. At the outbreak of the Revolutionary War, both sides made attempts to win Brant's support. His older sister Molly's very pro-British stance, and Brant's contact with his late brother-in-law Johnson were behind Brant's decision to support an allegiance with England.

Despite Brant's ill-feelings for certain British officials during the Revolutionary War, he remained a strong supporter of the British Crown and he demanded from everyone else strict adherence to the British nation. Brant was known to say: "I have learned to live as a good subject of the English, and to honor the King. A Mohawk must remain true to his beliefs. He cannot change them." Jeanne Meader Schwarz and Minerva J. Goldberg, *New York State in Story* (New York: Frank E. Richards, 1962), Book 2, p. 23.

In the aftermath of the Revolutionary War, Brant remained in Canada. In 1787, he translated the Prayer Book and St. Mark's Gospel into the Iroquois language. He also helped to establish the first Episcopalian Church in Upper Canada. On 24 November 1807, he died in Grand River, Ontario, Canada. For more on Brant see William T. Couch (ed.), *Collier's Encyclopedia* (New York: P. F. Collier and Son Corporation, 1955), Vol. 4, p. 24. For a picture of a painting of "Joseph Brant, the Mohawk chief" in uniform, see Esmond Wright (ed.), *The Fire of Liberty. The American War of Independence seen through the eyes of the men and women, the statesmen and soldiers who fought it* (New York: St. Martin's Press, 1983) between pp. 96–97; and William Leete Stone, *The Campaign of Lieut.Gen. John Burgoyne and the Expedition of Lieut.Col. Barry St. Leger* (New York: DaCapo Press, 1970, reprinted), between pp. 176–177. (Hereafter cited as *The Campaign*).

2   Campbell and Stone, *Siege and Battle*, p. 182.
3   William W. Campbell and William L. Stone, *Siege Fort Stanwix [Schuyler] & Battle of Oriskany* (New York: J. & J. Harper, 1831). (Reprinted Rome,

New York: Bropard Company, Inc., 1977), p. 181. (Hereafter cited as *Siege and Battle*).

4 Stone, *Siege and Battle*, p. 180.

5 Lossing, *Field Book of the Revolution*, Vol. 1, p. 237.

6 According to Stone, General Herkimer dispatched a messenger to Unadilla inviting Brant to meet him at that location. See William L. Stone, *Life of Joseph Brant—Thayendanegea Including the Indian Wars of the American Revolution* (New York: H. & E. Phinney, 1845), p. 181). (Hereafter cited as *Life of Joseph Brant*).

7 Cox was one of the directors of the Tryon County Committee of Safety.

8 Allan W. Eckert, *The Wilderness War: A Narrative* (Boston: Little, Brown & Company, 1967), pp. 109–110. (Hereafter cited as *The Wilderness War*). Stone, *Life of Joseph Brant*, p. 181, cites about 300 local militia from Colonels Cox, Klock, and Isenlord regiments. Lossing, *Field Book of the Revolution*, Vol. 1, p. 237, cites "Herkimer took with him three hundred Tryon county militia. In the meantime, Colonel Van Schaick marched with one hundred fifty men as far as Cherry Valley." (Ibid.)

9 Eckert, *The Wilderness War*, p. 110. According to Lossing, Vol. 1, p. 237, General Schuyler was very receptive to the idea of Herkimer meeting with Brant at Unadilla.

10 Eckert, p. 110. Campbell and Stone, *Siege and Battle*, p. 185, also cites four. Stone also cites that prior to this day Herkimer actually met with Brant on two previous occasions. Since nothing positive had been accomplished in their first meetings, Herkimer concluded that he might have to assassinate Brant. See Stone, pp. 184–185.

11 Lossing, Vol. 1, p. 238.

12 Ibid. Eckert, p. 110.

13 Lossing, Vol. 1, p. 238; Eckert, p. 110-1. Campbell and Stone, *Siege and Battle*, p. 183, cite Brant had close to 40 warriors within close proximity with many others nearby.

14 Ibid. Campbell and Stone, p. 184; Eckert, p. 111; Stone, p. 184.

15 Ibid. Lossing, *Field Book of the Revolution*, Vol. 1, pp. 238–239, acknowledges that the meeting was not on friendly terms.

16 According to Stone, *Siege and Battle*, p. 182, Brant was accompanied by 500 warriors. Lossing, Vol. 1, p. 237, cites "Brant came accompanied by five hundred warriors."

17 Eckert, p. 112.

18 According to Stone, p. 183, Brant was accompanied by Sir John Johnson and Captain Bull, a Loyalist officer.

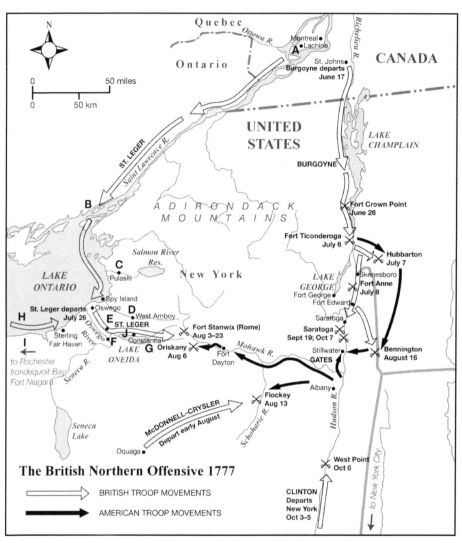

The British Northern Offensive 1777

⟶ BRITISH TROOP MOVEMENTS

⟶ AMERICAN TROOP MOVEMENTS

A. St. Leger departs Montreal/Lachine
   28 June–2 July, approx.
B. Carleton Island
C. Salmon River
D. Little Salmon River/South Branch
   (Proposed Route)

E. Old Block House *(Fort Brewerton)*
F. Three Rivers *(Seneca, Oneida, Oswego)*
G. Wood Creek
H. Walter Butler
I. Irondequoit Bay, Fort Niagara
J. Constantia

III

St. Leger Moves into the Western Wilderness

In July 1777, Carleton Island was manned by some British naval personnel attached to the island's regular British Army garrison. By mid-July, General St. Leger's entire force was to be assembled on the island, and early in the month the first contingents began to arrive, among them Barry St. Leger himself. Personnel problems, however, quickly arose. Though all commanders anticipate problems, in St. Leger's case, they never seemed to diminish.

Prior to reaching Carleton Island, the brunt of the Canadian Quebec Militia Company, commanded by Captain Hertel De Rouville, had suddenly deserted.[1] As General Burgoyne had by now learned, many miles farther to the east deep in the wilderness, and as St. Leger would soon learn, Canadian manpower—whether recruited for combat or support—was by and large unreliable.

Furthermore, from his discussions with the British military personnel based on Carleton Island, St. Leger learned that they not only regarded North American Indian warriors as ineffective fighters but, frequently, as a detriment. The British commander noted how the island's military men, stationed on the edge of a wilderness, miles away from any high-ranking military and civilian leaders of the British Empire, spoke more freely. Among the British leadership—in such cities as Montreal, Ottawa, Quebec, and in faraway London—the Indian was exalted as a superior forest warrior. Yet, whereas few would dare to criticize the Indian in front of those such as Sir Guy Carleton, the British Governor-General of Canada, or King George III, here, deep in the wilderness, a totally different opinion was aired. The soldiers considered them to be difficult to satisfy and quick to question anything and everything. In contrast to the military discipline the soldiers were used to, the Indians came and went as they pleased, acted as they pleased, and could not be trusted in combat. And they ate voraciously.[2] As St. Leger's force was in large part to be composed of Indian warriors, such comments would undoubtedly have caused the British general concern.

Even before Brant's meeting with General Herkimer on 27 June, Indian warriors from various American and Canadian tribes had begun to converge upon Oswego.[3] In July, Chief Joseph Brant arrived.[4] In addition to the Indians, pro-British Loyalists[5]—such as the Johnsons and Butlers—also arrived. Many warriors came to Oswego from the wilderness regions of present-day New York State—such as Oquaga or the areas around the Mohawk Valley—while others hailed from Canada. Those who came from Canada arrived via Fort Niagara following a brief stop at Irondequoit Bay.

Chief Brant, the Johnsons, the Butlers, and Royal Governor William Tryon had, until recently, been resident in the Mohawk Valley or in Tryon County.[6] Politically, Tryon County was a hotbed. Prior to the outbreak of the American Revolution, the county was controlled by one man: Sir William Johnson.[7] Born in Ireland, Johnson had immigrated to the North American continent in his youth. In time, he became the King's Superintendent of Indian Affairs.[8] Tryon County was named after Royal Governor William Tryon. Born in England, Tryon administered the Colony of New York for the British King and government.[9] Tryon also had a huge personal estate in the county.

In addition to administering Indian affairs, Sir William Johnson exerted his influence throughout the entire Mohawk Valley and far into the wilderness. Many settlers came to loathe Johnson, an Irishman, for being so loyal to a king and nation that had brutalized Ireland for centuries and was continuing to do so. His drinking and womanizing—he was rumored to have fathered 600 children—also affected his reputation. In July 1774 Sir William, infected with various diseases including syphilis, suddenly passed away. His son John—born from his marriage to Catherine Weisenberg—assumed control of the family's property, and Colonel Sir Guy Johnson, Johnson's nephew and son-in-law, became the Superintendent of Indian Affairs.[10]

Many of the inhabitants of Tryon County were of Dutch, Scots-Irish, and German descent. Many of the Scots-Irish were descendents of men and women who had fled to the New World to escape British persecution. Now, under British rule in the New World, they began to increasingly support those seeking an end to Britain's rule.[11] The settlers of Dutch and German ancestry also began to increasingly oppose Britain. After evicting the previous Dutch administration, Britain immediately imposed numerous laws, regulations, and rules detrimental to the longstanding inhabitants. As a result, these settlers sought a way of ending British rule. Among many of the Germans, the King was viewed as nothing but a brutal Germanic ruler.[12]

Yet, among the Dutch, German, and Scots-Irish, there were still those who voiced favorable sentiments toward England and the King. Many, however, did so out of uncertainty and fear. They felt that the newly established American nation would not prevail. Others supported the Crown because they were tenant farmers who owed their livelihoods to the Johnsons.[13] In addition, there were also the Loyalists who hoped the war would soon be over so that they would not have to become involved.[14]

Sensing increasing opposition and fearing for his life, Sir Guy Johnson fled from Tryon County to Canada on 31 May 1775.[15] He was accompanied by some Loyalists and Indians including Joseph Brant, John Butler and Walter Butler. A year later, in May 1776, Sir John Johnson also fled, accompanied by more Loyalists.[16] The Johnsons and their followers fled to Canada while many of the other Loyalists, including Lord Tryon, fled southward to New York City, which after General Howe's invasion and expulsion of George Washington's army in the summer of 1776 was under firm British control. With the departure of the Loyalist leadership from the Mohawk Valley, the Patriots seized total political control of the region. Soon, a political organization titled the "Rebels' Tryon County Committee of Safety" appeared.[17] Of historical significance is that this party was the very first pro-independence organization in Tryon County, and was one of the first in the Colony of New York. Among its notable members was the Patriot general George Clinton, who in 1777 would be elected New York State's first governor.

The Loyalists who fled either to Canada or New York City continued to agitate against the rebelling Patriots. They organized military units to assist the King's forces in suppressing the rebellion. John Butler and his son Walter raised Butler's Rangers, while Sir John Johnson organized a regiment officially titled the "King's Royal Regiment of New York,"[18] though, unofficially it was known as the "Royal York-ers," "Johnson's Greens," "Royal Greens," or "KRR."[19] Overwhelm-ingly, the volunteers who joined these units were Loyalists who had fled to Canada from Tryon County or its nearby environs. Initially, when some of the Loyalist leaders fled, they left their families behind. After all, they expected to return soon. Some even anticipated that upon their return they would receive a hero's welcome. But this never occurred. Angered at what the Loyalists were doing, the Patriots began to confis-cate their property. Among the estates seized by the Patriots were those of Lord Tryon, the Johnsons, the Butlers, and the Brants. As for the Loyalist families left behind, some were moved to new locations[20] while others were placed under house arrest. Such was the case with Joseph Brant's sister Molly, who was William Johnson's "widow."[21]

By the beginning of 1777, Canada had become a haven of refuge for the sizable number of Tryon County and Mohawk Valley Loyalists. Seeking to counter the Patriots, they flocked to the Butler and Johnson units. They not only wanted to return and recover what they had lost but also to punish those who had opposed the King. Until 1777, the struggle within and around the wilderness had largely been a war of words and politics,[22] but the Loyalists were not yet through. In Canada and Fort Niagara, they were now conducting formal military training. And the Patriots knew that it was just a matter of time before the King's supporters would attempt to return.[23]

In 1777, neither Fort Oswego nor Fort Ontario, standing on oppo-site sides of the Oswego River where it empties into Lake Ontario, were in usuable form. After both forts were sacked by a French and Indian army under Montcalm in 1756, with 1,700 prisoners carted off to Canada, the installations had fallen into disrepair. Work had resumed on Fort Ontario, which sat on the higher ground, in 1759, but little became of it. Despite plans to garrison the fort, it was seldom manned and became home only to rotting logs and abandoned buildings.[24] The ruins were located on the edge of a wilderness that stretched eastward into and through the Adirondacks into central and northern Vermont, southwestwards to Fort Niagara, eastward to the vicinity of Fort Stan-wix and south/southeastward to the current New York–Pennsylvania border. Here and there amid the endless trees, some tiny settlements existed where settlers, farmers, and trappers resided. Various sources claim that the population of the region was very small, yet there are indications that in some areas, which today encompass Oswego, Fulton, Syracuse, Auburn, Sterling, Fair Haven, Hannibal, as well as the shoreline region from Oswego to the present-day city of Rochester, the population was actually higher than generally believed.[25]

Many centuries earlier, the ice age had carved out the region later to be known as the Mohawk Valley. Adjacent to the northern edge of the valley stands the Adirondack Mountains, within and around which lie critical water routes such as the Mohawk River, Richelieu River, and the Lake Champlain/Lake George waterways. Numerous species of animals, birds, and fish existed within this wilderness, which for large stretches still existed in its primeval state.

Numerous creeks, streams, rivers, ponds, lakes, and swamps characterized the lay of the land. Most flowed year round, although some streams dried up in the summer months. From Oswego to the Mohawk Valley the land is characterized largely by deep gullies, ravines, natural fields, and rolling hills. The bulk of the wilderness, however, was heavily forested. In the forests, huge trees, some centuries old, reached high into the sky. The forest was composed of mixed trees—ash, beech, birch, black and pipe cherry, butternut, chestnut, elm, locust, maple (both hard and soft), oak, and willow, and various nut trees grew in abundance. Cedar and fur trees, such as pine and hemlock, were also found—especially abundant in the higher regions.

By 23 July, Fort Ontario contained an assortment of notable Loyalist and Indian leaders:[26] Sir John Johnson, son of Sir William, with his regiment the Royal Greens;[27] Colonel Daniel Claus, superintendent of the Canadian Indians;[28] and Colonel John Butler,[29] who commanded the unit that would later be referred to as "Butler's Rangers"[30] with his son, Captain Walter Butler. There was also Major Geoffrey Watts, who, besides being Sir John Johnson's brother-in-law, served as the assistant commander of the Royal Greens.

In addition to Chief Joseph "Captain" Brant, the Indian leadership arriving at Oswego included Chief Cornplanter of the Onondaga tribe; Chiefs Gucinge, Ghalto, Gisu-gwatoh, Cornstock, Sangerachta, and Blacksnake; and the Cayuga Indian agent named "John" Hare. These were just some of the more famous Loyalist and Indian personalities.

While in Oswego, Colonel Butler, much to his dismay and anger, learned that Daniel Claus would be in charge of the Indians. So upset was Butler by this development that on 26 July he wrote a formal letter of protest directly to Governor-General Guy Carleton. It is not known if the Canadian governor ever received the letter, but if he did, he took no action on the matter.[31]

Although different authors cite various figures, it seems likely that approximately 1,000 Indians from various American and Canadian tribes assembled at Oswego.[32] But an estimate is the only option, as no one ever properly registered the true Indian strength. Indeed, it may be argued that one of the major handicaps that plagued St. Leger (and even Burgoyne) was that from the outset they never knew what their true Indian strength was. The Indian force was comprised of tribesmen from the Mohawk, Seneca, Onondaga, Cayuga, Oneida, and Tuscaroroa tribes, and from Canadian tribes such as the Ottawas, Mississaugas, Hurons, and Chippewas. Others, such as some Algonquins, also hailed from Canada. Because these warriors came from so many different tribes, their gathering in Oswego truly resembled that of a rare inter-tribal conference. Brant arrived in Oswego with about 300 warriors.[33] Colonel John Butler, along with his son, brought another 300 in addition to their Loyalist fighters.[34] Another 400–500 Canadian warriors drifted in from various regions located to the west of Fort Niagara.

Colonel John Butler and the Ranger unit departed from Fort Niagara sometime in early July 1777. They moved on foot and first travelled to Irondequoit Bay, arriving around 15 July, where Butler assembled the remainder of his force, an additional influx of around 300 Indians. At Irondequoit Bay, on Saturday, 19 July, Butler received an order from General St. Leger to immediately dispatch 150 Indians to the main British force. These warriors were to be used for a surprise attack against Fort Stanwix; however it appears that the venture was cancelled as no such attack occurred.[35] Butler had to deal with the misgivings of his Indian force, a precursor to the problems that would occur when they reached Oswego. Having persuaded the Indians to accompany him, the combined force continued to proceed on foot to Oswego and traveled adjacent to Lake Ontario on an old Indian trail through the area that currently contains the towns and villages of Webster, East Williamson, Alton, Sodus Bay, Wolcott, Red Creek, Fair Haven, Sterling, and Fruit Valley.[36]

Many of the Indian warriors did not understand why they had been notified to appear in Oswego, and were beginning to voice displeasure and uncertainty. This was especially true of those who had just arrived from Irondequoit Bay. Informed about the planned campaign, they began to question it—some even expressed outright hostility towards the plan. Others, especially those resident in and around the Mohawk Valley, stated that they had no issues with their white neighbors, emphasizing that they had already concluded various mutual understandings and even treaties with the whites supporting the American cause. In these agreements the Indians had promised that they would not go to war against those supporting the Revolution, and the last thing the warriors wanted to do was break their word and thus leave their own families vulnerable to Patriot retaliation.

A number of the Indians openly questioned the wisdom of supporting the British Crown. Among them was Red Jacket, a youth approximately 18 years old. Red Jacket did not even understand why he was there. Someone had just talked him into coming along for what was to be a warriors' meeting pertaining to the upcoming hunting season. While growing up, on more than one occasion Red Jacket had heard from his elders how the British were only exploiting the Indians for Britain's advantage. No one, however, said anything about a war. Red Jacket felt very uneasy about what was going on.

Noting the Indian discontent, John and Walter Butler began to entice the warriors to fight for the British cause. Shouts and chants of "The King Is Rich! The Americans Are Poor!" along with promises of rewards for scalps and prisoners were used at Oswego, as they had been just days before at Irondequoit Bay.[37]

The disillusionment, however, was not just rife amongst those being encouraged to battle the Patriots, despite their own views or previous agreeements. To an extent, it also existed among those still favoring the British Crown, such as Joseph Brant. Despite his recent dispute with General Herkimer at Unadilla, and his proclaimed hatred of those rebelling against the Crown, by 1777 Brant, too, was becoming increasingly unhappy with British rule. So he began to complain, and was especially vocal about the lack of supplies for the Indians.

He argued that promises made by British officials in Montreal and at border posts, such as at Fort Niagara, were not being kept. Along with Brant, Colonel Daniel Claus was also unsatisfied. Claus was especially infuriated that at Oswego there was a lack of supplies because he had attempted to organize them before heading there. After encountering difficulties, Claus personally appealed to Governor-General Carleton, who had previously assured Claus that, "everything necessary would be provided and would be waiting at Oswego."[38] But this had not happened. There were very few supplies and Claus felt betrayed; worse, he was not only made to look incompetent to his fellow Indians, but he was also losing their trust and confidence. In addition, Claus, like others, did not hold the Butlers in high esteem, especially resenting young Walter Butler.

Noting the Indian discontent and fearing they would leave, Colonel Claus and Chief Brant, along with the Butlers, began to make new promises. They assured the Indians that supplies were forthcoming, and that George III was rich and could provide everything they needed.[39]

Repeatedly, the Indians were assured that the upcoming campaign would be an easy one. For them, no danger lay ahead. Easy loot and scalps were to be the reward for those who participated. To make their point, some of the Indians were brought forward, and in front of others they were provided with weapons, trinkets, or gold and silver coins.[40] As the items were being distributed, promises of more weapons, wealth, and rum were made. Yet, despite the partial distribution and rhetoric, Red Jacket remained unhappy; something was not right.

While the Butlers, Chief Brant, Colonel Claus, and others were soothing the ill-temper of the Indians and heaping new "promises" upon them, General Barry St. Leger was still on Carleton Island making his final preparations.

St. Leger's plans were based on an order issued 26 March 1777 by Lord Germain to Governor-General Carleton;[41] in turn, Carleton instructed General St. Leger to command the western force which would support General Burgoyne's offensive from the north. Lord Germain, however, did not just appoint a commander. He also stipulated what units St. Leger was to command along with their respective troop strengths. Such units and strengths were to consist of:

Detachment from the 8th Foot Regiment—100 soldiers
Detachment from the 34th Foot Regiment—100 soldiers
Sir John Johnson's King's Royal Regiment of New York—
    133 soldiers
German Anspach Jägers—342 soldiers.[42]

In addition to the above strength, Lord Germain's directive stipulated:

Together with a sufficient number of Canadians and Indians, and after having furnished him with proper artillery, stores, provision and every necessary article for his expedition, and secured to him every assistance in your power to afford and procure, you are to give him orders to proceed forthwith to and down the Mohawk River to Albany and put himself under the command of Sir William Howe.[43]

It is of interest how Germain established St. Leger's force. It is obvious that the 34th Foot Regiment was selected because it was St. Leger's personal regiment and he was well acquainted with it. However, it can only be surmised why only 100 soldiers were taken from each regiment. True, St. Leger's mission was one of a diversionary nature. Nevertheless, within the scope of the entire campaign, it had a vital role. In consideration of this, it appears that Germain did not give much thought as to the true strength St. Leger might need.

Lord Germain's directive also stipulated, "together with a sufficient number of Canadians and Indians." Yet, he failed to estimate a strength figure. It would have benefitted both Governor-General Carleton and St. Leger, insofar as gathering supplies and provisions, had Germain been more explicit in his guidance on the "number of Canadians and Indians." Upon receiving Germain's order, Governor-General Carleton simply passed it on to Daniel Claus to organize the irregular force. With no firm instructions as to how this was to be done, immense problems soon arose.

Lord Germain instructed Carleton to tell St. Leger that once he reached Albany, he was to "put himself under the command of Sir William Howe." Yet, at no time did Lord Germain ever write to General Howe informing him that he was to advance northward to Albany and, once there, assume command of the forces of both Burgoyne and St. Leger. Although the previous fall Howe had proposed an advance up the Hudson Valley with his army based in New York City, by the spring he had changed his mind and instead begun a move southward against Philadelphia.

Regardless of the reasoning behind Germain's stipulations, prior to departing Carleton Island, St. Leger officially had at his disposal only elements from the 8th Foot[44] and 34th Foot;[45] the King's Royal Regiment of New York;[46] and over 300 German Anspach Jägers.[47]

Notes

1   *"St. Leger's Attack"* in *Oswego Palladium-Times*, Tuesday, November 20, 1945, p. 4. On 27 August 1777, while in Oswego and in the aftermath of his defeat, St. Leger cited a "Quebec Militia" with a strength of 49. It is not clear, however, if the figure of 49 represented its survivors or the entire number found at the outset. Initially, this unit was to have a strength of no fewer than 100, but a combination of not enough willing volunteers, coupled with desertion, took its toll. See Gavin K. Watt and James F. Morrison, *The British Campaign of 1777* (Canada: Global Heritage Press, 2003), p. 17.

2   Carleton Island's critics were not an exception. In 1777, Lieutenant Colonel Mason Bolton, the British commandant of Fort Niagara, submitted a very detailed and critical report about the expense needed to maintain the Indians. Bolton was also critical of Colonel John Butler's spending costs towards the Indians. See Swiggett, *War Out of Niagara*, p. 117.

3   According to Lossing, Vol. 1, p. 239, "a few days after this conference [with Herkimer at Unadilla], Brant withdrew his warriors from the Susquehanna and joined Sir John Johnson and Colonel John Butler, who were [now] collecting a large body of Tories [loyalists] and refugees at Oswego, preparing to descent upon the Mohawk and Schoharie settlements."

4   To cite an example: "in July 1777, some Senecas and 40 western Indians arrived to Fort Niagara. Within days, they departed for Irondequoit Bay and Oswego." Barbara Graymont, *The Iroquois in the American Revolution* (New York: Syracuse University Press, 1972), p. 120.

5   Also known as Tories. As already mentioned, Tories were the Loyalists supporting England. (Hereafter Loyalist will mostly be utilized).

6   As for Royal Governor William Tryon, after fleeing to New York City he remained there until the end of the Revolutionary War. Just prior to the Patriots reoccupying the city in 1783, Tryon fled to England.

7   Jane Campbell, *Frontiers Aflame!*, p. 19.

8   Ibid.

9   At one time, William Tryon also served as the Royal Governor of North Carolina. See Ketchum, *Saratoga,* p. 270.

10 Campbell, p. 20.

11 Ibid. Campbell cites how their Scots-Irish ancestors brought much anti-British sentiment to the New World.

12 Campbell, pp. 20–22.

13 Ibid., p. 20.

14 Ibid.

15 Ibid., p. 20.

16 Ibid., p. 22.

17 Ibid.

18 Ibid., pp. 20–22.

19 Ibid.

20 Catalina Butler, for example, the wife of Colonel John Butler and their four

younger children, were transported to Albany and placed under arrest. (See Campbell, pp. 20 and 22). In such cases, it was usually a house arrest.

21 Although not arrested, Molly Brant was restricted in her movements. (In all sense it, too, was a house arrest.) In 1777, she fled. After a short stay at Oswego and Fort Niagara, she ended up in Canada and remained there until her death.

22 Some raiding, conducted by Loyalists and Indians acting under Loyalist encouragement, was already undertaken in the latter part of 1775 and 1776. In July 1776, for example, Ephraim Smith and his entire family were slaughtered in Cherry Valley.

23 See also Christopher Ward, *The War of the Revolution,* Volumes 1–11 (New York: The Macmillan Co., 1952), Vol. II, p. 481. Dale Van Every implies the Loyalists were not yet finished with the Patriots when he cites, "In New York the numerous and powerful frontier tories had been disarmed, dislodged, dispossessed, and driven into exile." See *A Company of Heroes. The American Frontier, 1775–1783* (New York: William Morrow and Company, 1962), p. 169.

24 Though in disrepair in 1777, by the conclusion of the war Fort Ontario would once again be rebuilt by the British.

25 It must be remembered that in the pre-Revolutionary years (and for some time in the aftermath of the conflict) no one ever conducted, at any time, an official or formal censuses. Though the new American nation did conduct a formal (and its first) census in 1790, it is doubtful that any census was ever taken in the wilderness in the 18th century.

We know something of some of the men who volunteered to fight from this region. Across to the east in Washington County, adjacent to Lake Ticonderoga, Captain John Armstrong organized a militia unit in 1777. In turn, this unit fell under the command of Colonel John Williams. Williams' sizable company was assigned to hold and strengthen Fort George (located to the west of Fort Ticonderoga on Lake George). But with the evacuation of Fort Ticonderoga in early 1777, Fort George was also evacuated and Colonel Williams' company was ordered to Fort Edward to reinforce Colonel Van Vort's Regiment. After retreating from Fort Edward, in the aftermath of 1777, Williams' company remained always on standby. It was utilized as a quick reserve force against roaming Loyalists and Indians conducting raids for the British.

Among those who served in this unit was a young volunteer named William McCoy. Born in June 1762 in Newfoundland, Canada, William was the son of William and Agnes McCoy, who had emigrated from Scotland. In time, they moved into the northern edge of present-day Washington County, which was then a wilderness region. From here, 15-year-old William McCoy enlisted. (For an interesting account about volunteer McCoy, see Hallie DeMass Sweeting, *Pioneers of Sterling, NY (Cayuga County).* (Red Creek: Wayuga Press, 1998), p. 13.

Another volunteer, James Wasson, enlisted into the 5th New York Regiment. He was born on 15 November 1763. It is believed he was born in Schenectady County (adjacent the wilderness region) but possibly, he was born farther to the north or west. When the 5th New York was decimated in October 1777 in the battles in the Highland's region of West Point, New York, Wasson, not yet 14 years of age, escaped. Wasson later served in the 1779 Sullivan expedition and, in 1780, joined Marinus Willett's force. After the Revolutionary War, Wasson received 200 acres of land in the town of Sterling for his military service. On 4 February 1847, he died in Sterling.

There is also the story of how two young men, in June or July 1777, approached Oswego to snipe on the Loyalists and Indians assembling on the grounds of the old fort. After conducting their attack, they proceeded back to the area that would later be known as Sterling. But a heavy rain began, and as the two proceeded to cross a creek in a deep ravine, they were caught in a flash flood and drowned. This story was related to the author by Mr. Robert Matson, a lifelong resident of Hannibal/Sterling. He had read about this incident years before in a local, privately owned family journal.

For many years, a story was passed from one generation to another within the Damewood and Butler families, which reside in present-day Auburn and Montezuma, that two of the Damewood ancestors—Captain Richard Damewood and his brother George—were Revolutionary War veterans. The mystery was finally unraveled on Tuesday, 23 June 1998, when a joint effort by inmate workers under the supervision of Lieutenant John Lamphere, a Cayuga County Sheriff, and county workers under Richard Smith, found a gravestone in an old cemetery located four miles to the west of Port Byron, listing him as "Capt. Richard Damewood/ Born Aug 18, 1759/ Died Aug 13, 1850." Captain Damewood was born in Montezuma, which in 1759 was in the wilderness. As for George, the captain's brother, sometime during the Revolutionary War, he was captured by a roving band of Indians. He returned years later after escaping, although he now had a "souvenir" for life. A ring, pierced through his nose by his captors, remained there forever. It could not be removed. For an interesting account of early settlers in the Montezuma–Port Byron area see "Revolutionary Vet's Grave Found in Montezuma" in *The Post Standard* (Oswego County Section), Wednesday, June 24, 1998, pp. A-1. See also "Echoes of War. Central New York's Connection to the Struggle for Independence" in *Herald-American, Sunday,* July 2, 2000, p. B-11).

26 According to Crisfield Johnson in *History of Oswego County, New York, 1739–1877* (Archives, Fort Ontario), p. 39, "There is some uncertainty about the details, but it is pretty sure that Sir Johnson, with his regiment of "Royal Greens," and Colonel Claus, Guy Johnson's deputy, came to Oswego as early as June, and began making preparations for the intended onslaught." On what date, exactly, Sir Johnson arrived to Oswego is not certain. It must be remembered that the Loyalist forces drifted in from var-

ious locations. It is known, however, that by the time Barry St. Leger arrived, the Loyalists were in place.

27 Sir Johnson's Royal Greens was the abbreviated title for "Sir Johnson's Royal Regiment of New York" or the "King's Royal Regiment of Tryon County in the Colony of New York." Raised in Canada in 1776/early 1777 the unit served in a number of places until its disbandment in Canada in June 1784. After being decimated at the siege of Fort Stanwix in August 1777, it was rebuilt in Canada from Loyalists fleeing into Canada in the aftermath of the Patriot wilderness victory of 1777. The Royal Greens participated in raids into the Wyoming Valley in 1778–79; fought at Klock's Field in October 1780, and at Jerseyfield in October 1781.

The unit was nicknamed the Royal Greens for the green coats they wore with their red and blue trimmings. A belt buckle depicting the Royal Crown adorned the front of their belts. Although a strength of 1,290 was registered at the conclusion of the war, it appears that this figure encompassed all of those who served in the regiment throughout its existence. See also Philip R. Katcher, *The Encyclopedia of British, Provincial, and German Army Units, 1775–1783* (Pennsylvania: Stackpole Books, 1973), p. 88.

28 Colonel Claus was delegated by the War Office in London to supervise General St. Leger's Canadian Indians recruited for the 1777 campaign. See "St. Leger's Attack" in *Oswego Palladium-Times*, November 20, 1945, p. 4.

29 Born in the Colony of New York, John Butler was a strong supporter of the British Crown.

30 Raised on the New York-Canadian border in 1777, Butler's Rangers was organized around six ranger companies from Loyalists who had fled to upper New York or Canada. The unit was commanded by Colonel John Butler. Posted to St. Leger's force, Colonel Butler also served as St. Leger's Adjutant-General. On 14 July 1777, Butler and his unit arrived at Oswego. Unofficially, John Butler's son, Walter—in the rank of captain—served as second-in-command. In July–August 1777, the unit suffered heavy losses at Fort Stanwix and in the Battle of Oriskany. Among the missing was Walter Butler, who was captured shortly afterward while probing into the Mohawk Valley. In the aftermath of the failed 1777 British campaign the unit was rebuilt from survivors augmented by the numerous Loyalists fleeing into Canada. Its losses were replaced and its strength actually rose to ten companies. On authority from Gov. Guy Carleton, It assumed the name Butler's Rangers in September. From 1778 until its disbandment in 1784, the unit's mission was to conduct raids into New York State. Its members wore a green jacket with trousers and leather caps. However, when raiding, frontier-type clothing was also worn. See also Stone, *Siege and Battle*, p. 68.

31 Graymont, *The Iroquois In the American Revolution*, p. 126. Carleton's inaction was undoubtedly affected by the fact that Daniel Claus was married to one of the daughters of Sir William Johnson (the former Superintendent of Indian Affairs) and was related to Sir John Johnson.

32 Eckert, *The Wilderness War*, p. 113. John F. Luzader, Louis Torres, Orville
    W. Carroll, *Fort Stanwix: Construction and Military History, Historic Fur-
    nishing Study, Historic Structure Report* (Washington, DC: U.S. Government
    Printing Office, 1976), p. 33, cites "According to tradition, 800 to 1,000
    Indians comprised his [St. Leger's] force." (Hereafter cited as *Fort Stanwix).*
    Luzader, *The Saratoga Campaign of 1777*, p. 31, cites "probably 800 Indi-
    ans;" Ward, *The War of the Revolution*, Vol. II, p. 482, cites "between 800
    and 1,000 strong;" Ketchum, *Saratoga*, p. 102, cites Burgoyne expected St.
    Leger to have between 400-500 Indians; Oscar Theodore Barck, *Colonial
    America*, p. 625, cites "1,000 Indians" and Colonel R. Ernest Dupuy and
    Trevor N. Dupuy, *The Encyclopedia of Military History, from 3500 B.C.
    to the present* (Revised Edition) (New York: Harper & Row, Publishers,
    1970), p. 714, cite a strength of "1,000."
33 Eckert, *The Wilderness War*, p. 114.
34 Ibid.
35 Graymont, pp. 123–124.
36 In the modern era, portions of this trail became the basis for highways Route
    104 and 104A.
37 Graymont, pp. 120–121. In fact, already at Irondequoit Bay Colonel Butler
    had assembled the Indians and promised them huge rewards if they sided
    with the Crown.
38 Ibid., pp. 118 and 124; Graymont, p. 118.
39 William L. Stone, *Life of Joseph Brant*, pp. 187–188; Lossing, *Field Book
    of the Revolution,* Vol. 1, p. 239.
40 Lossing, Vol. 1, p. 239, acknowledged also that in Oswego a number of
    promises were made to the Indians. Lossing also cites some "tawdry [showy
    and cheap] articles, such as scarlet clothes, beads and tickets, were then dis-
    played and presented to the Indians." (p. 239). But Lossing also writes that
    "to each Indian were then presented a brass kettle, a suit of clothes, a gun,
    a tomahawk and scalping-knife, a piece of gold, a quantity of ammunition,
    and a promise of a bounty upon every scalp he should bring in."
        Regarding this, Lossing erred. While some weapons, clothes, and pieces
    of gold and jewelry were issued, in general it was very limited and only
    issued to certain Indians. The warriors were actually promised that many
    more weapons, gold, clothing, and various items would soon be forthcom-
    ing. Promises were also made to the Indians that they would only view the
    capture of Fort Stanwix and would not be required to partake in the fighting.
    "After the fort will fall to the soldiers, you will be permitted to loot the fort."
        As for the kettles provided, according to *The Life of Mary Jemison*
    (written by Mary Jemison) (Published by James D. Bemis, Canandaigua,
    NY, 1823), some of the kettles were in use as late as 1823. According to
    Jemison, the Indians were strongly encouraged by the British to wage war
    with them against the Patriots. (See also Lossing, Vol. 1, p. 239).
        Mary Jemison's account is fascinating because it reveals not only the

war of 1777 from an Indian view, but also American Indian daily life prior to, during, and in the aftermath of the Revolutionary War.

As a little child, Jemison was captured near Fort Duquense near present day Pittsburgh, Pennsylvania. She was raised among the Indians. Although later on in life she had numerous opportunities to leave the Iroquois Indian Nation and return to white society, Jemison (as most others who resided with the Indians), refused to do so. Educated by missionaries, she was married to a chief and, in 1777 was residing within the Seneca tribe. As a member of the Indian Council of Mothers, Jemison opposed the Wilderness War of 1777 and voiced a strong opinion against siding with the British. Unfortunately—indeed, tragically—for the American Indians, despite its best efforts, the Council of Mothers no longer wielded the authority it had previously held. The Council of Mothers also failed, in 1777, to halt the eruption of the civil war among the Iroquois. Jemison witnessed the horror of the Wilderness War and its cruel aftermath. Her writings are a true tribute to the events of that era. She passed away in 1825 at the age of nearly 90.

41 *Revolutionary War Diaries Relating to Oswego.* (Unpublished text found in Fort Ontario Archives.) (Hereafter cited as *Oswego Revolutionary War Diaries.*)

42 *Oswego Revolutionary War Diaries*, p. 3; Reverend Reed, "Units At Fort Ontario" in *Fort Ontario*, p. iv; Eckert, *The Wildness War*, p. 115; and Stone, *Siege and Battle*, pp. 218–220, identifies the 8th and 34th Foot Regiments as well as the order of march to Fort Stanwix. Luzader, *Fort Stanwix*, p. 33, acknowledges the units and cites the 8th and 34th each provided 100 soldiers and 342 Germans were committed, but Luzader cites these were Hanau Chasseurs (light infantry or Jagers) and "a company of rangers under Walter Butler" and "Sir John Johnson's Regiment (the [Royal] Greens)." Though Luzader did not provide a personnel strength for Butler's or Sir Johnson's units, Luzader acknowledges "exact figures of St. Leger's strength cannot be established, but an estimated 700–800 white troops and, according to tradition, 800 to 1,000 Indians comprised his force." (Ibid.).

43 *Oswego Revolutionary War Diaries,* p. 4.

44 The 8th King's Regiment of Foot was initially raised in 1685 and was known as the Princess Anne of Denmark's Regiment of Foot. In 1702, the regiment was redesignated the Queen's Regiment of Foot and in 1716, as the King's Regiment of Foot. In 1751, the regiment received its "8th" numerical designation. In 1768, the entire 8th Foot arrived in Canada where it was immediately subdivided and stationed in various areas. Four of its companies were stationed in Niagara; three in Detroit; two at Michimackinac, Canada; and one in Oswego. But the company stationed in Oswego was soon recalled to Lachine, Canada. In 1777, this entire company with a reinforced strength of 100 soldiers was assigned to support General St. Leger.

45 The 34th Regiment of Foot was raised in 1702. It served under the names of various Colonels. But in 1751, the regiment received its numerical desig-

nation of "34." Cumberland was its home station. In May 1776, the 34th
arrived at Quebec, Canada. Lieutenant Colonel Barry St. Leger assumed
command of the 34th from Lieutenant Colonel Samuel Townsend in 1776.
In 1777, its flank companies served in Burgoyne's army; another 100 soldiers
were posted to General St. Leger and the rest of the 34th Foot remained
behind, stationed in Canada throughout the Revolutionary War. The companies serving with Burgoyne surrendered in Saratoga; while the majority
of those deployed with St. Leger perished at Fort Stanwix, Oriskany, or during the retreat back to Canada. Upon his return to Canada in 1777, St. Leger
remained with the 34th until the end of the war.

46 Also known as the Royal Greens. Although initially Lord Germain stipulated
a strength of 133 was to accompany St. Leger, in actuality, Sir John brought
two full companies along with a sizable number of individuals from other
companies totaling no fewer than 300 and possibly as many as 350. Watts
and Morrison, *The British Campaign of 1777*, p. 237, cite that on 6 August
the King's [Royal Greens] Regiment of New York had a strength of 301.
However, this strength did not include the reinforcement of over 100 Loyalists, commanded by Captain Jacob Miller, which arrived on 15 August to
St. Leger's army and were directed into the regiment. See "Recruiting During
the St. Leger Campaign" in *The British Campaign of 1777*.

47 Initially, in Canada, it was proposed to utilize the German Hanau Chasseurs
unit. This outfit, however, was never committed. The Anspach-Beyreuth
Regiment was composed of the 1st Anspach Battalion and the 2nd Anspach
Battalion. Each battalion was authorized a strength of 570 personnel of
which 27 were officers and 543 noncommissioned and private personnel. A
typical infantry company consisted of 4 officers and 97 other ranks.

In June 1777, the Anspach-Beyreuth Regiment (now just simply referred
to as the Anspach grenadiers), arrived in New York City; however, 300
Anspach grenadiers were immediately transferred to the vicinity of Montreal, Canada, and posted to St. Leger. All of them accompanied St. Leger,
as well as some German personnel from other units. In total, St. Leger had
around 350 German soldiers. As for the Anspach units in New York City,
in November 1777 they were sent to Philadelphia. Watt and Morrison,
"British and German Regulars," in *The British Campaign of 1777*, p. 31,
cite that in Oswego, there were 342 Germans of all ranks. Of this strength
one company of 89 soldiers was from the Hesse Hanau Jager Regiment. A
jäger (hunter) detachment was also dispatched to the Oriskany ambush site
in the early night hours of 6 August. (Ibid., p. 23).

The German contingent that accompanied St. Leger suffered very heavy
losses. Although no formal records exist as to their exact casualties, the German personnel captured by the Northern Army in 1777 all revealed heavy
losses. One individual who was more than happy to surrender on the edge
of Lake Oneida to the pursuing Americans revealed that he was the sole survivor of a group of 20 German soldiers.

IV
—————

The Patriots Advance into the Western Theatre

—————

As events were unfolding on both Carleton Island and in Oswego, farther to the east at Fort Stanwix, in the vicinity of modern-day Rome, New York, other major events were underway.

In March 1777, Major General Philip Schuyler, commander of the Northern Department, ordered Colonel Peter Gansevoort[1] to Fort Stanwix. Gansevoort's mission was to strengthen the fort, and extend his mobile defense perimeter—if possible—northwestward to Oswego,[2] defend the Mohawk Valley, and halt any British attempts to advance from the west and penetrate deep into the newly forming New York State.

Fort Stanwix stood between the Mohawk River and Wood Creek. Between these two water routes existed a portage road known as the "Oneida Carry." Boats and canoes were manually transported over this "carry" from one waterway to another, not unlike the modern practice of switching trains to continue onward to one's destination. The Oneida Carry was a vital strategic spot, the control of which could block an opponent's water transit route between western and eastern New York. Prior to 1758, four forts existed in the same area: Fort Craven and Fort Williams stood on the western bend of the Mohawk River; Fort Newport stood on the southern edge of Wood Creek immediately adjacent the portage road; and Fort Bull stood one-and-a-half miles southwest of Fort Newport on Wood Creek.

Further control is what motivated the British to construct Fort Stanwix in 1758. Standing right in the midst of this portage, all traffic could be halted to and from Wood Creek and the Mohawk River, as well as into and out of the Mohawk Valley.

Constructed by British Army General John Stanwix at a cost of 60,000 pounds, Fort Stanwix was a large fort, as well as a marvel of military engineering.[3] Prior to the Revolutionary War, the fort had never experienced any action, although British troops stationed there were able to effectively monitor the critical portage and river system during the French and Indian War. Following the collapse of French rule in 1763, the British withdrew their military garrison from Fort Stanwix; however, the fort was occasionally utilized as a center for Indian affairs. In 1768, for example, the Iroquois and British government concluded the Boundary Line Treaty there, which cleared the way for further Colonial expansion to the west.

With the eruption of the American Revolutionary War in 1775, America's Continental Congress, realizing the importance of Fort Stanwix, ordered the Northern Department to refortify the site.[4] The Americans were also urged by the Oneida Indians to defend Fort Stanwix[5] because rumors of a British attack via Lake Ontario were rife well before 1777.

Therefore, General Schuyler was ordered to repair and strengthen the old fort and erect additional works, if necessary, along the Mohawk River. In response, General Schuyler and Northern Army headquarters dispatched Colonel Elias Dayton to repair the fort and prepare additional defense positions. However, the Colonel, who arrived at Fort Stanwix on 23 July 1776 with his 3rd New Jersey Regiment of the Continental Line from the Northern Army, did not stay there very long. Some work was done on the site, but it was far from completion. Dayton's situation was complicated by the fact that the personnel serving in the 3rd New Jersey were under a contract and their service time was to expire on 31 December 1776.

Knowing this, on 5 October 1776, Schuyler wrote to Colonel Samuel Elmore who, with his Connecticut soldiers, was in the German Flats, warning him that his unit might have to move to Fort Stanwix to replace the 3rd New Jersey and prepare the site for defense. On 9 October the order was issued, and on 17 October 1776, Colonel Elmore arrived at the fort. Elmore's unit, however, only had the strength of a weak battalion of about 200 soldiers. Upon their arrival at Fort Stanwix they realized there was not enough cold-weather housing and the first snows had already begun to fall. Therefore, Elmore released a part of his battalion back to the German Flats to winter near Burnet's Field. Concerned about Elmore in Fort Stanwix, on 21 December 1776, General Schuyler ordered General Henry Glen, the Northern Army's Quartermaster, to immediately send the garrison an eight-month supply of beef, flour, soap, and candles. On 28 December 1776, the Continental Congress again ordered: "That Fort Stanwix be strengthened, & other fortifications be made at proper places near the Mohawk River. . ." The Congress regarded this as an urgent matter when they added, "to be executed this winter."[6]

At the end of March 1777, General Schuyler ordered Colonel Peter Gansevoort to Fort Stanwix, and he arrived on 3 May with an advance party of about 25 soldiers of the 3rd New York Continental Regiment[7] and assumed command of the fort. Approximately a week later, Colonel Elmore departed.[8] Several weeks after Gansevoort's arrival, on 29 May,[9] Lieutenant Colonel Marinus Willett[10] arrived with the bulk of the 3rd New York and a small element from the 9th Massachusetts Continental Regiment. Willett and Gansevoort were not only ardent Patriots but were both well known for their aggressiveness. Knowing that such leadership was especially needed in the central/western wilderness region, this was undoubtedly why they were chosen by Schuyler for the dangerous command.

By the end of May, Gansevoort was positioned in Fort Stanwix with the 3rd New York Continental Regiment (minus one company), with a strength of 400 soldiers;[11] 50 men from the Massachusetts 9th Regiment, commanded by Lieutenant Colonel James Wesson;[12] and 100 New York militiamen.[13] Approximately 550 marched westward with Willett, though various other sources cite a strength of 750.[14] At the close of May, Gansevoort's troop strength probably stood at about 600.

En route to Fort Stanwix in late April 1777, Colonel Gansevoort knew that he had a difficult mission to perform. And time, always a critical factor, was not on his side. Upon entering the fort the Patriot commander immediately saw that despite some efforts to improve the place, hardly anything had been accomplished. The Americans immediately went to work, putting right the effects of fourteen years of neglect.

Gansevoort renamed the installation "Fort Schuyler," but the name never stuck. Throughout 1777 and the entire Revolutionary War, almost everyone continued to refer to it as Fort Stanwix. During this time, other forts were also repaired or constructed in the Mohawk Valley and adjacent regions, and one of these, constructed in the vicinity of present day Utica, New York, was also named Fort Schuyler. To prevent confusion, even if unofficially, Fort Stanwix's name remained. (Hereafter, the fort will only be referred to as Fort Stanwix.)

Upon arrival, the Americans found that heavy snows had collapsed roofs and walls; trees and brush were growing around and inside the compound; while wild animals inhabited the buildings. Portions of the exterior walls had weakened, and here and there had even begun to collapse, and stagnant water filled the fort's wells.

The vegetation around the fort needed to be cleared in order to create open fields of fire in case of attack. It was necessary for fireplaces and living quarters to be cleaned, remortared, and even rebuilt. In addition, the ramparts had to be strengthened. Aside from all this, security and patrols still needed to be maintained, training had to take place, and communications with the Northern Army in Albany had to be kept secure.

When Colonel Gansevoort was ordered to Fort Stanwix, he was also instructed to rehabilitate the old Fort Oswego as well. However upon arrival at Fort Stanwix, Gansevoort quickly concluded that shifting some of his troops to Oswego, some 60 miles away, would not only be positioning them deeper into a wilderness region—thus stretching them thin and exposing them to danger—but would also significantly weaken his entire force. Realizing he needed every soldier that he could muster, he kept his command together in Fort Stanwix. In the end, Gansevoort's reasoning proved correct because had any personnel been dispatched to Oswego, they undoubtedly would have been lost to the British and Indian confluence there, and during St. Leger's investment of Stanwix, there would have been inadequate troops to defend the fort.

As the defenders of Fort Stanwix were rapidly preparing for war, unknown to them, on Carleton Island, General St. Leger was also undertaking preparations. And his first key objective was Fort Stanwix.

Notes
1   Peter Gansevoort was born in Albany, in the British Colony of New York on 17 July 1749. In 1775, with the rank of major, he participated with the

Patriot expedition to Canada. In 1776, he was promoted to full colonel. In 1778, the Congressional Congress formally thanked him for his efforts, especially at Fort Stanwix. In 1781, the State of New York promoted him to Brigadier General. On 2 July 1812, he passed away at age 62.

2   Major Tharratt Gilbert Best, *A Soldier of Oriskany* (Boonville, NY: The Willard Press, 1935), p. 11.

3   Ibid. "Historic Structure Reports" in Luzader, *Fort Stanwix*, pp. 121–200.

4   Mark M. Boatner, "Fort Stanwix" in *Landmarks of the American Revolution*, p. 248. According to Lossing, Vol. 1, pp. 236–237.

5   Graymount, p. 177.

6   Boatner, p. 248.

7   The 3rd New York Regiment of 1777 (not to be confused with the 3rd New York Regiment of 1775) was organized between November 1776 and early 1777. From 21 November 1776 until 1 January 1781, the 3rd New York Regiment was commanded by Colonel Peter Gansevoort. During the Wilderness War of 1777, this regiment served from the Highlands to the western edge of the wilderness. On 1 January 1781, it was disbanded by a General Order. Its officers were incorporated into the 1st New York Regiment of 1775 and the 1st New York Regiment of 1776. See also Fred Anderson Berg, *Encyclopedia of Continental Army Units. Battalions, Regiments and Independent Corps* (Harrisburg, PA: Stackpole Books, 1972), p. 85. See also Luzader, *The Saratoga Campaign of 1777*, p. 31.

8   Luzader, *Fort Stanwix*, pp. 23–25; Graymont, p. 45. One of the reasons Elmore's unit was ordered out of the fort was because Northern Army headquarters wanted to build his independent battalion to a strength of 350–400 and be trained for special needs. Repositioned in the vicinity of Albany, Elmore's battalion was strengthened, and during the Wilderness War of 1777 played a vital role as a rapid reaction force.

9   29 May 1777 is when William Willett, the son of Colonel Willett, cited as the date his father arrived to Fort Stanwix to defend the fort. This date is also cited by Colonel Willett in his transcript of memoirs relating to the Revolutionary War. See *A Narrative of the Military Actions of Colonel Marinus Willett* (New York: G. & C. & H. Carvill, 1831. Reprinted New York: New York Times & Arno Press, 1969), p. 42. Other sources cite 28 May as the date of the arrival of the main body. See Luzader, *Fort Stanwix*, p. 27; and Private William Colbrath, *Days of Siege. A Journal of the Siege of Fort Stanwix in 1777* (New York: Publishing Center for Cultural Resources, 1983), pp. 11–12.

10   Born on 31 July 1740 in Jamaica, Queens County, on Long Island, Marinus Willett was the son of a farmer. In 1758, he joined the British Army and served with General Abercrombie in the disastrous battle at Fort Carillon (Ticonderoga) on Lake Champlain. Shortly after, Willett succumbed to an illness and he was transferred to recuperate to the newly built Fort Stanwix. Returning to New York City in the aftermath of the French and Indian War,

Willett enrolled in The King's College, from where he eventually graduated.

Prior to the Revolutionary War Willett began to favor the Patriots. In late 1775, he joined a militia unit and, in 1776, the Northern Army. He served in the Patriot expedition to Canada. In Canada, Willett proved to be a highly aggressive commander who quickly won the trust of his men. Transferred to the Highlands in 1776, Willett served in the 3rd New York Continental Regiment of 1777 as Gansevoort's assistant and was second in command. Willett quickly turned the 3rd New York into a crack outfit and at Peekskill in March 1777, successfully repulsed a heavy British attack. Willett also served at Fishkill, and in addition to continuing to train, was assisting in constructing a fortifications system on Constitution Island and other sites in what in near future years would become the nation's Military Academy at West Point. Willett played a crucial role in achieving for the Patriots a victory in the Wilderness War of 1777. In 1778–79, he served with General Washington and fought at the Battle of Monmouth.

After the Revolutionary War, Willett served as New York City's Chief-of-Police. In 1897, he was elected the city's mayor. In the 1820s, he served as President of the Electoral College. Very interested in social services and the needs of its citizens, Willett established relief centers and a city medical clinic and hospital to assist the needy. He donated much of his own money for this center and was involved with it until his peaceful death on 23 August 1830 at the age of 91.

11 The 3rd New York Regiment was a combat-experienced regiment. The regiment was raised in the Highlands and many of its recruits hailed from the region and the towns of Fishkill and Poughkeepsie. Initially, the regiment was posted on and around Constitution Island in the Highlands (now a part of West Point, New York). In March 1777, Willett commanded the unit because Colonel Gansevoort, its top commanding officer, was not present. On 22 March 1777, as the regiment was conducting regimental drills, a rider suddenly appeared. It was an express order from Brigadier General Alexander McDougall who was the commanding officer of the Northern Army's southern front, which encompassed the entire Highlands. General McDougall ordered Lieutenant Colonel Willett to immediately march to the high ground overlooking Peekskill, New York, which was coming under attack by a British force directly from New York City. Immediately the regiment moved from its parade field to that location. Linking up with General McDougall at about 3 p.m., Willett assessed the situation and proposed to attack immediately. General McDougall, however, opposed the idea. The commander of the Highlands wanted to wait for the arrival of a called-up militia unit.

Finally, General McDougall consented. The militia unit had still not appeared and it was getting dark. With McDougall advancing on Willett's left, Willett advanced forward. Although Willett's regiment had to overcome two sizable fences posing as obstacles, his attack was well executed. Willett's troops launched a successful bayonet charge. For the loss of two killed and a handful wounded, Willett repulsed the British. Amongst the items recovered on the field of battle was a British officer's blue camlet cape. This cape, secured by Captain Abraham Swarthout, a company commander in the 3rd New York, would later be taken to Fort Stanwix where its cloth would be utilized in sewing a flag.

On 23 March, Willett returned to Fort Constitution. He remained there until 18 May recruiting and training personnel. On that day, the 3rd New York Regiment was ordered by the Northern Army's headquarters to move immediately to Fort Stanwix. Placing the entire regiment on three sloops, he reached Albany on 21 May. Transferring his force onto bateaux, Lieutenant Colonel Willett reached Fort Stanwix on 28/9 May 1777. Lowenthal, *Marinus Willett. Defender of the Northern Frontier*, pp. 21–23. (Hereafter cited as *Marinus Willett.*)

12 Luzader, *The Saratoga Campaign*, p. 31. Lieutenant Colonel James Wesson, however, was not among the soldiers. According to Lieutenant Colonel Fairfax Downey, *Indian Wars of the U.S. Army, 1776–1865* (New York: Doubleday and Company, 1962), p. 13, "The 3rd New York and the 9th Massachusetts Regiments were the backbone of Fort Stanwix's garrison." (Hereafter cited as *Indian Wars.*) At this time, a part of the 9th Massachusetts had arrived at Fort Stanwix. Likewise, one company from the 3rd New York, commanded by Captain Thomas DeWitt, remained behind in Fort Dayton. DeWitt's mission was to conduct security operations. In short time, DeWitt and his company would rejoin their parent regiment at Fort Stanwix just before the arrival of St. Leger, and participate in the fort's defense. As for Lieutenant Colonel Wesson, he was now commanding Fort Dayton and, along with a number of Continental soldiers from the 9th Massachusetts, would assist in protecting the Mohawk Valley. It should be noted that during the siege of Fort Stanwix, elements of the 9th Massachusetts remained in the vicinity of Fort Dayton.

13 These militiamen hailed mostly from the Mohawk Valley. A large number of them, however, soon departed to return home. Though it is known that a number were caught in the siege, the greater number of them had left before St. Leger's arrival.

14 This strength would rise. Initially, approximately 500 marched to Fort Stanwix in May and, upon their arrival, were greeted by Colonel Gansevoort, the fort's commanding officer. But this strength also included the 100 militiamen, most of whom, as mentioned above, would soon depart. But on 30 July, 150 soldiers arrived followed by another 200 on 2 August. Among the returnees was the company commanded by Captain DeWitt with its strength of 50 soldiers. (DeWitt's company belonged to the 3rd New York Regiment). Hence, why various authors cite a figure of approximately 750 defended Fort Stanwix. Ward, *The War of the Revolution*, Vol. II, p. 483; Leckie, *The Wars of America*, p. 173, cites "about 750 men under Colonel Peter Gan-

sevoort and Lieutenant Colonel Marinus Willett." Martha Byrd, *Saratoga*, p. 71, cites 750 Continentals; and Stone, *The Campaign*, p. 168, cites "The command of Colonel Gansevoort now consisted of seven hundred and fifty men, all told."

V

St. Leger Assembles His Army

Prior to St. Leger's departure from Lachine, Colonel Daniel Claus had conferred with Sir Guy Johnson at Fort Niagara, near Buffalo in western New York.[1] In his discussion with Sir Johnson, Claus questioned the reports that, "Fort Stanwix was a picketed place with only 60 men manning the position."[2] Claus informed Sir Johnson that it had recently been brought to his attention by Colonel John Butler, the commanding officer of the Loyalists at Fort Niagara, that Fort Stanwix's troop strength was significantly higher than believed, and that the fort was undergoing major repairs. How Butler obtained this information is unknown, perhaps it was obtained by one of his scouts.

Doubting Sir Johnson's reports and desperate to find the truth, Claus met with a small party of Iroquois warriors, mostly Cayugas, outside of Fort Niagara on Wednesday, 18 June.[3] Amongst the Indians stood Odiserunery and Hare. They and their ten warriors were tall, strong, and adorned with war paint. Claus told them he wanted them to go to Fort Stanwix, scout it out, and capture four or five men from the fort. They should then return to Oswego with their prisoners.[4]

Having understood their mission, Odiserunery and Hare signaled to the others to follow them, and the group quickly disappeared like wildcats into the wilderness.

Claus was not the only one seeking information. So, too, was Colonel Peter Gansevoort. In June, a man from Canada was arrested in the Mohawk Valley as a "spy." He had revealed "that a detachment of British troops, Canadians and Indians, was to penetrate the country by way of Oswego and the Mohawk Valley to join Burgoyne when he reached Albany."[5] So Gansevoort knew that sizable numbers of Indians, augmented with Loyalists, were assembling in Oswego, and their numbers were growing daily. As often was the case whenever and wherever Indians congregated, Loyalists and British were nearby. Knowing that it was just a matter of time before Fort Stanwix would be attacked and that his position—deep in New York's wilderness—was a precarious one, it was imperative for Gansevoort to know as much as he could about enemy strengths, dispositions, and intentions. Likewise, information about their commanders and leaders would also benefit the defenders. And, of course, any information obtained by Gansevoort would be immediately passed on to the Northern Army's high command in Albany. It was imperative for General Schuyler and the other commanders to know what was happening.

On 28 June, Gansevoort met with an Oneida[6] warrior, Ahnyero, to ask him to undertake a vital mission. A lifelong resident of the Mohawk Valley, Ahnyero was, by profession, a blacksmith. He also had another name: Thomas Spencer. Because Colonel Gansevoort himself had long been a resident of the Mohawk Valley, the two had known each other for many years and were close friends. Gansevoort knew he could trust Spencer to bring him accurate information.

Understanding the situation, Spencer volunteered to go to Oswego. Dressed in Indian clothing he could easily infiltrate the crowds assembling in Oswego, and gather whatever information was needed. Spencer was fluent in Iroquois and French, and though half-white, knew that he could fit in. Gansevoort was concerned for Spencer's safety if he was captured by St. Leger's men, or Brant's, but the half-breed was adamant he would not be caught. They agreed that Spencer would send back runners to Fort Stanwix with any information he gained.[7]

News of the fall of Fort Ticonderoga to Burgoyne's army reached St. Leger on 17 July, eleven days after it happened.[8] Why it took so long for St. Leger receive the news has never been explained. While the wilderness did pose an obstacle to communications, news and information among the Patriots moved much more swiftly: no matter how far a message, an urgent letter, directive, or order had to go, in most cases—at best within four or five days—it was delivered. Unfortunately for the British, they never developed an effective communications system amongst their various commands.[9] In the end, this weakness would be one of the main factors in their defeat in 1777.

Having been informed of the fall of Fort Ticonderoga, St. Leger decided to move rapidly. Possibly, he even harbored thoughts of reaching Albany before Burgoyne. To increase morale, he announced to his troops the fall of the famous Fort Ticonderoga, site of a horrific battle during the French and Indian War. Determined to reach Albany as fast as possible, St. Leger organized an advance guard and issued orders that it was to depart at 4a.m. on 18 July;[10] he also ordered all of his commanders to be ready to move on one hour's notice.[11]

In addition to issuing orders to his advance party, St. Leger began to provide guidance to his remaining force. Provisions for forty days were to be immediately loaded into the bateaux. Lieutenant Collerton was ordered to prepare and load the artillery ammunition and to issue 50 cartridges to each of the first 500 departing soldiers. To feed the force, bakers were assigned to each unit with orders to prepare a six-day supply of bread. Unit commanders were to notify the deputy commissary general of any specific needs or essentials required by them no later than 10 p.m.

Yet, on the very day that the confident St. Leger was preparing to depart, General Nicholas Herkimer was issuing a draft proclamation. Herkimer intended to raise a strong militia force to counter the British invasion.

At 4 a.m. on Saturday, 19 July, amid the rising mist on Carleton Island, General St. Leger's advance guard boarded their bateaux and began to row out. The advance consisted of the entire officer corps of the 8th Foot Regiment,[12] all of the officers from the 34th Foot Regiment,[13] 80 soldiers from each of the two regiments,[14] a number of Canadian Rangers,[15] and a number of Canadian Indians from the Mississauga tribe along with some Indians from the Iroquois Confederacy.[16]

Spearheading the advance guard was Captain Potts, an experienced British officer. The plan was that the advance guard would deploy, and then several days later St. Leger's entire force would depart. The two forces would rendezvous in Oswego, and the combined force would advance eastward to Fort Stanwix to capture the fort, strike into the critical Mohawk Valley to secure it for the Crown, and, somewhere in the vicinity of Albany, link up with Burgoyne and Howe. Following the link-up, St. Leger would place himself and his entire command under General Howe.

However, based on what he thought he knew, St. Leger now decided that perhaps it would be best to attack Fort Stanwix as soon as possible. He decided that going to Oswego would waste time, and so he planned that instead he would now land his Carleton Island force at the mouth of the Little Salmon River.[17] In the meantime, a part of the force from Oswego would link up with him at the mouth of the river. Once united, the force would proceed up the south branch of the Little Salmon, which would take them southeast towards Fort Stanwix. St. Leger could then either travel a short distance south overland to Wood Creek[18] to follow it directly east toward Stanwix, or just march through the wilderness in a southeasterly direction toward the fort. The rest of the force at Oswego would proceed toward Fort Stanwix to rendezvous there with the advance.

St. Leger's new plan was based on the information that Fort Stanwix was weakly manned and fortified. He reasoned that he would only need his infantry, some of the Indians, and Loyalist rangers. Everything else, such as the artillery and baggage accompanying him from Carleton Island, would continue down to Oswego. With light forces, he could move rapidly through the wilderness to conduct a quick surprise attack on Fort Stanwix to capture its weak garrison.[19] Afterwards, St. Leger's guns, wagons, most of the horses, provisions, and remaining personnel coming in from Oswego would link up with him, and with his command united and strengthened, he would then attack into the Mohawk Valley.

Theoretically speaking, the plan was excellent. But before he could proceed with his new plan, a series of problems arose which forced him to revert back to his original one. Abandoning the plan wasted time, and St. Leger would soon learn the tragic consequences that arose from lost time—especially in the wilderness.

Before St. Leger could depart, Colonel Claus suddenly appeared at Carleton Island.[20] Accompanied by a group of about 150 Indians, he also brought something of special value to St. Leger: prisoners. The small group of warriors led by Odiserunery and Hare dispatched to Fort Stanwix in June had returned to Oswego with several Patriot soldiers. After debriefing the Iroquois scouts and interrogating the prisoners, Claus was unhappy with what he had learned. Feeling that perhaps St. Leger himself should hear the news firsthand, Claus canoed the prisoners from Oswego up to Carleton Island.

One of the prisoners was a Lieutenant Caspar, who told St. Leger of the current state of affairs at Fort Stanwix. But the British commander refused to believe that almost 700 soldiers, mostly regular Continental troops, were now manning the fort and that it was in the process of being repaired. The 700 soldiers, combined with any militiamen and sympathetic Indian warriors who might also have appeared since the lieutenant's capture, would make a sizeable force. Angered about what he was hearing, St. Leger threatened the young man with torture, attempting to force the truth from him. Despite the threats, Caspar was sure of his facts.[21]

Claus informed St. Leger that in previous interrogations of Lieutenant Caspar, he had learned that the current commander of Fort Stanwix was Colonel Gansevoort. But more disturbingly, he had learned that the Patriots not only knew that the British were coming, but that they had identified Fort Ontario at Oswego as a staging base, and St. Leger as the commanding officer. St. Leger wanted to know how Gansevoort could know all this detailed information, but the lieutenant denied any knowledge of its source. St. Leger then interrogated the rest of the prisoners, but they all corroborated the information the lieutenant had given.

Colonel Claus, his warriors, and their prisoners were not the only ones to arrive at Carleton Island. Following the first large Canadian defection, additional Canadians had been quickly recruited and dispatched to join the assembling force. More Indians, mostly from the Canadian Mississagua tribe, also appeared. But because no formal records were ever kept, and the Indians came and went as they pleased, it was difficult to keep a proper accountability of their strength and whereabouts.

On 19 July, within a day of the delivery of his prisoners, Claus was ordered by St. Leger to return to Oswego.[22] With him went Sir John Johnson with his regiment of Royal Greens, the Canadians who had just arrived,[23] and most of the Indians on the island.

On 22 July St. Leger departed Carleton Island and proceeded toward the mouth of the Little Salmon River. As his force rowed to the mouth of the stream, they passed a tiny island covered in trees and brush.[24] Pulling their boats and bateaux up on the shore of Lake Ontario, they didn't worry about anyone watching, as they were operating deep in the wilderness, far away from any people.

But on this little island lived one man, Mr. Silas Towne. He was much more than just a local settler; he was a fur trapper, hunter, and woodsman. Towne knew the wilderness thoroughly, from the eastern shores of Lake Ontario to Lake Champlain. He knew the shortcuts through the woods into the Mohawk Valley, and—a true woodsman—he could move quietly and swiftly. He was also a patriot, sympathetic to the American cause. So as St. Leger's force rowed past, Towne noted everything with his eagle eyes, registering how many soldiers, Indians, and support personnel he saw, and how many cannon, bateaux, and canoes. He noted their uniforms, weapons, and equipment—nothing escaped him.

As St. Leger journeyed southward, more Indian warriors were arriving in Oswego. Sangerachta, the Seneca chief, arrived with 200 of his warriors.[25] In addition, Joseph Brant gathered up 300 more from several tribes.[26] Other warriors, individually, in pairs, and in small parties, also appeared. Together with those who had arrived previously, an impressive strength of no fewer than 800–1,000 warriors were now assembled.[27]

Yet, upon arrival, the issues supposedly resolved previously in Irondequoit Bay and in Oswego regarding the Indian role in the campaign and what materiel support they were to receive resurfaced once again. Dissatisfaction and disillusionment continued to run high among many of the warriors.

In an effort to quell the Indian discontent, Brant, Claus, Colonel Butler, his son Walter, and Johnson—who had just arrived from Carleton Island with his Royal Greens—assured the Indian warriors that they had nothing to fear, and that in short time their needs would be taken care of.

But just as the Indians were being brought under control, from out of nowhere, thousands of raven birds mysteriously appeared, darkening the sky over the old Fort Ontario for several days. In Indian folklore, the raven is perceived as a messenger of death; indeed during this period many Americans—both native and of European descent—viewed the raven as the Devil's servant delivering death and doom. A mystical bird, the raven is revered for its strong spirit and bravery. Some American Indian traditions respect the raven as a symbol of creation and natural order, but even then, the bird is still regarded as an omen of misfortune. The presence of so many of these birds began to unnerve the assembled warriors. In turn, the premonitions of the Indians began to impact negatively the Loyalists in Oswego. Ugly feelings of defeat, doom, and death set in.[28]

Captain Tice, who served as an aide to General St. Leger, arrived in Oswego on 24 July.[29] He came from the mouth of the Little Salmon River where St. Leger's former Carleton Island force was now located, and brought a message for Colonel Claus from the general.[30] The communiqué ordered Claus to take a sizable number of Oswego's Indians and a number of the Loyalists immediately to the mouth of the Little Salmon, where they were to meet up with the main body. Tice would guide Colonel Claus to the rendezvous site. The rest of the force gathered at Oswego—Sir John Johnson's Royal Greens, Butler's Loyalist rangers, the artillery, most of the Canadians, and a number of the Indians—would proceed from Oswego eastward to Fort Stanwix to link up with the rest. St. Leger stipulated that Colonel Butler was to command the forces marching eastward. As for equipping the Indians, this would be done in the location of the Three Rivers where the Seneca, Oneida, and Oswego Rivers merge together.[31]

Refusing to believe the Patriot prisoners, and still convinced that Fort Stanwix was weakly manned, St. Leger had concluded that he could capture the fort with light forces minus the artillery. In fact, he thought he would not even need the bulk of his Indian and Loyalist strength. Realizing that the larger and heavier Oswego-based force would require more time to move through the wilderness, St. Leger anticipated a link-up shortly after his capture of the fort. Then, with his entire force marching eastward, he would advance through the Mohawk Valley. En route, he would gather up additional Loyalists, eventually marching into Albany at the head of a strong column, impressing Burgoyne and Howe.

Before Tice left Carleton Island for Oswego, the twenty-five or so remaining Indians accompanying St. Leger became not only argumentative but threatening.[32] In an effort to placate them, he ordered that rum be issued, as he believed the alcohol would have a relaxing effect. Unfortunately for St. Leger, the opposite occurred. As Claus later acknowledged in his September report:

> The Indians with him were very drunk and riotous, and Captain Tice, who was his [St. Leger's] messenger, informed me that the brigadier ordered the Indians a quart of rum apiece which made them all beastly drunk.[33]

In the meantime, as St. Leger was awaiting the arrival of Colonel Claus and Joseph Brant and attempting to control the Indians at the mouth of the Little Salmon River, Captain Tice was experiencing trouble in Oswego. After receiving St. Leger's message, Claus immediately began to organize a sizable force to proceed northward to the mouth of the Little Salmon. Claus ordered Butler to take the remaining Indians and Loyalists to the site of the Three Rivers, and to to wait there until Claus appeared.[34] But as Claus and Butler prepared to depart, Brant spoke up.

Mindful of the mood of the Indians gathered at Oswego, Brant urged Claus not to go, fearing that if Claus departed for the Little Salmon River, many of the Indians would leave. He felt that if St. Leger arrived with his entire force in Oswego, it would truly impress the Indians, and if St. Leger would issue them some extra gifts, it would encourage the Indians to remain and support the British offensive. He argued that St. Leger was not far away, and that it would not be difficult for him to come to Oswego, and in doing so solve the problems that were incentivizing the Indian warriors.[35] Agreeing with Brant's logic, Claus ordered everyone to stay put. Unable to entice Claus into departing, Captain Tice reboarded his canoe to return to St. Leger.

On hearing that Claus was not coming, St. Leger was furious. But he realized he had no alternative but to head to Oswego, and issued the order to pull out. As the dark skies engulfed the peaceful shoreline of Lake Ontario, the remainder of St. Leger's force rowed away to Oswego. Unknown to St. Leger, their actions were still being monitored. Shortly after the last boat had left, Silas Towne moved. Cautiously, ensuring that if anyone had remained behind he would not be seen, he moved through the water to the rocky shoreline and hid in the bushes until he was entirely certain that no one was around.

Finally satisfied that it was safe, Towne slowly stood and set off at a crouched run into the thick forest, aiming for his next destination— Fort Stanwix.

Approaching the Oswego shoreline at dawn on 25 July, General Barry St. Leger was still fuming about Claus' refusal to move to the mouth of the Little Salmon River. As his boat neared the shore, a cacophony of shrill cries and war whoops suddenly rang out. Amid the screams and chants, muskets were fired into the air. Whether the reception was spontaneous or planned is unknown, but it served its purpose. As St. Leger's troops rowed to the shore, they were impressed by the performance, just as the watching Indians and Loyalists were impressed by the arriving British force. Finally brought together, St. Leger's assembled force was an awesome sight.

Amongst those celebrating stood the entire Indian and Loyalist leadership: Colonel Daniel Claus; Colonel John Butler and his son, Captain Walter Butler; Sir John Johnson; Major Geofrey Watts and his brother, Captain Stephen Watts; Captain Angus McDonald; Lieutenant Donald J. (John) McDonald; Chief (Captain) Joseph Brant; Chief Ghalto; Seneca leaders Chief Gu-cinge and Chief Blacksnake; Onondaga leader Chief Cornplanter;[36] Chief Sangerachta; and Seneca leader Chief Gisu-gwatoh. However, one important figure, Sir Guy Johnson, was not present.

Citing "poor health" as an excuse, Guy Johnson, who was intended to accompany St. Leger's force, stayed behind in Canada. But perhaps this was for the better because in the eyes of many, Sir Guy was nothing but a problematic, hot-tempered minister who was not only failing the Indians but also the entire British leadership. He had been deputy to his uncle, Sir William Johnson, and had become Superintendant of Indian Affairs upon the latter's death in 1774. Unlike his predecessor, Sir William, Guy Johnson was a weak and incompetent administrator. Since late 1774, supplies to the Indians had been slow in coming and the supplies that were provided were never enough. Sir Guy was also corrupt, and so could never properly account for his expenditures. He was also a drunk, and when in the bottle was totally obnoxious. Joseph Brant had had firsthand evidence of this on 27 February 1777 when, desperately seeking supplies, he had personally visited Sir Guy in Montreal. Nothing was accomplished; Sir Guy was not only highly intoxicated and very argumentative, but also belligerent. Unable to reason with him, Brant left, but from that day on, he despised Sir Guy.[37]

To a large extent the Loyalist leadership was actually a family affair. Sir John Johnson was the son of Sir William Johnson, who had recently passed away in 1774, with Guy being William's nephew (and John's cousin). Joseph Brant was of course related to Sir John Johnson via his sister, Molly. Colonel Claus was married to one of Sir William Johnson's daughters. Major and Captain Watts, via various relatives, were related to both the Butlers and Sir John Johnson.

Stepping onto the rocky shoreline with his adjutant-general, Major Wesley Ancrom, St. Leger was thrilled with this reception. Immediately approached by various Loyalist and Indian leaders such as Colonel Daniel Claus, St. Leger was introduced to the key players who would accompany him on his expedition to Albany. He was also briefed on the current situation, and Claus explained why he had been unable to follow the order to relocate some of the Oswego-based force to the mouth of the Little Salmon River. Understanding the situation, St. Leger decided not to assail Claus. Though probably still unhappy that some time had been lost, and in terms of distance his advance to Fort Stanwix from Oswego would now be farther than from the mouth of the Little Salmon, St. Leger was still confident of success.

Impatient to depart eastward, St. Leger ordered that an assembly be held that evening, and everyone was to attend. Information needed to be disseminated, but St. Leger also reasoned that such a congregation would enable his British and German soldiers, Loyalists, and Indian warriors to get to know each other better. It was also on 25 July that St. Leger officially designated Colonel Claus to command the Indians.[38]

That evening, at around 8 p.m., the force assembled in the open field adjacent to the old fort. A makeshift stage had been constructed, and throughout that evening various Loyalist leaders and Indian chiefs spoke, and high-sounding proclamations were made. St. Leger also issued some gifts to the Indians. Highly appreciated by the warriors, this gesture was especially welcomed by those pressing for loyalty to the British Crown. In addition to dispensing gifts, promises were made that more would be forthcoming. Intoxicated with their gifts and pleased that additional presents were en route, and finally satisfied with the promises made them about the campaign ahead, the Indians howled with delight and war whoops. The screams and howls emitting from the thousand Indians—bolstered by the cheers, chants, and gunfire of the Loyalists and European soldiers—could have been heard far and wide over the peaceful waters of Lake Ontario.

Following another chorus of shouts, screams, and war whoops, Colonel John Butler stood up. Fluent in the Iroquois language, including several of its dialects, the senior Butler commanded attention from the gathered warriors. Raising his arms and hands upward for silence, he began to speak, as his son, Walter, stood nearby. Despite the fact that father and son would be campaigning together, it was no secret that their relationship was not the best. With silence achieved, the elder Butler began to speak. In simple words, supported with gestures, he told the assembled warriors that the army was marching on Fort Stanwix, but stressed that the warriors were simply expected to watch the fort fall. They were not expected to take part in the attack. Once the fort had fallen, the Mohawk Valley would be open, and the warriors could then make war on the inhabitants however they wished, with "twenty pounds worth of gifts from the King" for every scalp.[39]

Madness filled the air; screams shattered the tranquility of the night. As the warriors raved, numerous tomahawks and spears were raised upward.

Watching Butler carefully as he spoke was a warrior, Cohdah, known as "Colonel" Louis. Half-black and half-Indian, Louis' father was a trapper of African-American descent who married an Indian woman in the wilderness. Following in his father's footsteps, Louis also trapped. Well over six feet in height, Louis was physically very strong. Agile, as most trappers were, he also knew the entire wilderness, for he had trapped from the Adirondacks to the Ohio Valley. A free man, he was proud of his status and lifestyle. But along with other trappers, Louis had also experienced his share of hardships under British rule, especially in recent years.

Under Dutch rule, Louis' ancestors had managed to secure freedom and live as they pleased. British laws, however, had restricted much of that liberty. Louis was unable to marry outside his race, possess a gun, own property, or operate a business. True, within the wilderness, Louis could—as his father did previously—avoid most of the new laws. But when the British passed the Appalachian Act of 1763, Louis and the other trappers were tremendously affected. In fact, the numerous laws and regulations consistently imposed by the Crown were destroying his entire way of life. In the true sense, he was nothing but a slave under British colonial rule.

As he listened to the words of John Butler, Louis knew that they were lies. He knew that the Butlers were nothing but pawns of the British Crown and Empire. They were there only to exploit the Indian and those whites stupid enough to follow them. Louis also knew that the Butlers despised blacks, and both supported slavery.

Louis was so deep in thought that at first he did not even feel the Oneida scout Thomas Spencer's hand upon his shoulder attempting to attract his attention. Louis and Spencer were old and close friends, virtually brothers. In fact, their mothers were from the same tribe. Spencer asked Louis if he was ready and Louis slowly nodded.

As Butler began to conclude his speech, amid a frenzy of war whoops and screams, Louis retreated into the trees and set a quick course for Fort Stanwix. Along with the information brought by Silas Towne, Louis' observations would prove vital for Colonel Gansevoort and the defenders of the Mohawk Valley. Knowing that his friend would be at Fort Stanwix in a couple of days, Spencer prepared to stay with the British-led forces until they commenced their march, spying on them for a little longer.

A few days later, at Fort Stanwix, Colonel Gansevoort had debriefed Silas Towne, "Colonel" Louis, and the other messengers previously dispatched by Spencer, and he was satisfied. At last, he truly knew what the British were conspiring and what his men would be up against.

Prior to the American Civil War, an intelligence service did not formally exist within the American army. By and large, the gathering and spreading of intelligence was solely a commander's responsibility. While General George Washington would, for example, share what intelligence he had with his subordinates, matters pertaining to intelligence were still largely a local or regional commander's problem.

For example, if a commander such as Colonel Gansevoort received an order to fortify and defend a place like Fort Stanwix, he would have to carry out the order. He would be provided with supplies and reinforcements as best as possible, but when it came to intelligence he would have to seek out his own information.

In the event that General Schuyler or even General Washington received some bit of information that they reasoned would benefit Gansevoort, they would surely pass it on. Unfortunately, neither within General Washington's main Continental Army nor within the entire Northern Army did an intelligence gathering and briefing cell formally exist. Therefore, the onus was on local leaders such as Gansevoort to collect their own intelligence. How they would utilize it and to whom it would be passed on was left to their discretion.

Though no formal intelligence service existed within the Northern Army and the Northern Department, information did pour in. From New York City, Albany, New Hampshire, and Vermont, and from Canadian cities such as Montreal and Quebec, much critical and accurate information did find its way into the headquarters of the Northern Army, and even directly to General Washington. On occasion, it was even passed on to the American Continental Congress.

This was despite the tremendous distances involved, and the fact that much of the fighting in New York and Vermont occurred in the wilderness. Partly, this was attributable to the fact that in rural areas, no matter how remote, information could move rapidly via a network of army scouts, trappers, settlers, and friendly Indians. From populated centers under British control (such as New York City) agents, spies, and couriers brought forth information. As the fighting intensified and the Northern Army commenced deep raids into the enemy's rear, its personnel were instructed how to seek out information. In time, whatever was observed or heard made its way into the headquarters of the Northern Army. In actuality, during the Wilderness War of 1777, the Patriot commanders of the Northern Army were blessed with a significantly higher degree of professional intelligence gathering and distribution than that which their British and German counterparts possessed. By the conclusion of 1777, it may be surmised that the Northern Army had a very capable intelligence network.

Fueled with new information and knowing for certain that General Barry St. Leger—with a mixed force of European soldiers, Loyalists, Indians, and Canadians—would be knocking on the gates of Fort Stanwix in his push into the Mohawk Valley, Colonel Gansevoort immediately sent the information east to the Mohawk Valley's militia forces and to General Schuyler's headquarters in Albany.

As the word spread that the British were invading from the west, from Oswego to Albany, some men and women began to make preparations to leave. Others were not inclined to flee, and instead prepared to resist. Among the latter was General Nicholas Herkimer, a militia commander from Tryon County.

Notes

1   *"St. Leger's Attack,"* p. 4.
2   See also *"St. Leger's Attack,"* p. 4; and Graymont, p. 125.
3   *The Wilderness War,* p. 102.
4   Eckert, *The Wilderness War,* p. 103.
5   Benson J. Lossing, *The Pictorial Field-Book of the [American] Revolution* (NewYork: Harper & Brothers, Publishers, 1860, Volumes 1–11) (hereafter cited as *Field Book of the Revolution* with proper volume), Vol. 1, p. 241.

6   Some have also cited that Ahnyero or Thomas Spencer was actually a half-breed.

7   Eckert, *The Wilderness War*, p. 112.

8   *"St. Leger's Attack,"* p. 4.

9   To cite an example: well before the British even commenced their campaign of 1777, a series of letters were exchanged among various British military commanders and civilian officials on how to conduct the operation. Besides a lack of urgency in establishing priorities and clear-cut directives, what also compounded the problem was the time factor. Frequently days (if not weeks and months), went by before a letter or messenger appeared. In turn, responses to letters and inquiries were oftentimes slow and, it was not uncommon for a response to lack proper and clear-cut guidance.

10   *"St. Leger's Attack,"* p. 4. St. Leger subsequently ordered the advance guard's departure to commence on 0400 hours 19 July. Why this change occurred has never been explained. Possibly, they just needed an extra day to get ready.

11   Ibid.

12   *"St. Leger's Attack,"* p.6.

13   Ibid.

14   Ibid.

15   Ibid. Not all of the Canadians deserted. Precisely how many Canadians departed with St. Leger's advance guard on 19 July is not known.

16   Ibid. Among them were Indians from the Cayuga, Seneca, Mohawk, and Onondaga tribes. It is not known if any Oneida or Tuscarora Indians were on Carleton Island. The exact number of Indians on Carleton Island was never recorded. As for the Canadian Indians, most accompanied St. Leger from Lachine although a small number drifted into Carleton Island. As for the Iroquois, most arrived at Oswego from their respective tribes, though a number came via Fort Niagara.

17   The Little Salmon River is not to be confused with the Salmon River.

18   From the vicinity of Fort Stanwix, Wood Creek flows westward and empties into Lake Oneida.

19   According to Eckert, *The Wilderness War*, p. 451, fn. 112, St. Leger's route via the Little Salmon River would have been very difficult, especially since he would be hauling his artillery and supplies. Eckert holds the view that "almost surely the entire expedition would have become bogged down between present West Amboy and Constantia." (Ibid.)

Taking the entire force, to include the artillery, wagons, horses, and baggage through the rough wilderness terrain with no roads or sizable trails, would have caused St. Leger considerable difficulties. He would have been forced to clear and widen any existing trails, perhaps construct entire sections of road, build bridges, fell trees, etc. This would have forced St. Leger to move at a snail's pace. In consideration of the time factor, Eckert's observation is very true.

However, as verified by Eckert, St. Leger did harbor the idea of advancing swiftly through the wilderness solely with light forces to capture Fort Stanwix. (Ibid., p. 114. See also *"St. Leger's Attack!"* p. 4). A movement with light forces through the wilderness minus its artillery, baggage, wagons, horses, and heavy equipment could have been accomplished. And had Fort Stanwix been weakly manned, a surprise attack with light forces could have secured the fort.

20 Graymont, p. 118. The possibility also exists that Claus came to Carleton Island seeking supplies.

21 See Eckert, *The Wilderness War,* p. 113.

22 *"St. Leger's Attack,"* p. 6.

23 According to *"St. Leger's Attack!"* p. 6, "a company of Chasseurs lately arrived [at Carleton Island and] accompanied Claus as well." *"St. Leger's Attack"* also identifies the company as being a "company of French Canadian rangers and boatmen" commanded by a Captain Rouville.

   Chasseurs (a French word also meaning huntsman) denotes light cavalry or infantry trained for rapid movement. Undoubtedly, this was a Canadian mercenary company of some sort. Its exact strength is unknown but it appears to have been around 100 fighters because it is known that Canadian combat personnel were utilized during the siege of the fort and at the Battle of Oriskany.

24 Currently, the site is still known as "Spy Island." In actuality, it is not an island but a small brush-covered peninsula that juts into Lake Ontario near the mouth of the Little Salmon River. However, when the lake's water level rises, the isthmus part is covered by water except for the most outermost point which is just several feet higher in elevation; hence, at certain times of the year it is an "island." The site is at Mexico Point and may be viewed by the public. Adjacent to the Little Salmon Rivers southern (or western) bank is the Village of Texas.

25 *"St. Leger's Attack,"* p. 6.

26 Ibid.; Eckert, p. 114.

27 *"St. Leger's Attack,"* p. 6; Eckert, p. 114.

28 Ann Bailey Dunn, "Raven: Majesty and Myth" in *The Conservationist* (New York: Latham Publishing Co., April, 1999), p. 3.

29 This date was cited by Colonel Claus in early September 1777 in the aftermath of St. Leger's retreat to Fort Ontario following his unsuccessful attempt to capture Fort Stanwix. Graymont, p. 124, cites 24 July 1777 as well.

30 Claus, John Butler and Sir John Johnson all held the rank of colonel at Oswego. Who was the top ranking and commanding officer in Oswego prior to St. Leger's arrival is not known. Possibly, there was no senior ranking officer officially in charge. The fact that St. Leger sent his order to Colonel Claus would seem to indicate that he regarded Claus as the senior officer.

31 Located about 5 miles to the northwest of Syracuse, presently a small hamlet known as Three Rivers exists there. Nearby is the town of Phoenix.

32 *"St. Leger's Attack,"* p. 6. According to Graymont, pp. 124–125, intoxica-
    tion had set in among the Indians and some of the warriors even began to
    rampage. Therefore, St. Leger requested Claus' immediate presence to con-
    trol the Indians.

33 *"St. Leger's Attack,"* p. 6.

34 Graymont, p. 125.

35 Eckert, p.114. Regarding "stores and gifts," it is known that prior to the
    commencement of St. Leger's march and throughout the siege of Fort
    Stanwix, the "Indians [were] encouraged by generous presents and their bel-
    ligerency stimulated by liberal issues of rum." See also Dale Van Every, *A
    Company of Heroes: The American Frontier, 1775–1783*, p.114.

36 According to Eckert, p. 115, Cornplanter was the subcommander, or second
    in command of the Indians, following Brant. Cornplanter's relationship with
    Brant, however, was poor. In fact, at Irondequoit Bay, Cornplanter had had
    a large argument with Brant because he opposed the idea of supporting the
    British campaign of 1777. See also Donald A. Grinde, Jr., *The Iroquois and
    the Founding of the American Nation* (New York: Indian Historian Press,
    1977), p. 85.

37 Eckert, pp. 88–89. Brant's low opinion of Sir Guy, incidentally, was shared
    by many others. Colonel John Butler, for example, also despised Sir Guy.

38 Eckert, p. 115, acknowledges that Claus carried the title of Superintendent
    of Indian Affairs during this time. This occurred because of Sir Guy John-
    son's absence and because earlier Sir Guy himself had abdicated his respon-
    sibility in the role.

39 Eckert, p. 116. In *The American Revolution*, Vol. III, p. 377, author George
    Bancroft cited that previously at Irondequoit Bay Colonel Butler had assured
    the Indians that there would be no hindrance on the warpath, and they
    would have only to "look on and see Fort Stanwix fall." According to Colin
    G. Calloway, *The American Revolution in Indian Country. Crisis and Diver-
    sity in Native American Communities* (M.A.: University of Cambridge,
    1995), p. 33, cites "the British invited Iroquois warriors to come and see
    them whip the rebels at the siege of Fort Stanwix." (Hereafter titled *Revo-
    lution in Indian Country*). Likewise, "Promised gifts . . . persuaded hundreds
    of Indians to join St. Leger at Oswego." See Lowenthal, *Marinus Willett*,
    p. 26.

VI

General Herkimer's Preparations for War

Nicholas Herkimer, born in 1728,[1] resided in the area known as the German Flats. Founded in the Mohawk Valley, German Flats was named after the Palatine Germans who first arrived in the New World in 1708 via New York City.[2] Overwhelmingly, these people hailed from the region of the Palatinate in Germany's Rhine Valley.[3]

Initially, many of the Palatine Germans were bonded, or indentured, servants.[4] These were immigrants who contracted to work for a period of time for various British officials or companies found in the New World. A man or woman too poor to book passage on their own might choose to sign a contract—also known as a deed—with a sponsor in North America. Their sponsor could be a well-established farmer, landowner, a businessman, or someone who simply needed one or two persons to assist in a household for a period of time. Upon their arrival, they worked for a period of time for the individual or firm that had paid their way until the debt was erased. Indentured servants tended to represent Europe's poorest; however, once free of their bond, many went on to become prosperous in their new land.

Poverty, however, was not the sole factor in leaving one's homeland. Many of these Germans were also tired of the constant internal strifes and civil wars raging between the various noblemen living within the Palatine district. Dejected, exhausted, and seeking land and peace, they began to look for new places in which to settle. Since Europe had little to offer, the Palatine Germans eyed the New World.

In 1712, the Palatine Germans who had first arrived in 1708 began to migrate inland. Some headed into western and southern New Jersey, others entered Pennsylvania, while others headed north to Albany. Many of the talented artisans and craftsmen settled in Albany, quickly enriching the town with their skills; others, however, sought land. Wanting to farm, they pushed farther westward into the wilderness.

In 1723, twenty German Palatine families were residing on the eastern fringes of the Mohawk Valley.[5] They settled in the vicinity of Stone Arabia on the edge of the great wilderness. By 1725, ninety more families from the Palatinate had appeared.[6] Also seeking land, they pushed farther into the frontier of the Mohawk Valley. Among them were the Herkimers. And here, within the area that came to be known as German Flats,[7] in a small settlement known at the time as Burnets-field,[8] Nicholas Herkimer was born.

After attending a local school, Herkimer followed in the footsteps of his father, Johann, a well-known Mohawk Valley farmer and trader. Johann owned over 5,000 acres of land south of the Mohawk River, and in this location, in approximately 1752, he established a sizable farm, and in 1764 he built a fashionable two-story English Georgian-style mansion, which stands to this day.[9]

Always interested in the military, Herkimer joined the Schenectady Militia and was commissioned a lieutenant on 5 January 1758. That same year, when the French and Indians attacked the Palatine settlers, Lieutenant Herkimer commanded a namesake fort. From Fort Herkimer he played an instrumental role in protecting the various settlements and farms in his area, and he rose in rank.

In addition to farming and trading, politics became an issue in the Herkimer household. As verified by the Johnson papers, the Herkimers began to oppose British rule years before the American Revolution had even commenced.[10] By 1770, Nicholas was firmly embracing the American Revolutionary cause. A man of both civilian and military prominence, he was elected to head the newly formed Tryon County Committee of Safety in 1775. In addition to being one of the wealthiest landowning farmers in the Mohawk Valley, he was also earnestly involved in both the activities of the German community and in political affairs. On 5 September 1776, the New York State Convention elevated Herkimer's rank to that of brigadier general in the state militia,[11] and he was ordered to take action against both Sir John Johnson and Chief Joseph Brant.[12]

Prior to the critical events of 1777, General Herkimer had written a series of letters to the Northern Army and the Continental Congress. In these he requested that regular Continental Army units be sent to assist in the defense of the Mohawk Valley and its frontier. But the Continental Congress, burdened with its own problems and convinced for the moment that the British would not attack from the north, did not regard the wilderness frontier as a threatened area.[13]

Prior to General Burgoyne's crossing over from Canada, and St. Leger pushing out from Lachine to Carleton Island, General Herkimer, accompanied by some militia soldiers, had been patrolling the region between the eastern Mohawk Valley and Albany.

Cherry Valley and Cobbleskill were also covered. Herkimer was acting on reports of Loyalists and Indians who were supporting the Crown, but wherever he and his men showed up, no threat existed. Regardless, Herkimer's show of force cannot be totally discredited. His pursuits afforded him an opportunity to train his militia, they demonstrated to the local populace that an armed force was on hand to protect them, and they showed those who held secret sympathies for the Crown that local Patriot forces would not tolerate any Loyalist activity.

On or shortly after 26 July, General Herkimer learned that a sizable British force had landed in Oswego and within days would be advancing eastward. Herkimer was not surprised by this news because he had known since the latter part of June that many Indians and Loyalists were converging in the area. In response to this upcoming threat, Herkimer had already issued a proclamation announcing a manpower draft for Tryon County on 17 July.[14] Of historical significance is that his draft proclamation was the very first one ever issued in the State of New York.

The proclamation was based on a very moving appeal. Printed on numerous leaflets and displayed on public billboards and buildings, Herkimer's draft notice stated:

TO ALL CITIZENS OF TRYON COUNTY, NEW YORK
Whereas it appears certain that the enemy of about two thousand, Christians and savages, have arrived at Oswego with the intention to invade our frontiers, I think it proper and most necessary for the defense of our country—and it shall be ordered by me as soon as the enemy approaches—that every male person being in health, from 16 to 60 years of age in this

our country, shall, as is duty bound, repair immediately with arms and accoutrements to the place to be appointed in my orders, and will then march to oppose the enemy with vigor as true Patriots, for the just defense of their country.

And those that are above 60 years, or really unwell and incapable to march, shall assemble there also, at the respective places, when women and children will be gathered together, in order for defense against the enemy if attacked, as much as lies in their power.

But concerning the disaffected and those who will not directly obey such orders, they shall be taken, along with their arms secured under guard, to join the main body.

And as such, an invasion regards every friend to the country in general, but of this country in particular, to show his zeal and well-affected spirit in actual defense of the same.

All the members of the committee as well as those who, by former commissions or otherwise, have been exempted from any other military duty, are requested to appear also, when called, to such place as shall be appointed, and join to repulse our foes.

Not doubting that the Almighty Power, upon our humble prayer and sincere trust in Him, will graciously succour our arms in battle for our just cause, and victory cannot fail to our side.

> NICHOLAS HERKIMER, Brig. General
> Commanding
> Tryon County Militia[15]

Simply worded, Herkimer's proclamation was explicit in guidance. What is important to note is that an enemy strength "of about two thousand" strong is identified. Possibly, Herkimer received this figure—which was correct—from the headquarters of the Northern Army, which, in turn, received it from the commanding officer of Fort Stanwix, Colonel Gansevoort. As this estimate was close to the number that St. Leger actually commanded, then it appears that Colonel Gansevoort's spies were doing their job very well.

Herkimer's proclamation, however, was not to be taken lightly, because at the very moment he was appealing for support, General

Burgoyne with a larger British force was steadily advancing southward toward Albany. Fort Ticonderoga, Skenesborough, Fort Edward, and Hubbardrton, along with a number of other forts and settlements, were now in British hands. The road to Albany, both from the north and west, was open. Recognizing the dangerous situation, the residents of the town of Deerfield,[16] located about fourteen miles to the southeast of Fort Stanwix, fled eastward. Refugees were pouring into Albany from the north, east, and west. Deep in Pennsylvania, General George Washington himself was monitoring the wilderness crisis.

In response to Herkimer's draft proclamation, many men and even some women stepped forward. Although many hailed from Tryon County, other volunteers came from the upper Hudson Valley—from Albany, various parts of the Mohawk Valley, and from the foothills of the Adirondack Mountains, the northern Catskills, and the Schoharie Valley. An examination of the Oriskany roster[17] reveals individuals from various European nationalities and of all ages. They hailed from different professions, occupations, and educational backgrounds. A number had served previously in the British or French army. A good percentage had been associated with local militias. For many others, however, this would be their very first military experience.

Some joined because they were patriotically minded, while others joined only to defend their families, farms, and businesses. Many were motivated by the draft proclamation or entered Herkimer's militia because of fears that if they did not appear they might be ridiculed or accused of being a Loyalist. Possibly, some feared arrest. Others enlisted solely because family members, along with close friends and neighbors, had done so. Possibly, some sought to escape from boredom or a dissatisfied way of life, and were motivated by the search for action, adventure, and excitement.

It must be noted, however, that the Oriskany roster is not totally accurate. The names of many who served were never recorded. Individual militiamen also came and went. Regardless, in its own way, the roster represents all of the brave men and women who served the Patriot cause during the terrible Wilderness War of 1777.

From the Bellinger family, a total of twelve family members appeared. All four Diefendorf brothers volunteered: two served as captains, one as a sergeant, and one—undoubtedly the youngest—as a private. Three Dunlap brothers and five Dygert brothers enlisted.

Colonel Frederick Visscher (spelled sometimes also as Fisher) along with two cousins who utilized the Fisher spelling—Captain John Fisher and Harmon Fisher—also enlisted. American Indians are also found among the names, among them Atyataronghta Louis, an Oneida Indian in the rank of lieutenant colonel. In addition, Jacob Alter, John Huyck, Frederick Iser, Nicholas Hill, Peter Bargy, Lieutenant Nicholas Petire (Petrie), Major John Bliven, Jacob Peeler, John Countryman, Christian Schellsbush Schell, John Spore, Henry Sanders, John Visger, and Jacob Youker were among the numerous volunteers. Thirteen-year-old Jan (John) Van Eps, from Hoffman's Ferry in the vicinity of Schenectady, was the youngest volunteer, managing to enlist by claiming to be sixteen years of age.

Requiring an assembly area, General Herkimer chose Fort Dayton,[18] located about thirty miles to the east of Fort Stanwix.[19] The fort was also deep in the Mohawk Valley. General Herkimer's intent, once his force was assembled, was to march westward to commence an operation against St. Leger's army somewhere in the vicinity of Fort Stanwix.

As General Herkimer was preparing to march westward, General St. Leger was dispatching a reconnaissance force in his direction. Commanded by twenty-four-year-old Lieutenant Herleigh Bird, a highly aggressive and mission-minded officer, the force consisted of several British personnel, some Loyalists, and a number of Indians. Their mission was to probe eastward all the way to Fort Stanwix and report back along the way as to what was happening. Departing Oswego in the mid-afternoon of 26 July, this force was the very first one to deploy eastward.

It is important to note that at this point, St. Leger had no knowledge of General Herkimer and his activities, while Herkimer—along with the leadership of the Northern Army—was fully aware of St. Leger, the force he was leading, and his mission. Indeed, St. Leger would have been shocked if he had known what the Patriots knew about him.

Notes

1   In Germany, the name was possibly spelled as Herkheimer, Herheimer, or Herkhammer. The spelling of the name as Herkimer was conceived in America and probably originated in the Mohawk Valley. Other sources identify a Johan Jost Herchheimer as an ancestor from the German Palatinate. See New York State Pamphlet "Herkimer Home" in *State Historic Site, Little*

Falls, New York, Central Region. (Published by the Office of Parks, Recreation and Historic Preservation.)

An examination of the various letters found in James Sullivan, *The Papers of Sir William Johnson* (Albany University Press, 1922) (hereafter cited as *The Papers of Sir William Johnson*), reveal spellings of Harkemar, Her Heimer, and Herchheimer. And it is known that Nicholas Herkimer's father, Johan Jost Herkimer, occasionally used his middle name of Jost in place of Johan. (For an example of this see the letter of August 1756, to Sir William Johnson signed by Jost Herch Heimer and John Conrad Franck.)

2 The former region of Palatinate, Germany, was divided into two regions: the Lower and the Upper Palatinate regions. The Lower or Rhenish Palatinate bordered the left bank of the Rhine River as it flowed northward toward France through southwestern Germany and the region extended northward to present-day Heidelberg and Mannheim; the Upper Palatinate was in an area to the west of the Bohemian Forest. The city of Regensburg was located within this area. (See *Collier's Encyclopedia*, Vol. 15, p. 373.) The two regions were merged into one state, Bavaria, in 1777.

3 William H. Watkins, "Slavery in Herkimer County. African Americans Were Here in the Valley From the Beginning" in *Legacy* (New York: Published by Herkimer County Historical Society), Issue No. 3, 1990, p. 6. (Hereafter cited as "Slavery in Herkimer County.")

4 A contract might, for example, work as such: a young man in Europe would sail to New York City in the New World. The owner of a shipping company, requiring his services, would pay for his ticket and travel expenses. Upon arrival, the indentured servant would work for a certain period of months or even several years for the owner of the shipping company, for example, as a dockworker. (Usually the work period was agreed upon prior to arrival). At first, the pay would be minimal. After working off the debt, the indentured servant would either leave or, if he or she decided to stay on, would remain with the employer as a steady worker and no longer as an indentured servant.

However, problems did sometimes arise. An indentured servant might be harshly treated or expected to do much more work then what initially was agreed upon. Or after their work period was concluded, an indentured servant might be told that he or she could not leave. When this happened, indentured servants sometimes had no alternative but to flee. If they fled, it usually was westward into Pennsylvania, or northward into a wilderness region.

Unfortunately, indentured servants were sometimes mocked, ridiculed, and looked down upon. Ugly racist quotes such as "white slaves" and "riff-raff" were heralded against them. But for those who arrived as indentured servants, by and large the majority became useful, successful, and prosperous citizens. Many even became supportive of the American Revolution; and two former indentured servants signed the Declaration of Independence.

5   Watkins, "Slavery in Herkimer County," p. 6.
6   Ibid. Stone Arabia is located northwest of the current city of Amsterdam, New York. Amsterdam lies on the northern bank of the Mohawk River.
7   Also spelled as German Flatts. Currently, the towns of Utica, Little Falls, and Herkimer are located in this area. German Flats, which became the home of the German Palatine settlers, ran alongside the southern bank of the Mohawk River and encompassed a stretch of land from the west to east of approximately 10 miles between present-day Utica and the town of Little Falls. See also Mark M. Boatner, "German Flatts" in *Landmarks of the American Revolution. People and Places Vital to the Quest for Independence* (Harrisburg, PA: Stackpole Books, 1992), pp. 249–250. (Hereafter cited as *Landmarks of American Revolution.*) Despite the British defeat in 1777, from 1778 until 1781 German Flats did experience a series of raids by Loyalists and Indians.
8   Now known as Herkimer.
9   Though the Herkimer house survived the Wilderness War of 1777 and the raids conducted upon German Flats in the following years, in time the house was abandoned. It is now a state historic site open to the public. See John G. Waite and Paul R. Huey, *Herkimer House. An Historic Structure Report* (New York State Historic Trust), 1972.
10 See letter of Horatio Gates dated 8 August 1756 to Sir William Johnson in *The Papers of Sir William Johnson* (Vol. II, pp. 534–535). (At this time Horatio Gates was a British Army officer serving in North America.) According to Waite and Huey, p. 6, "Johan Jost Herkimer refused to help open a new road by land to Oswego, and he strongly resented the British garrison in his house near German Flats, called Fort Herkimer." The Herkimers also found "a British officer named Horatio Gates seemed especially obnoxious." (Ibid.). By May 1772, "the Herkimer family had become angry with Sir William Johnson and, the situation worsened as the Revolution approached." (Ibid., p. 9). See also *The Papers of Sir William Johnson*, Vol. III, p. 468. Though Sir William passed away in July 1774, Herkimer despised both Sir William's son, Sir John, and Sir William's nephew, Sir Guy.
11 A predecessor organization that helped to establish the State of New York in 1777.
12 *Collier's Encyclopedia*, Vol. 10, p. 21.
13 This view was initially held in 1775 and into 1776. By late 1776/early 1777, the Continental Congress viewed the northern theater differently.
14 *Revolutionary War Dates*, p. 5; *"St. Leger's Attack!"* p. 6; Ward, *The War of the Revolution*, Vol. II, p. 482. According to Ward, "Herkimer issued a brief but vigorous and stirring proclamation." See Stone, *Siege and Battle*, p. 215. According to Stone, Herkimer also ordered, on 17 July, the arrest of all non-compliers and those who were pro-Loyalist. According to John R. Alden, *A History of the American Revolution* (New York: Alfred A. Knopf, 1969), pp. 319–320, "Brigadier General Nicholas Herkimer, the militia

commander of Tryon County—that County covered the settlements of western New York—asked every Patriot male between the ages of sixteen and sixty to prepare to take up arms." According to Alden, General Herkimer also "called for the arrest of all tories." (Ibid.)

15 Eckert, pp. 117–118.

16 This settlement, adjacent to the Mohawk River, is now a part of the city of Utica and Yorkville.

17 A roster of names is also cited in Stone, *Siege and Battle*, pp. 1–14, Index section. It is important to note, however, that this roster is neither complete nor accurate.

18 Initially, Fort Dayton was known as Fort Herkimer. A log blockhouse, it was built during the French and Indian War but had fallen into ruin. In 1776, Colonel Elias Dayton decided to build a new fort at the site. Constructed in 1776, Fort Dayton was slightly upgraded in 1777. In actuality, it was not a fort but a strong blockhouse position that could hold a sizable number of defenders and civilians. It was from Fort Dayton that Herkimer commenced his military march to relieve Fort Stanwix in 1777. This blockhouse fort is now a state historic site and is located in the present-day village of Herkimer.

Neither the previous Fort Herkimer nor the later Fort Dayton should be confused with the Fort Herkimer Church. This position, which began to be built around 1730 to replace a log church initially built in 1723, remained unfinished for decades. Even during the French and Indian War it had not been completed. But in 1767 General Herkimer's father, Johan, completed the structure. Prior to 1767 it had also been utilized as a trading post, church, and, if necessary, a fortification. Fort Herkimer Church was located about 5 miles east of Fort Dayton. In 1777, no military actions were noted there, but on 13 September 1778, local inhabitants successfully defended themselves at that site from a Loyalist-Indian raid. (See also Boatner, pp. 237–238 and p. 243.)

19 In 1777, Utica did not exist.

VII

St. Leger's Advance to Fort Stanwix

As General Herkimer was mobilizing a militia force and preparing to march west to Fort Stanwix, General Barry St. Leger's combined British-Indian army was preparing to march east. Not wanting to lose any more time and anxious to arrive at Fort Stanwix, St. Leger quickly completed his final preparations to march.

Fort Stanwix was on high alert. On the afternoon of 27 July, their readiness was tested when from the woods they heard the firing of four guns. The men ran with muskets and rifles to key points within the fort. By now, each and every soldier knew what position he was to man. A drummer boy beat the call to arms. This incident was recorded by both Colonel Gansevoort and Major Willett. As the men watched, a young girl ran over the recently cleared open area in front of the fort. As she ran, she zigzagged to make it difficult for her assailants to take aim and fire at her.

When her pursuers, several warriors, broke out of the woodline, the garrison fired at them, and the girl managed to reach the fort and safety. Wounded, she was taken to Doctor Hunloke Woodruff, the 3rd Continental Regiment's chief doctor and surgeon, who removed two musket balls from her shoulder.[2]

From her, the garrison learned that she, along with two other much younger girls, had been picking wild raspberries when Indian warriors suddenly pounced on them. A detachment was dispatched to search for the other two. The girls were found not far from the fort, tomahawked and scalped.[3] The fate of these young innocents underlined what everyone already knew: that out here within the wilderness, the war would be a vicious struggle with little honor, dignity, or concerns for human decency.

On Monday, 28 July, General St. Leger commenced his march from Oswego with the bulk of his force.[4] Crossing the Oswego River over to its southern bank, he assembled his men at what currently is the corner of West First and Oneida Street.[5]

To maintain security and tactical control in the dangerous wilderness, St. Leger organized his force to suit the situation. Leading were the Indians, in five columns.[6] Each column was single file, the warriors spaced apart. The task of these leading columns was to spot any danger, whether enemy or natural. In the event an enemy force was encountered, the Indians were not to engage them but were to halt in place and report their observations. Once warned, St. Leger could respond appropriately.

Approximately 460 paces to the rear of these columns marched the advance guard with a strength of exactly 60 marksmen, detached from Sir Johnson's regiment of Royal Greens.[7] Major Watts commanded this force[8] and their mission was to engage any Patriot forces encountered.

Following the advance guard was the main body. The left wing (positioned on the northern edge), comprised the 34th Foot Regiment; the right wing (on the southern edge), comprised the 8th (King's) Foot Regiment minus one of its companies, which remained behind to assist and protect the supply and baggage personnel.[9]

General St. Leger and his staff were positioned in the center between the two wings. This allowed St. Leger to have firm tactical control of his entire army. In the event that any enemy forces were met, the plan was that the advance guard would pin them down while the main body and rearguard maneuvered around and behind them. The bulk of the rearguard was composed of Loyalist forces. The remaining soldiers of Johnson's Royal Greens along with Butler's Rangers, some Indians, and most of the German soldiers were also positioned in the rearguard.

Of interest to note is that St. Leger actually placed the brunt of his strength into the rearguard, whereas usually it is found in the main body. No explicit reason for this is cited. Though right from the outset neither the 34th nor the 8th Foot were at full strength, possibly St. Leger regarded these two British regiments to be the most elite of his entire force and for that, felt that he would not need any more personnel within his main body.

Besides the Indians in the front and rear, additional Indians also ringed the entire force on all sides, providing extra security. St. Leger's force, which would be moving solely on foot, had to move through the wilderness as quickly and safely as possible.

Yet, even as British and German drummers were heralding the order to commence forward, his force had long been infiltrated by an enemy. It was Ahnyero, or Thomas Spencer. Covered in war paint and shrieking the cry of battle, Spencer stepped forward with the rest into the wilderness.

By now Spencer was fully aware of the various weaknesses in St. Leger's army. For starters, there was no strong accountability of its personnel. In this polyglot force there was no morning or evening roll call. Many of the Indians, along with some of the Loyalists and Canadians, came and went at will. Knowing this, Spencer could personally exploit the weakness to his advantage. His plan was simple: he would accompany the force until they stopped to rest for the night. After everyone was bedded down, he would slip into the darkness. Once in the woods, nothing and nobody could stop him. Within one or two days at most, he would be inside Fort Stanwix. There, he would personally brief Colonel Gansevoort as to what was happening. In the meantime, Spencer kept his eyes and ears open for more information.

Late on this day, Lieutenant Bird, who had departed Oswego two days previously, reached the site of the Three Rivers. So far, his force had moved swiftly with no problems. But now, the Indians began to differ with Bird on what was to be done and they proffered new demands. As Bird encamped at Three Rivers, seventy to eighty of the Indians revolted.[10] Stealing two head of oxen, they refused to proceed further until they had feasted.[11] Angered by their insubordination, Bird left them behind and continued with the remaining Indians toward Oneida Lake.[12] Though in his message of 29 July Bird cited problems with the Indians, he added that he was still proceeding rapidly toward Fort Stanwix.

On that Tuesday, 29 July, the remainder of St. Leger's force departed Oswego. Prior to his departure, the British general had explicitly ordered that this force was to depart no later than on the afternoon of 30 July. This second column encompassed the support troops, Canadian work personnel, and British naval men, and they took with them all the baggage—the artillery, numerous cases of bullets and musket balls, gunpowder barrels, horses, wagons, tools, tents, field tables with chairs, lanterns, extra clothing, blankets, barrels and cases of food rations, and, of course, the barrels of rum. However, the most important item—the money chest—had not been left in the hands of the support personnel. Instead, St. Leger ordered that it be placed upon a small two-wheeled cart, which was pushed along through the wilderness with the main body.

Unlike the force that marched out on 28 July, this support column would travel mostly by water. The force which moved out on 29 July was accompanied by one company from the 8th Foot,[13] commanded by a lieutenant whose last name, oddly enough, was "Colonel"; Captain Rouville's remaining Canadians; six squads of the Royal Greens; and the Royal Artillery commanded by Lieutenant Glennie.[14] The task of the soldiers and Loyalists accompanying this force was to not only protect it but to assist in its movement. St. Leger's small quantity of artillery numbered two 6-pounder and two 3-pounder cannon, and four 4.4-inch mortars.[15] Forty artillerymen manned the guns.[16] Lieutenant Anderson J. Wilkerson was in charge of the loading and unloading of the baggage onto the bateaux. Boat commanders were instructed that, excluding an emergency, their boats were not to fall back or be put ashore.

Some Indian warriors, traveling by canoe, were also dispersed throughout this force. Because this heavily laden column was moving by boat, it was anticipated that it would travel more slowly than the one marching overland. Along the way, several waterfalls would have to be negotiated. Though none of the falls were very high, at each one, the boats would have to be grounded and unloaded. The boat and its cargo would be hauled overland around the falls, and, once the boats were back into the water beyond the falls, they would again be loaded up before the journey could resume.

The water transport detail was by no means an easy assignment. Along with the waterfalls, various other natural obstacles—huge floating logs and fallen trees—posed hazards. As the Oswego and Oneida Rivers and Wood Creek flow westward and northward, the boat operators would actually be paddling and rowing against the current. However, unless a major rainstorm erupted, serious problems were not anticipated because in the summer months, the water currents move slowly.

The detachment would be traveling up the Oswego and Oneida Rivers to Oneida Lake's western shoreline and from there, directly east across the lake to Wood Creek, which empties into its eastern side. They would then follow Wood Creek almost its entire length, to the vicinity of Fort Stanwix. This would take longer than the main force's march through the wilderness, but St. Leger expected them to appear shortly after the capture of Fort Stanwix. Records do not reveal who commanded this group, but since Sir John Johnson was the highest ranked person found within this contingent, possibly St. Leger designated him to be the commander.

Nothing and nobody was to remain behind in Oswego—each weapon, piece of equipment, soldier, and warrior would go. St. Leger would need every man and gun in his expedition, though he was also expecting a strong Loyalist reinforcement after entering the Mohawk Valley. As in the case of Burgoyne, St. Leger had been assured that "the countryside is rife with the King's supporters."[17] The British were hoping that with the arrival of regular British Army troops into the Mohawk Valley, a strong sentiment in favor of the King would arise. With its populace rising in support of the British, the critical Mohawk Valley would be under firm British control. St. Leger had also been previously assured by the Johnson family, who were the largest landowners in the Mohawk Valley, that most of the settlers were loyal to the King. St. Leger was also assured that although "the people had not yet taken up arms [against the patriots], they would cooperate with the British once St. Leger and his troops marched victoriously down the Mohawk Valley."[18]

Exactly how many European soldiers, Loyalists, Canadians, and Indians constituted the entirety of St. Leger's force is not certain, as figures differ. Personnel strengths range from approximately 1,700 to over 2,000.[19] Probably St. Leger himself never knew his exact strength. In the European armies of that era, commanders were not held as accountable for their troop strength figures as they now are. It must also be remembered that St. Leger's force was largely comprised of irregular fighters. Because no one really had—nor could they have had—any firm control over them, these warriors came and went as they pleased. Regardless, it may be accurately surmised that St. Leger possessed a military strength of nearly 2,000 personnel.

Ketchum cites 200 British regulars, 200 provincial Loyalists, 300–

400 Germans, and 400–500 Indians.[20] Ward cites 100 British regulars apiece from the 8th and 34th Foot Regiments for a total of 200, 133 Loyalists in Sir John Johnson's Royal Greens, a company of Loyalist Rangers under Colonel John Butler, and about 350 German Hanau Jagers. Some Canadian irregulars, along with axmen and other non-combatants, were also included.[21] "The Indian contingent, commanded by Joseph Brant, maintained a strength between 800 and 1,000 warriors."[22] Bird cites, "some 400 British and German regulars and 400 or so loyalists," and "between 800 and 1,000 Indians."[23] Furneaux cites, "200 British infantrymen; 100 German chasseurs; 100 tory [loyalist] rangers under Colonel John Butler; a tory regiment commanded by Sir John Johnson, and about 900 Mohawk and Seneca Indians."[24] The Oswego Palladium Times cites, "400 Hessians, mostly Wurttemburg Chasseurs, 200 [British] regulars from the 8th and 34th Regiments, Captain Rouville's company of French Canadian rangers and boatmen, and about 200 Royal Greens."[25] To this strength at Oswego were added 300 Mohawks and 500 other Six Nations Indians, mostly Senecas, Cayugas, and Onondagas.[26] However, the Indian figure would increase. Following the Indian Council at Three Rivers,[27] additional warriors joined St. Leger's force as it proceeded via the Three Rivers.[28]

Eckert, similar to Ward, states that St. Leger's force included, "100 experienced regulars from both the 8th and 34th Foot, Sir John Johnson's 133 strong Tory regiment, one company of Tory rangers under Colonel John Butler, 350 Hanau Jaegers, 50 Canadian irregulars and almost 200 axmen, boatmen, and support non-combatants,"[29] and "1,000 Indians."[30] Wilcox cites that General Burgoyne himself mentioned a strength of "roughly seventeen hundred regulars and auxiliaries, half of them Indians" for St. Leger.[31]

Lieutenant Bird's reconnaissance force had left Oswego ahead of the main force on 26 July. His mission was to probe toward Fort Stanwix, report back on what he was observing, and if possible, secure the Lower Landing site located about a quarter of a mile directly to the south of the fort on the north bank of the Mohawk River, where it bends sharply. The Lower Landing served as a communications line between Fort Stanwix and the Mohawk Valley.[32]

Lieutenant Bird's force consisted of 30 Loyalist riflemen from the Royal Greens and about 200 Iroquois.[33] The Iroquois scout John Hare, now with the rank of a lieutenant, accompanied Bird, and was also in command of the Indians. Amongst Hare's warriors was a renowned long-range rifle shooter named Ki. Reaching The Three Rivers[34] on Monday 28 July, and wanting to inform his general what was happening, Lieutenant Bird dispatched an Indian warrior back to St. Leger's main group with a message on 29 July.

As St. Leger's three forces moved into the wilderness, minor combat actions were now taking place from Oswego to Fort Stanwix. In themselves, these actions revealed that an attack against Fort Stanwix was imminent.

Prior to St. Leger's arrival in Oswego on 25 July, a number of Loyalists and many more Indians had already preceded St. Leger to Oswego. In actuality, the first Indians began to congregate in June 1777. With no firm guidance and seeing that for the moment no activities were underway, some of the warriors had banded together to conduct raids.[35] Forming into teams ranging from three or four men to groups of up to 30–40 warriors, they disappeared into the wilderness. The raiders sought scalps and booty. Although in 1777 the area around Fort Stanwix was still formally a wilderness, small numbers of settlers were residing in the area. These settlers, along with any soldiers from Fort Stanwix caught off guard, were targeted. Such occurred in the case of Captain Lawrence Gregg and Corporal Asmon Madison.

In late June a party of 150 soldiers, including Captain Gregg and Corporal Madison, were dispatched to Wood Creek to chop down and drop some trees into the water as a barrier. The creek was quite narrow in several places, and the plan was that the tree obstacles would bar anyone from moving up the creek from Oneida Lake.

Shortly after arriving at the work site, Captain Gregg decided to go duck hunting. The captain's actions were in clear violation of Colonel Gansevoort's orders forbidding soldiers to separate themselves from any sizable and well-armed party. After instructing Lieutenant Caspar[36] to "take charge of the work detail" Captain Gregg, accompanied by his dog Cricket and Corporal Madison,[37] proceeded into some marshy ground to do their hunting. Because they were not very far from the fort, they also reasoned the risk was low. Spotting some ducks, they moved towards them, but they never got close. Suddenly, the crack of two muskets—fired almost simultaneously—shattered the day's tranquility. Corporal Madison was dead before he even hit the ground. Struck in the lower back, Captain Gregg went down as well. The musket ball just barely missed his spine, yet still, the ball went in deep and Captain Gregg fell to the ground, unable to stand or run.

The first warrior to approach drove his tomahawk deep into Madison's head, shattering his skull. A second warrior appeared and scalped the corporal with his knife. The first warrior then crossed to Captain Gregg, still holding his tomahawk, red with the corporal's blood. But instead of driving it into Gregg's head, he cut a gash above his ear. The warrior then took his knife and cut a circular incision around the top of his head. Gregg must have realized what was coming, but he had to feign dead, or his demise would be immediate.

The warrior placed his foot behind Gregg's neck, and gripped the captain's hair. In one quick motion, the scalper jerked the captain's head backwards. Fortunately for Captain Gregg, the warrior was very proficient in the art of scalping. Within a split second, as the captain's head was jerked backward, a "popping" type of sound was heard. Now, all of Captain Gregg's hair, with his scalp attached, was torn off.

Satisfied with what he had done, the scalper raced off, leaving Gregg in agony on the ground. Perhaps, if he had had some more time, the warrior would have removed one or both of Captain Gregg's ears. But the gunshots had resonated through the woods, alerting other Patriots. The warriors knew that other soldiers were in the vicinity and possibly feared that they were already on their way. Firmly grasping the two scalps, the warriors disappeared into the wilderness.

As for the scalp torn from the captain's head, it would soon be stretched on a willow or birch hoop to be dried out in the sun. Afterwards, the inside of the now dried-out, exposed skin would be painted "red." In itself, the red color would indicate that the scalp was obtained from an officer; additionally, one "black spot"—to depict gunpowder—was painted in the center of the red. To a scalp buyer, the red color and the black spot indicated that the scalp had been removed from an officer who had been shot.[38] An officer's scalp would fetch more money.

Had the warriors realized Captain Gregg was still alive, he would have been killed with the tomahawk before being scalped. But in the aftermath, a small image of a tomahawk, rather than a black spot, would have been painted in the center of the red scalp. To a scalp buyer, this would indicate that the officer had been killed up close rather than with a gunshot.

During the Wilderness War of 1777, scalps were always purchased.

They were bought either directly from a scalper or from a middleman scalp buyer. Once enough scalps were accumulated, they were packed into bundles, each containing 90–100 scalps. Once about ten or twenty bundles of scalps taken by Loyalists were assembled, the scalp shipment went directly to Canada, usually to cities such as Montréal or Quebec. As for those who were scalped by the Patriots in 1777, their scalps usually ended up in Albany. From there, the dried-out and painted scalps were sometimes delivered to various New England ports and sent overseas.

It should be noted that British soldiers did not scalp. Various British commanders, however, viewed the practice differently. Some, like General Howe opposed it totally, while others—such as Burgoyne—tried to restrict its usage, though usually without success. Still others, such as St. Leger, encouraged the use of scalping as a weapon of terror.[39] It appears that German soldiers also refrained totally from scalping.[40]

On the American side, though scalping was never officially endorsed and many Continental commanders prohibited its practice, it is known that some Continental soldiers, along with some militiamen and Indian warriors serving with the Patriots, did scalp. Timothy Murphy, a celebrated riflemen serving in Colonel Daniel Morgan's brigade, was one such individual.

It must be noted that in the Wilderness War of 1777, scalping was a rampant habit undertaken by both sides. Though an ugly practice, it was waged indiscriminately. It was not just soldiers and warriors who were targeted. No racial lines were drawn as to who scalped whom and who could be scalped. Loyalists scalped the Patriots as well as their women, children, and Indian supporters, while Patriots scalped the Loyalists and Indians; Indians scalped whites, blacks, and many of their fellow Indians, even some who hailed from their own tribe. During the Revolutionary War, scalping occurred throughout the continent but in certain regions it was more widespread, as during the vicious Wilderness War of 1777. By the time the struggle of 1777 concluded in the northern region, many individuals would be scalped.[41] The vast majority of individuals scalped were already dead, and most of those who weren't died shortly afterward, although a few, including Captain Gregg, lived to tell the tale. Gregg was saved by his dog Cricket. The dog had run off when the men were attacked, but he then returned to his master leading soldiers to come to his aid.[42]

Captain Gregg's wounds were, indeed, very serious, and in that era, a number of doctors would not have even attempted to treat such a patient because they lacked the knowledge and expertise to treat such grave wounds. But Dr. Woodruff was not an average surgeon. He had joined the 3rd Continental Regiment on 21 November 1776, serving as its regimental surgeon until January 1781. He had arrived at Fort Stanwix with Lieutenant Colonel Willett. Woodruff removed the musket ball lodged beneath the captain's heart and lungs, and cleaned and bandaged his head injury. A report read:

> He [Captain Gregg] was a most frightful spectacle. The whole of his scalp was removed; in two places on the forepart of his head the tomahawk had penetrated the skull; there was a wound on his back with the same [tomahawk] instrument, besides a wound in his side, and another through his arm with a musket ball.[43]

The doctor knew that very few scalping victims survived because infection usually set in and killed them. In the event that a victim did survive, the physical, psychological, and mental anguish would always remain. Never would their hair grow back; and survivors were known to wake up in the middle of the night, covered with sweat, screaming as if they once again were being scalped. Against the odds, Captain Gregg survived. He witnessed the victory of 1777 and the conclusion of the Revolutionary War. In time, he even resumed a command position.[44]

On 30 July, an Oneida Indian appeared to Colonel Gansevoort bringing a wampum belt and a letter from the chiefs of Caughnawaga, an Oneida village. In their letter, the chiefs assured the American defenders of Fort Stanwix that the Indians of Caughnawaga were determined to keep the peace with the Americans. But it also contained some vital information. The letter stated that St. Leger's army had reached the Three Rivers. From there, two detachments were now probing ahead of the main body. One detachment was organized around a strength of eight men, and the other around 130.[45] The detachment of eight were to secure prisoners while the larger group was to cut communications along the Mohawk River.[46] Colonel Gansevoort, however, was not the only one to receive this warning. The Oneidas added that they had been warning other military commanders, and still others would soon be warned as well, even the Northern Army's high command in Albany.

That same day, Colonel Gansevoort received a reinforcement of 200 troops. Of these, 150 were from the 9th Massachusetts Regiment whose Major, Ezra Badlam, commanded the entire body. This strength arrived from farther eastward in the Mohawk Valley.[47] Major Badlam had been dispatched by Colonel James Wesson, the commanding officer of the 9th Massachusetts who, at the time, was also commanding Fort Dayton. Colonel Gansevoort's remaining company of 50 soldiers, commanded by Captain Thomas DeWitt, also came in. Initially, DeWitt's company had been posted at Fort Dayton with a mission to assist local militia in conducting training and security operations after Willett brought the majority of the 3rd New York Continental into Fort Stanwix proper.[48] Major Badlam also informed Gansevoort that additional supplies and reinforcements were presently en route up the Mohawk River on two large bateaux, and that in several days, a Lieutenant Colonel Robert Mellon would arrive at the Lower Landing. With Major Badlam's arrival, Colonel Gansevoort's strength rose to at least 700 soldiers.[49] Needless to say, this reinforcement raised both the fighting strength and spirit of those defending Fort Stanwix, and simply knowing that additional supplies and reinforcements were en route further raised morale. Also on that same day,[50] General Herkimer's militia army began to assemble in Fort Dayton.

Reaching Wood Creek on 31 July, Lieutenant Bird's British force now stood approximately fifteen miles to the west of Fort Stanwix. At Wood Creek, he linked up with Lieutenant John Hare and 36 of his Indians who had been probing ahead.[51] St. Leger's main force had now reached the Three Rivers, where St. Leger received Bird's message of 29 July.

For Lieutenant Bird, however, the situation again clouded. He had planned to push out on 1 August, but his Seneca warriors refused. Fearing uncertainty, they demanded that the entire force remain in place until some of their warriors had an opportunity to scout out Fort Stanwix. Only the Canadian Mississaugas were willing to proceed forward.

Assembling the Seneca Indian chiefs, Lieutenant Bird attempted to resolve the issue but to no avail. He could not change their minds; no one would depart until their warriors had seen the site for themselves.

Bird was furious, but grudgingly he accepted the will of the Seneca chiefs. He told them he was prepared to wait just one day—at daybreak on 2 August, he would proceed to Fort Stanwix whether the Senecas were ready or not. Fearing the Senecas would prove to be ineffective, Bird quickly dispatched another message to St. Leger.[52]

Emerging from the woodline at mid-morning on 1 August, three Oneida Indians approached Fort Stanwix. They reported that in the vicinity of Oneida Lake, they had encountered several non-Iroquois Indians. These warriors informed the Oneidas that over 100 Indians were currently congregated at the old Royal Block House. Built decades earlier as a small British Army outpost in the vicinity of where Wood Creek flows into the eastern edge of Oneida Lake, the position was no longer in use. According to the Oneidas, the non-Iroquois informed them that the assembled Indians were awaiting the arrival of a sizable mixed British, German, Loyalist, and Indian force that was coming in from Oswego. Once assembled, their intent was to immediately attack Fort Stanwix.

As Lieutenant Bird was fuming and dispatching another message to St. Leger from Wood Creek, Lieutenant Colonel Robert Mellon, accompanied by 100 soldiers aboard two large bateaux filled with cargo for Fort Stanwix's garrison, was approaching.[53]

In response to the letter received on 30 July from the Oneida chiefs of Caughnawaga, and the warning provided on 1 August by the three Oneidas that a sizable raiding force was nearby, along with the information submitted by "Colonel" Louis and Ahnyero's Indians, Colonel Gansevoort quickly formed a rapid response force. Commanded by Captain Frederick Christian Von Benscheten,[54] his mission was to provide outer security to Fort Stanwix. Upon the arrival of the two bateaux, his task was to protect their crews, the soldiers coming in, and the cargo. A highly patriotic and aggressive commander, Von Benscheten organized a force of 100 crack fighters.[55] In addition to being excellent shooters, Von Benscheten ensured that each fighter was proficient with a tomahawk. He knew that in the hands of a skilled user, the tomahawk was a highly lethal weapon.

Gaining entry into Fort Stanwix in the very early morning hours of Saturday, 2 August, Ahnyero, aka Thomas Spencer, was immediately ushered into the headquarters of Colonel Gansevoort. He reported that St. Leger and his force would be arriving the following day, or even late the same day. He warned that they were strong, and had artillery. He then left the fort to travel on to General Herkimer in the German Flats and warn him as well.[56]

Eager to move at the crack of dawn, Lieutenant Bird was up well before the first birds began to chirp. Thoroughly disgusted with the sequence of events and the fact that an entire day had been needlessly lost, the lieutenant gathered up his force and began to press forward. For Bird, 2 August would prove to be a monumental day.

Bird knew that he could not just run right up to the fort. For the first several miles he could move somewhat rapidly, but afterwards, he would have to proceed with caution. Bird dispatched another messenger to St. Leger, who by now was not far behind.

That same day, in the late afternoon, St. Leger responded to Lieutenant Bird's message of 29 July.[57] St. Leger wanted to let Bird know that he was beyond the Three Rivers and quickly approaching. St. Leger's response would also assure the young lieutenant that all was going well. The general wrote:

Sir:
I, this instant received your letter containing the account of your operations since you were detached, which I with great pleasure tell you have been sensible and spirited; your resolution of investing Ft. Stanwix is perfectly right; and to enable you to do it with greater effect I have detached Joseph (Thayendanega) [Brant] and his corps of Indians to reinforce you. You will note that I have nothing but an investiture made; and in case the enemy, observing the discretion made, should offer to capitulate, you are to tell them that you are sure that I am well disposed to listen to them: this is not to take any honor out of a young soldier's hands, but by the presence of the troops to prevent barbarity and carnage, which will ever obtain where Indians make so superior a part of a detachment; I shall move from hence at eleven o'clock, and be early in the creek.

I am, Sir, your most obt. and humble ser't.
(Signed) Barry St. Leger
[For] Lieut. Bird, 8th Regt.

At approximately 5 p.m. Lieutenant Colonel Robert Mellon's two heavily laden bateaux pulled in to the Lower Landing.[58] After beaching, Mellon's force soon began to unload the supplies with assistance from some of Fort Stanwix's soldiers. Quickly placed upon wagons, the supplies were immediately moved to the fort; simultaneously, during the unloading, Von Benscheten's specialized fighters were ringed all around, providing close security. All of the supplies,[59] along with another 100 soldiers from the 9th Massachusetts, were quickly moved into the fort.[60] Now, Fort Stanwix's personnel strength stood at approximately 850.[61]

As all of this was happening, Lieutenant Bird was observing. From his concealed position behind some brush, he was furious that he had been unable to intercept this newly arrived shipment. One of his tasks—in addition to dispatching reports to St. Leger—was to secure the landing site in order to intercept any Patriots coming in. As for the reports, this had been done; otherwise, however, Lieutenant Bird had failed in his mission.

Of course, Bird knew that none of this was his fault. He had done the best he could. The Lower Landing had not been secured in time, and the supplies had not been intercepted because of the time lost en route, and this was strictly attributable to the Indians. Between their feasting, bickering, and their insistence on scouting out Fort Stanwix, which in the end proved to be unnecessary, Bird estimated that he had lost nearly two days.

Suddenly, Bird noticed Lieutenant Hare signaling. Looking toward the Lower Landing, Bird saw what the Indians were up to. The boatmen and soldiers who had unloaded the boats had departed for the fort, but the two bateaux captains, along with three crewmen, had stayed behind. Though they had been instructed to leave, apparently they felt no danger. As they fumbled about in their craft, Hare and his Indians crept closer and closer.

Suddenly, Hare signaled with his arm. Screaming as they surged forward, the Indians struck rapidly. Within moments one man lay dead and the others were captured. Among the captured was Captain Martin, the commander of the two bateaux.[62] Delighted with their success, Hare and the others unleashed victorious war whoops.

Assembling those around him, Bird ordered them to stay put. "We will stay here until St. Leger arrives." Bird could do no more, and accompanied by a handful of Sir Johnson's Royal Greens, he went looking for Hare and his captives, intending to insure that the prisoners were not tortured.

Until 2 August 1777, the Wilderness War in the western region had been characterized mostly as a war of movement intermixed with some skirmishing, raiding, and scalping. Unlike much farther to the east, where north of Albany and south of West Point in the Highlands major clashes had not only occurred but were still underway, the western region had been relatively quiet. But the curtain was beginning to rise on the fiery hell that would engulf the wilderness. As the night settled over the defenders of Fort Stanwix and the men settled down for rest, most were oblivious that the following day would bring forth a new chapter for those serving in the western theater of the Wilderness War of 1777.

Notes

1   According to Willett, the incident occurred on 3 July. (See Stone, *Siege and Battle*, p. 228). However, it is obvious that he either erred or he got this particular incident confused with some other incident that occurred on 3 July 1777.

    In actuality, the date of this incident was Sunday, 27 July. In a letter personally written by Colonel Gansevoort to Colonel Van Schaik and dated 28 July 1777 from Fort Stanwix, Colonel Gansevoort opened the letter with the words: "Dear Sir – Yesterday, at 3 o'clock in the afternoon, our garrison was alarmed with the firing of four guns." ("Yesterday" implies 27 July). Continuing on, Gansevoort cited "three girls, who were out picking raspberries, were brutally attacked of which two were lying scalped and tomahawked." Colonel Gansevoort also denounced the attack by adding:

    "I had four men with arms just passed that place, but these mercenaries of Britain come not to fight, but to lie in wait to murder; and it is equally the same to them, if they can get a scalp, whether it is from a soldier or an innocent babe." For the entire short but detailed letter see Jeptha R. Simms, *History of Schoharie County and Border Wars of New York* (Albany: Munsell and Tanner, 1845), p. 232.

2   Recovering rapidly, in the following weeks she would remain with the fort's defenders. The daughter of a former British army officer who had settled in the vicinity of Fort Stanwix in the 1750s, the girl was born and raised in the wilderness. She would not only witness firsthand the ordeals of the Wilderness War of 1777, but would participate in the fort's defense. The girl would serve as a nurse, cook, baker, and, to the fort's higher command, stenographer. She would be one of the eight young women to endure the entire siege of Fort Stanwix.

3   One of the killed was the daughter of a former British artillery officer who,

after recovering from his wounds suffered during the French and Indian War, remained as an invalid. Deciding not to return to England, he settled in the area of Fort Stanwix. Lossing, Vol. 1, p. 252, fn. 6, cites the girls had been gathering blackberries when attacked. "Two were killed and scalped, but the third escaped." The murdered girls were wrapped in a tarp and buried behind the fort.

4   Regarding what day 28 July actually was, different authors cite different days. Stone, *Siege and Battle*, p. 220, cites 28 July as being a Tuesday. Eckert, *The Wilderness War*, p. 117, cites 28 July as a Monday. *"St. Leger Attacks!"* p. 6, cites 28 July as being a Sunday. In actuality, the calendar of 1777 reveals 28 July as being a Monday. In a letter titled "Colonel John Butler to Carleton" and dated 28 July 1777, Butler acknowledged that for seven days he motivated the Indians until "they accepted the hatchet [tomahawk]." See Bancroft, *The American Revolution*, Vol. III, p. 377.

5   Today, a marker designates this location. Lossing, Vol. I, p. 241, says that the entire force based in Oswego moved out and provides a diagram of their Order of March. See also Stone, *Siege and Battle*, pp. 218–220. On p. 219, a picture depicts how the army's different units were positioned as they marched.

6   Lossing, Vol. 1, p. 241.

7   Lossing, Vol. 1, p. 241.

8   Ibid.

9   Ibid. The entire contingent of the 8th Foot "Kings" Regiment did not march out on 28 July. A small part remained behind to assist and protect the supply and baggage personnel detachment that departed on the following day, 29 July 1777.

10   Ibid. According to Johnson, *History of Oswego County*, p. 40, at Three Rivers 70 to 80 Mississaugas appeared. But they declined to proceed any farther that day. Their canoes were filled with meat from two oxen and the Indians were determined to have a feast. (Ibid.)

11   *"St. Leger's Attack,"* p. 6; and Johnson, p. 40. Where the Indians obtained the two oxen is not known. It is known that Lieutenant Bird did not possess any oxen because the cumbersome and slow moving animals would have hindered the fast pace he established. Because St. Leger's army did not possess any oxen, they were undoubtedly stolen from some local homestead that was raided.

12   Presently the town of Constantia located in Oswego County.

13   Stone, *Siege and Battle*, pp. 217–220. Lossing, Vol. 1, p. 241, cites that the regular troops encompassed both the British and German personnel.

14   Furneaux, *The Battle of Saratoga*, pp. 106–107. On 14 June 1777, St. Leger ordered "the party of artillery under Lieutenant Glennie to be reinforced immediately by a corporal and twenty men from the 8th, 34th, and King's [Loyalist Green] Royal Regiment of New York. 8th and 34th Regiments will give five each and New York Regiment ten. The 8th Regiment will give the

corporal." On that same day, St. Leger also appointed an adjutant and quartermaster for the artillery. See *Revolutionary War Dates*, p. 4.

15 Furneaux, pp. 106–107; Martha Byrd, *Saratoga. Turning Point*, p. 70; Oswego Times, *"St. Leger's Attack,"* p. 6; and Ward, Vol. II, p. 482. According to Ward, the mortars were small "Cohorns," also known as "Royals."

16 Furneaux, pp. 106–107. *"St. Leger's Attack,"* p. 6, says that the 40 artillerymen were already positioned in Oswego.

17 According to Furneaux, p. 107, the nature of St. Leger's expedition was actually more political than military. According to Byrd, p. 69, "without Loyalist support his [St. Leger's] chances for success would not be high" and "clearly, the expedition's success or failure would be determined to a large extent by factors outside St. Leger's control—the support of local Loyalists and the conduct of his Indian auxiliaries." (Ibid., p. 70.)

18 Ibid., p. 69.

19 According to T. Harry Williams, *The History of American Wars From Colonial Times to World War I* (New York: Alfred A. Knopf, 1981), p. 67, "[St. Leger] gathered a force of 875 regulars and 1,000 Indians." (Hereafter cited as *History of American Wars*.) Williams also cites St. Leger's rank as that of a "Colonel" when, in actuality, St. Leger was a lieutenant colonel temporarily promoted to brigadier general.

    "St. Leger Attacks," p. 6, cites "a total of about 2,000 men including 40 artillerymen gathered at Oswego to participate in the expedition. This number was increased a few days later by other members of the Six Nations who joined the Indian group at Three Rivers." Byrd, p. 106, cites the totals: 200 British infantrymen; 100 German chasseurs; 100 Tory Rangers commanded by Colonel John Butler; 900 Mohawk and Seneca Indians commanded by Joseph Brant; and a Tory (Loyalist) regiment (its strength not cited) raised by Sir John Johnson. Stone, *Siege and Battle*, p. 218, cite "all told, the army of St. Leger consisted of seventeen hundred men—Indians included." Ward, Vol. II, p. 482, cites "his [St. Leger's] white men numbered 875 of all ranks. The Indian contingent, under Joseph Brant, between 800 and 1,000 strong." Eckert, p. 115, cites "a combined force of approximately two thousand men." Ketchum, *Saratoga*, pp. 102–103, cites St. Leger was to command "more than 1,200 effectives." Lossing, Vol. I, p. 241, cites "1,700 hundred strong came up Oneida Lake." And Bancroft, Vol. III, p. 377, cites St. Leger's force exceeded 750 white personnel and, as verified in a letter by Colonel Daniel Claus to British Secretary Knox, "more than 800 [Indians] joined the white brigade of St. Leger." (Ibid.). Colonel Dupuy, *Encyclopedia of Military History*, p. 714 cites "Arriving to Oswego, St. Leger, with 875 British, Tory, and Hessian troops and 1,000 Iroquois." Dupuy also says the Indians were commanded by Joseph Brant. (Ibid.)

20 Ketchum, pp. 102–103.

21 Ward, Vol. II, p. 482.

22 Ibid.
23 Byrd, *Saratoga*, pp. 69–70. Byrd cites that the regulars also included the 40 artillerymen and that St. Leger's expedition included nine small cannons (p. 70).
24 Furneaux, p. 106.
25 *"St. Leger's Attack,"* p. 6.
26 Ibid.
27 Where the Oneida and Seneca Rivers converge together, and from here the Oswego River, fed by the waters of the two other rivers, begins its flow northwestward into Lake Ontario right past the old Fort Oswego.
28 *"St. Leger's Attack,"* p. 6.
29 Eckert, p. 115.
30 Ibid.
31 William B. Willcox, *Portrait of a General, Sir Henry Clinton*, p. 146.
32 Regarding this, there appears to be some discrepancies as to why Bird's mission arose. According to *"St. Leger's Attack,'"* p. 6, "Bird left Oswego 27 July. . . and preceded to Oswego Falls where they camped that night. They were followed next day [28 July] by the main army." And Johnson, *History of Oswego County,* pp. 39–40, cites "27 of July the Advanced Guard set forth." According to Eckert, p. 119, St. Leger "chose Lt. Bird to push ahead rapidly with an advance detachment and try to take the Lower Landing at Ft. Stanwix, thus preventing the supplies getting through." St. Leger's decision was supposedly based on information received on 21 July from an Indian who had appeared from the east. This Indian had been dispatched by Molly Brant. At this time, she was still deep in the Mohawk Valley and was monitoring Patriot activities. According to Brant, who interviewed the Indian, two large bateaux filled with food, clothing, gunpowder, and ammunition were proceeding up the Mohawk River and shortly would be arriving at Fort Stanwix. Therefore, St. Leger dispatched Bird to intercept these supplies. (Ibid.)

Regardless of what the real motive was, in a strict military sense it was a tremendous advantage for St. Leger to have dispatched a strong probing force ahead of his main body. Such a force would not only have kept the main body informed as to what was occurring up ahead, but Lieutenant Bird's force could have also been used as a striking force to overcome any small Patriot forces or positions barring the route to Fort Stanwix.
33 Eckert, p. 119.
34 As a result, various authors have cited 26 July as the date when St. Leger commenced his advance. See Graymont, p. 126.
35 According to Lossing, Vol. I, p. 252, "before the fort was invested by St. Leger, the Indians, in small parties, annoyed the garrison, and frequently attacked individuals when away from their dwellings." Captain Lawrence Gregg, Corporal Asmon Madison, and the three civilian girls picking berries are prime examples of what Lossing referred to. Lowenthal, *Marinus Willett,*

p. 26, cites ". . . advance Indian scouts were seen lurking around Fort Stanwix before St. Leger's arrival. Captain James Gregg, a corporal and three
girls were identified as victims."

36 This was the same Lieutenant Casper who within weeks would be captured
and delivered to Carleton Island where he would be personally interrogated
by St. Leger. Of interest is that Colbrath, in *Days of Siege*, p. 16, cites how
on "July 3d Ensign Spoor being Command with 7 men cutting sods for the
Fort, were Attacked by a Party of Indians who killed and Scalped One,
Wounded and Scalped another and took the Ensign and 4 Men Prisoners."
Because Ensign was sometimes the rank that in those days depicted a Lieutenant, possibly "the Ensign" Colbrath was referring to within this particular
group was Lieutenant Caspar.

37 Regarding the name of the corporal, there appears to be some confusion.
According to Eckert, p. 107, the corporal's name was Asmon Ball. But in a
report titled, "Col. Gansevoort to Gen. Schuyler (Extract)" and dated "June
26, 1777," Colonel Gansevoort identifies a Corporal Madison. In consideration that Colonel Gansevoort was on the scene and submitted the report,
presumably the corporal's last name was Madison. Colonel Gansevoort also
wrote that Captain Gregg "was shot through his back, tomahawked, and
scalped, and is still alive."

Of interest is how Colonel Gansevoort included in his opening sentence
". . . that Captain Gregg and Corporal Madison, of my regiment, went out
a gunning yesterday morning, contrary to orders." Clearly, Gansevoort
wanted to make it absolutely clear to the commander of the Northern Army
that this incident occurred through no fault of his. Possibly, Gansevoort even
feared that General Schuyler might hold him accountable and negligent for
not properly controlling his troops. Though informed of this matter, General
Schuyler never pursued it and he continued to hold Gansevoort in high
esteem. (For the entire report see Stone, *Siege and Battle*, p. 226.)

According to Colbrath, *Days of Siege*, p. 16, "Capt. Grigg [Gregg] and
Corporal Madison [Madison]. . . were Attacked by a party of Indians who
wounded and Toma-hawk'd them and Scalped them. The Captain was alive
when found but the Corporal Dead." Colbrath's entry is dated June 25th.

38 Simple colors and symbols were established to denote a particular scalp. For
example: dried skin painted white depicted an infant. Skin painted yellow
with red tears indicated the scalp came from a mother; green, with a red hoe
symbol in the center of the skin, indicated a farmer killed on a field. If he
had been killed in a house or barn, the inside of the scalp would have been
painted brown with a red hoe. The green indicated a field and brown the
color of a log cabin. The hoe was the symbol of an agricultural worker. If a
settler had been killed in a field or woods, a black ax symbol would be
drawn in the center of the skin. And so it went. For a more detailed description of how scalps were identified, see Eckert, p. 450, fn. 110.

39 St. Leger, however, made no effort to stop or curb it. In fact, he used scalping

as a terror weapon and even offered a bounty of 20 British pounds for each scalp brought in.

40 During the author's extensive research, he never uncovered any accounts or reports of German military personnel involved in scalping. Even torture was ruled out. However, German personnel—when ordered to do so—did kill prisoners. In the event this was done, a victim was usually shot. But even this was kept to a minimum. Though brutal physical punishments were known to be inflicted by the Germans, in most cases these were administered against a fellow soldier accused of an infraction of some sort; incidents of German soldiers looting and burning the homes and property of known Patriots (and even Loyalists) also occurred. But usually when this happened, the German soldier was following orders.

41 This was especially true if a bounty was placed on a scalp.

42 Lossing, Vol. I, p. 252; Eckert, p. 109. Eckert, pp. 109–110, credits Cricket for saving Captain Gregg's life. Lossing, Vol. I, p. 252, fn. 6, also credits the dog for saving his master's life.

43 These words are actually a part of a report submitted by Doctor Woodruff in the immediate aftermath of his operation, but Lossing, Vol. I, pp. 252–253, fn. 6, cites that Doctor Thacher conducted the surgical operation on Captain Gregg and wrote this description. But this medical officer was serving much farther to the east, and he was never in Fort Stanwix prior to, during, or after the siege. In a personal discussion with the historical staff at Fort Stanwix, it was acknowledged that Doctor Woodruff, who served as the garrison's chief medical officer, was in fact the doctor who performed the difficult operation on Captain Gregg. The possibility also exists that Doctor Thacher and Woodruff knew each other. In the aftermath of the conflict of 1777, perhaps both doctors met somewhere and exchanged their experiences. Since Dr. Thacher recorded Doctor Woodruff's observations in his personal medical journal, possibly Lossing drew an incorrect conclusion.

44 Because the captain's actions resulted in the needless death of a soldier and in his own personal suffering, charges of negligence, incompetence, and failure to obey the orders of a commanding officer could have been placed against him. However, Colonel Gansevoort decided that he would not pursue the matter any further. In consideration that the captain had suffered enough, and for the rest of his life would know that his actions resulted in the death of a young man, perhaps Gansevoort concluded that this was sufficient punishment. A lack of time to thoroughly investigate this matter further and the arrival of St. Leger's army, which escalated the war into full fury, were undoubtedly additional factors as to why the issue was concluded.

45 "St. Leger's Attack," p. 6.

46 Ibid.

47 "St. Leger's Attack," p. 6. Luzader, Fort Stanwix, p. 36, also cites that "the fort's commissary, a man named Hanson, arrived the same day with word

that seven bateaux, loaded with provisions and ammunition were on their way upstream."

48 Watt and Morrison, "Defenders of the Mohawk Region" in *The British Campaign of 1777,* Vol. I, p. 104, cites "one [of the companies] of the 3 NY and Badlam's 150 men, marched for Stanwix." (The company from the 3rd New York would have been Captain DeWitt's company.) According to the authors, Fort Stanwix's strength was now raised to eleven companies (Ibid.)

49 This strength, however, would again rise in the next several days. According to a July 1777 personnel strength return of the 3rd New York Continental Regiment, a total strength of 453 was cited in the garrison. (Watt and Morrison, *The British Campaign of 1777,* Vol. I, p. 154.) Of these, 41 were officers (excluding Colonel Gansevoort), 62 were non-commissioned officers, and 349 were privates (Ibid.). Doctor Thacher and his two medical orderlies are also included. However, the August return revealed a strength of 444. (Ibid.) A total of eight line companies: 1st—Von Benscheten; 2nd—DeWitt; 3rd—Jansen; 4th—Swarthout; 5th—Aorson; 6th—Gregg; 7th—Tiebout; and 8th—Bleecker (Ibid., p. vi). But this regimental strength did not include the fort's one artillery company detached from Colonel John Lamb's Continental Artillery Regiment. (When the 3rd New York Continental Regiment deployed to Fort Stanwix from the Highlands, 36 artillerymen from Lamb's artillery unit, a unit also stationed in the Highlands, were attached to the 3rd New York. Colonel Lamb, a veteran of the Canadian campaign, commanded—as per General Washington's orders—the artillery at West Point in the Highlands.) See Lieutenant Colonel (Ret'd) William L. Otten, Jr. *Colonel J.F. Hamtramck: Captain of the Revolution. His Life and Times,* Vol. I, 1756–1783 (Texas: D. Armstrong Co., Inc., 1997), p. 260. And neither the July or August 1777 personnel strength rosters include the approximately 300 soldiers from the 9th Massachusetts, nor the remaining militiamen and messengers numbering over 100.

50 Ward, Vol. II, p. 484.

51 "*St. Leger's Attack,*" p. 6, cites 31 July as the date when Bird's advance party linked up with the 36 Indians commanded by Lieutenant Hare's force near Wood Creek.

52 "*St. Leger's Attack,*" p.6.

53 Lossing, Vol. I, p. 242, cites 100 soldiers arrived. According to the Journal of William Colbrath, *Days of Siege,* p. 24, "Four Batteaus arrived, being those the Party went to meet, having a Guard of 100 Men of Colonel Weston's Regiment from Fort Dayton under the Command of Lieut-Col. Millen [Mellon] of that Regiment." However Eckert, p. 119, cites that Colonel Mellon brought along 200 soldiers. But in his memoirs, Lieutenant Colonel Willett cited that "two hundred men who guarded the bateaux, were commanded by Lieut.-Colonel Mellon of Col. Weston's regiment." See *A Narrative of the Military Actions of Colonel Willett,* p. 50. Luzader, *Fort Stanwix,* p. 37, cites "one hundred men of the 9th Massachusetts Regiment"

arrived on that day. Watt and Morrison, *The British Campaign of 1777*, Vol. I, p. 104, cite "LtCol Mellon and 100 men, soon came up the Mohawk. Mellon's guard and all of the supplies entered the fort only minutes before St. Leger's advance sealed off the lower Valley."

54 See also "*St. Leger's Attack!*" p. 6. Some sources identify Von Benscheten's rank as that of a lieutenant. Regardless, it is known that in 1777 he attained the rank of captain.

55 "*St. Leger's Attack,*" p. 6.

56 Eckert, p. 120, cites that the Patriots were provided ample warning. According to Luzader, *Fort Stanwix*, p. 36, the Patriots in Fort Stanwix were well supplied with accurate information right up to the last moment of St. Leger's arrival on 3 August. "Oneidas and Mohawks sent messages to the fort informing the commander of the progress of St. Leger's column and the whereabouts of Indian parties" (Ibid). During this entire time Ahnyero's scouts had not only been reporting to Fort Stanwix but to General Herkimer as well. In turn, this information was immediately relayed to General Schuyler, the commander of the Northern Army.

57 "*St. Leger's Attack,*" p. 6.

58 Both Lossing and Colbrath cite that the men and provisions that arrived on 2 August had been dispatched by Lieutenant Colonel Wesson from Fort Dayton and this group was commanded by Lieutenant Colonel Mellen. (Mellen's name has also been spelled as Mellon). As for Colonel Wesson, he and his regiment would soon see, in September and October of 1777, action at Bemis' Heights in the vicinity of Saratoga. Wesson's name has also been spelled as Weston, Wesson, and Wessen. (See Lossing, Vol. I, p. 242, fn. 1. However, on the main text p. 242, Lossing spells it as Wesson. But Colbrath, *Days of Siege*, p. 24, spells Weston).

59 The supplies of these two heavily loaded bateaux tremendously assisted the defenders. Now, the defenders of Fort Stanwix had sufficient provisions for six weeks. (Lossing, Vol. I, p. 242.)

60 Lossing, Vol. I, p. 242. Luzader, *Fort Stanwix*, p. 37. Personal discussion with Mr. William Sawyer.

61 Though the exact true strength of Fort Stanwix will never be known and the strength of 750 is customarily the accepted figure, in actuality if one cited the entire personnel strength of the Continentals, militiamen, boat personnel, and the 8 women, nearly 850 were inside Fort Stanwix. (Personal discussion with Mr. William Sawyer.)

62 According to Eckert, p. 122, one boatman was killed and four others were captured. "*St. Leger's Attack,*" p. 6, cites that four bateaux (and not two as cited in other accounts), pulled in and that three boatmen suffered wounds. The one boatman that was shot, stabbed, and scalped, succumbed to his wounds shortly afterwards. "The master of the bateaux was taken prisoner and one man was reported missing after this assault." (Ibid.)

According to *Narrative of the Military Actions of Colonel Willett*, p.

50, the enemy attacked after the last supplies were safely delivered. "These boats arrived about 5 o'clock, p.m., on the second day of August; and the stores were immediately conveyed into the fort. At the instant the last loads arrived, the enemy appeared on the edge of the wood near where the boats lay; and the captain who commanded them, remaining behind after all the rest had left, was taken prisoner." (Ibid.)

Colbrath, *Days of Siege*, p. 24, cites ". . . at the [Lower] Landing, that two of them were Wounded, the master of the Batteaus taken prisoner and one man Missing."

Exactly how many prisoners were taken is not known. Accounts vary, but it is known that after the supplies were delivered safely, an attack occurred. This attack occurred only after Captain Von Benscheten's soldiers, providing security and assistance, withdrew. Why someone, or even a handful, remained behind or possibly returned is not known.

According to Stone, *Siege and Battle,* p. 229, the supplies were delivered safely into the fort. But shortly after, the captain of the two bateaux was captured. As for the number of boats that arrived, it was actually two large bateaux.

VIII

The Siege Begins

At noon on Sunday, 3 August, with St. Leger and his men just hours away, Colonel Gansevoort called for a full military assembly inside Fort Stanwix. Excluding those manning the ramparts and the few such as Captain Gregg, who were lying in the hospital, the bulk of the fort's 800-plus soldiers listened to their commanding officer.

Precise figures for the garrison of Fort Stanwix in August 1777 do not exist, but with additions over the summer its overall strength had increased to around 850. It comprised around 450 Continental soldiers from the 3rd New York, some 300 Continentals from the 9th Massachusetts, 36 artillerymen from Colonel Lamb's artillery regiment, a few of the 100 militiamen who had arrived in May, a handful of boatmen, messengers who had come in and were now caught in the encirclement, and eight women.[1] From this point on these women, too, were officially involved with the defense of Fort Stanwix.[2] By the time the siege was lifted, all eight would have played an instrumental role in repulsing the enemy.[3]

Being the commander that he was, Peter Gansevoort was sincere and spoke straight to the point. He acknowledged that the fourteen pieces of artillery in the fort did not have much of an effective range,[4] and that he had received word that the artillery being brought along by the enemy was more powerful; but he made it clear that if the enemy attempted to storm the fort, the fourteen pieces would be of tremendous value. The 28-year-old commander also praised the efforts of Lieutenant Colonel Mellon for bringing in the extra supplies, gunpowder barrels, and ammunition. Thanking his troops for their efforts so far, he encouraged them to continue to excel.

Colonel Gansevoort, however, did warn his troops that their supply of lead for producing bullets was very low. Much of the ball they had received was too large and needed to be remade, so for the time being at least, the colonel limited his soldiers to no more then nine rounds per day.[5] Needless to say, Gansevoort's men knew what this meant: "make every round count!" Though more ammunition would have been most welcome, Gansevoort's soldiers—especially those who possessed a rifle—prided themselves on the fact that most of their bullets hit their intended targets anyway. Gansevoort exhorted them to shoot only when a sure target was in sight, and shoot to kill.

Ordering his entire command to the position of attention, Colonel Gansevoort first saluted them, then dismissed them with the shout, "By the grace of God, we are going to defend this place!"[6]

As Gansevoort was addressing Fort Stanwix's assembled garrison, about thirty miles farther to the east in Fort Dayton, General Herkimer's militia army was continuing to assemble. Compared to the Continental troops and even the militia personnel serving in Fort Stanwix, General Herkimer's volunteers were by and large a motley force. Many lacked discipline and training; some appeared with outdated firearms. They were dressed in bits and pieces of uniforms, homespun farm clothes, buckskin shirts and pants, and deer- and moose-skin smocks. Raccoon caps, old military hats, and dress or floppy headpieces covered their heads. Footwear ranged from moccasins, knee length fur or deerskin boots, "Sunday shoes" (worn only for church), to regular leather boots or shoes. A few even showed up barefoot in the belief that they would be issued footwear upon appearing.

Their ages ranged from as young as thirteen to those in their forties and fifties, but by and large, the men were healthy and strong. Many stood between five-and-a-half to six feet in height. They could march great distances with ease, and the weather did not affect them. Many were skilled woodsmen. Some could throw a knife or tomahawk with deadly accuracy.

Most possessed muskets, but a sizable number were armed with rifles. Some appeared with both a musket and rifle, and many of those armed with rifles were crack shots. They could hit targets up to and beyond 300 yards and could reload a rifle while on the run. Many were hunters who knew the importance of the theory "one shot, one kill."

Various hand weapons were also brought along. Different types of swords and bayonets from the French, British, and even the Dutch and Spanish armies were noted. Long knives, many homemade, were brought along. Here and there, a militiaman displayed his so-called "scalping knife." Various Indian spears were also exhibited. Five to seven feet in length, and tipped with a well-constructed sharp steel head adorned with beautiful feathers, the spears were exhibited with grace. And almost every militiaman was armed with the traditional weapon of the wilderness: the tomahawk.

Among them, various degrees of military expertise existed. A number of the volunteers had previously been associated with a militia unit. Others, however, had served at one time or another in the British Army, such as during the French and Indian War. A small number were veterans of the 1776 Long Island and New York City battles or had soldiered in the Canadian campaign during the winter of 1775–76. Former Indian fighters, who had previously fought either in Pennsylvania or somewhere out west, were found. From amongst the more professional and skilled personnel, General Herkimer selected a number of officers and sergeants. However, some of the volunteers appeared in groups with their own leaders. Such was the case with Nathaniel "Nat" Foster who, from December 1776 through early January 1777, had fought with General Washington at Trenton and Princeton. He had returned home, but now found himself going into action once again. He led forty other volunteers, most of them veterans of Washington's winter offensive—and now dubbed "Dare-Devils"—into Fort Dayton.[7]

On 3 August, General Herkimer began to organize his force into some semblance of order. The 800-plus volunteers were organized into four separate regiments, each of about 200 men.[8] Colonel Isaac Paris, along with Colonel Peter Bellinger, commanded the Kingston-German Flats District Regiment; Colonel Ebenezer Cox commanded the Canajoharie District Regiment; Colonel Jacob Klock commanded the Palatine District Regiment; and Colonel Frederick Visscher commanded the Mohawk District Regiment.[9] All four of these units were officially formed on 3 August 1777 at Fort Dayton.

It appears that General Herkimer did not have a formal staff section. He did, however, have some close advisors, such as Colonel Samuel Campbell. In addition to being a native of the area, Campbell had also previously served as a staff officer in a regular Continental

Army regiment, and had been posted by the Northern Army into the Mohawk Valley region to assist General Herkimer. Colonel Campbell was also one of the few who wore a Continental Army uniform.

Initially, General Herkimer's intent was to commence his march on 3 August. But because volunteers were still coming in, he decided to wait until the following day before setting out. In the meantime, the slight delay would afford his commanders the opportunity to acquaint themselves better with their commands, and the extra time would be utilized for any final preparations.

As General Herkimer was assembling, organizing, and preparing his force, farther to the west, General St. Leger's combined army was converging upon Fort Stanwix. By late morning, the British general stood approximately two miles from the fort. At a river portage called Deowainsta[10] adjacent to Wood Creek, St. Leger disembarked. He was now aware of Lieutenant Bird's failure to secure the Lower Landing, and that Fort Stanwix had just been reinforced and resupplied. But being a confident and resourceful commander, St. Leger reasoned that once he appeared on the scene, his presence would soon rectify the situation.

Barry St. Leger, however, was not going to show up after his journey from Lake Ontario like a tired dog dragging his feet. The British general was going to march in with style. He was contemplating how he might even induce the rebellious Americans into surrendering simply by a show of force. Thus, orders were issued to shave, clean up, and change into proper, clean uniforms; flags were to be unfurled, the band soldiers were to uncase their instruments, and the units were to be formed into columns with drummers posted up front. The Indians were also ordered to clean up and put on fresh war paint. They were told that when the force neared the fort, a signal would be given, upon which the warriors were to unleash a massive volume of noise. For the next two hours, St. Leger prepared for his grand appearance. Psychological warfare was to be his first gambit.

Meanwhile, inside Fort Stanwix, anxiety levels rose, and from the ramparts and rooftops, eyes strained in every direction—especially westward—looking for first sight of the enemy.

At first, the drumbeats were barely audible. But as the columns neared, the drumming became increasingly more loud and clear. The British were coming. Tightening their hands around the stocks and barrels of their muskets and rifles, the men continued to strain their eyes. At approximately 3 p.m., St. Leger's columns finally appeared.[11] Emerging from the wilderness' woodline, the columns marched in precise military order.

The British were dressed in their scarlet red and white uniforms; Sir John Johnson and his Royal Greens and the Germans wore green uniforms, while Butler's Rangers appeared splendid in their green jackets, light-colored trousers, and leather caps. Covered in war paint and holding their guns, war clubs, spears, bows, and tomahawks, the Indians assembled in the open. For extra sensationalism, the warriors were arranged into a number of groups placed alongside the various conventional forces. Virtually each man and woman within the fort observed this glamorous entry. Even those assigned to the work detail of strengthening the fort dropped their tools and clambered upon the ramparts to view the spectacle.

Once out in the open, the columns began to deploy. They fanned into lines that swung around to enclose the fort.[12] The units maneuvered as the drums were beating, bugles were blaring, and flags were waving. Once the fort was entirely ringed by the colorful army bristling with weapons, the drummers and buglers ceased to play. No one moved; every unit and group stood frozen in place. A deep eerie silence set in—but not for long.

Suddenly, an Indian chief lifted up a knife in one hand and a tomahawk in the other. Raising his head upward, he unleashed a scream. Instantly, nearly 1,500 throats roared in unison. Inside Fort Stanwix, chills went up a number of spines. Colonel Gansevoort knew for certain that the waiting was over. And surely, before the end of the day, St. Leger would demand the surrender of the fort.

Suddenly, the defenders realized that they had no flag! As they viewed the British flag amongst the numerous enemy regimental banners, they realized that an American one had never been issued[13] so one was hurriedly cobbled together. The stars and white stripes were cut out from a white shirt, the red stripes were made from a woman's red petticoat,[14] and the flag's blue background was cut from a blue cloak captured by Willett's troops after they had repulsed a British attack in Peekskill the previous March.[15] The flag was proudly sewed by the women defenders of the fort,[16] and as soon as it was ready, hoisted high upon a pole mounted on the front rampart. Willett wrote:

The Flagg was sufficiently large and a general Exhilartion [of] Spirits appeared on beholding it Wave the Morning after the arrival of the enemy.[17]

Convinced that he had inflicted a major psychological blow upon the defenders of Fort Stanwix, General St. Leger sent forward a messenger under a large white flag with a letter designed to induce the garrison into surrender. Delivered by one of his officers, St. Leger's statement was an exceptionally long and high-sounding manifesto. Besides being "a rather pompous proclamation,"[18] it also meandered from the subject at hand.

Indeed, it may even be argued that St. Leger's statement was more of a request than a demand. Between references to "God," "the King," "the Mercy of the King," "the Roman Church," "the profanation of religion," "justice, devastation, famine, wrath," and so forth, St. Leger's surrender request made no sense of any kind. Marked by exaggerated self-importance and flowery script, it was even difficult to understand.[19]

While the message was being read inside the fort and St. Leger's representative was eagerly awaiting Colonel Gansevoort's response outside the main gate, St. Leger's soldiers and Indians continued their vigilance. Their mere presence, reasoned the British commander, would surely induce the defenders to capitulate.

Despite St. Leger's impressive martial display and his high-sounding manifesto, however, he did not have to wait long for a response because the Americans had no intention of surrendering. It has been suggested that St. Leger erred by exhibiting his large Indian force. There had been cases where a fort's personnel had surrendered, following promises of safe passage, but were then set upon by Indian warriors, and the defenders could easily imagine a similar fate as they looked out at the massed tribesmen with their weaponry.[20] However, though sometimes the sight of Indians compelled a garrison to resist, in the case of Fort Stanwix it would have made no difference because, Indians or not, Gansevoort and Willett would still have refused to give in.

His request for surrender rejected, St. Leger gave the order to withdraw into the forest. From now on, there would be bloodshed!

Because it was late and St. Leger had not yet formulated a plan of attack, the remainder of the day and evening was spent settling in the troops and planning a new strategy. Whenever a military commander advances and encounters resistance from a defensive position, he has a number of options available. In the event that an offer of surrender is refused, a commander may decide to bypass the surrounded position—provided, of course, that he can do so. If he decides to bypass the obstacle, he must ensure that the surrounded force will not pose a threat to his rear. If, in fact, it is determined that the isolated force will pose a threat, then the commander must eliminate it, using either time to wear down the garrison or brute force to overcome it quickly.

Some have argued that St. Leger should have simply bypassed Fort Stanwix and continued to march directly into the Mohawk Valley. After all, the Valley was St. Leger's main objective, and once it was traversed, he would have been able to link up with Burgoyne. However, St. Leger was in no position to simply bypass Fort Stanwix.

For starters, the fort—despite its unfinished repairs—was a much stronger and better fortified position than he had expected; furthermore, the number of defenders were many more than the British had estimated. Also, the regular Continental troops were of high quality, and a very firm and aggressive leadership existed behind the installation's walls.

Had St. Leger decided to bypass the fort and leave behind a token force, in short time the defenders would have realized it. Though St. Leger outnumbered his opponents at Stanwix by at least two to one, the margin was insufficient for him to split his own force. Had the garrison emerged against a fraction of the invading army, it could have engaged and scattered those besieging the fort, cut the enemy's communication and supply line, and destroyed those still coming in. Afterward, they could have pursued the remainder of St. Leger's force, pinning his advance units against Herkimer's and other Patriot columns further up the Mohawk Valley.

St. Leger was in no position to leave behind a minimal or token force to contain a well armed and protected garrison of over 800 men. Had his force been larger and stronger, particularly with more regular troops and artillery, it would have been a different story. But because his strength was limited, and about half his manpower consisted of loosely led and ill-disciplined Indians, St. Leger could not divide his force to simultaneously conduct a siege of a strong fort and an offensive action into the Mohawk Valley. Because it would have been suicidal for St. Leger to continue marching with only 800–900 men deep into the

Mohawk Valley to reach Albany, in the end he only had one recourse: to proceed with a siege.

For tactical control and efficiency, St. Leger established his camp and headquarters tent about half a mile to the east of Fort Stanwix. From there, he would command operations against the fort or against any potential relief column.

Late that evening, as St. Leger was contemplating how to conduct the siege, deep in the German Flats, Molly Brant was giving hurried instructions a Mohawk warrior. Living near Fort Dayton, where General Herkimer was assembling his force, Joseph Brant's sister had accumulated much useful information on the local Patriot forces from other Loyalists, from her personal observations, and from simply asking friendly questions. Indeed, the fact that much information that should have remained secret was allowed to become public knowledge was a key failing of both sides during the Wilderness War of 1777. Conversing softly in their native language, Molly gave the young warrior explicit instructions:

> With all haste, go to my brother. Tell him that General Herkimer has assembled his army here. Tell him there are 800 men. They are going to march against St. Leger's army tomorrow. Most of all, be sure to tell him that instead of continuing to come up the north bank of the river until they reach Fort Stanwix, Herkimer plans to cross over the river at Deerfield and camp at old Fort Schuyler. Then continue up the south bank along the trail to Oriskany.[21]

At Fort Stanwix, noting Colonel Gansevoort's troops placing additional sod upon the buildings, St. Leger's Indians and Loyalists, along with some British and German troops, began to take potshots against them. Shots were also fired from the redoubts quickly thrown up by St. Leger's men during the night of 3–4 August.

Most of the shots missed but some casualties were noted. Among St. Leger's sharpshooters was the celebrated Indian marksman named Ki, who had previously accompanied Lieutenant Bird's force. Ki rarely fired but when he did, he seldom missed. Being a hunter throughout his life, Ki was a crack shot with his rifle and could easily strike targets at ranges of 300 yards and beyond.

His technique was to first perch himself high up in a tree for a better field of observation. Well concealed amid the tree's foliage, Ki would "hunt" for those on the ramparts. Because of shooters such as Ki, the defenders of Fort Stanwix could not expose themselves in their efforts to improve the fort. Noting several outbuildings that had been constructed outside of Fort Stanwix, the Indians set fire to them during the night, leaving the fort standing alone.

In preparation for a full siege, St. Leger arranged his forces to surround the fort. To the east, he established his main camp. British and German camps were also positioned in the vicinity of his headquarters, and the artillery camp was positioned northeast of the fort. In a wide semi-circle, from the battery positions around to Brant's main Indian camp at the Lower Landing to the south of the fort was the Indian line, reinforced with outposts manned by both British and German regulars. Eastward and between Brant's and St. Leger's camp was positioned Sir John Johnson's camp of Loyalists.[22]

However, though St. Leger had fully surrounded the fort, the bulk of his artillery, baggage, and supplies, were still far to the rear. St. Leger had noted that Wood Creek had been blocked by the Patriots, particularly at narrow points, with large obstacles such as trees. Since it would be very difficult and time-consuming to clear the creek, he opted to have a road constructed. This temporary road would be constructed along an old Indian and trapper path for approximately sixteen miles from the mouth of Fish Creek where it empties into Wood Creek toward Fort Stanwix. Although some Indians were possibly tasked to work on this project, by and large it was the job of the British and German regulars, along with some Loyalists, to build this road. According to Eckert, "all but about 250 of his men"[23] were detailed to assist in its construction. Grabbing whatever tools and ropes they had, they proceeded westward to clear and widen the path. As they marched off, the crack of rifle and musket fire and war whoops filled the air.[24]

Notes

1   Ibid. In personal discussions with Mr. William Sawyer and Mr. Craig Davis, curators at Fort Stanwix, both acknowledged that though no precise figure exists, it appears that around 850 were at the fort when St. Leger appeared.

2   Linda Grant DePauw, *Four Traditions. Women of New York During the American Revolution* (Albany, NY: New York State American Revolution Bicentennial Commission, 1974), p. 23. (Hereafter cited as *Four Traditions.*)

3   DePauw, *Four Traditions*, p. 23.
4   Eckert, p. 123.
5   Eckert, p. 123, cites that Colonel Gansevoort issued the order for expending no more than nine rounds per day.
6   Ibid.
7   A.L. Byron-Curtiss, *The Life and Adventures of Nat Foster: Trapper and Hunter of the Adirondacks* (Utica, NY: Thomas J. Griffiths Press, 1897). (Reprinted 1976 by Harbor Hill Books, Harrison, NY, p. 22.)
8   Lieutenant Colonel Downey, p. 19, cites a strength of 800 militiamen.
9   "*St. Leger's Attack*," p. 8; Eckert, pp. 124–125; Watt and Morrison, "Tryon County Militia Brigade" in *The British Campaign of 1777*, pp. 173–182. Watt and Morrison also cite, in addition to names, the numbers: Colonel Cox's 1st "Canajoharie" Regiment; Colonel Klock's 2nd "Palatine" Regiment; Colonel Visscher's 3rd "Mohawk" Regiment; and Colonel Bellinger's 4th "Kingsland German Flats" Regiment.
10 Deowainsta was an Iroquois name. (See also Eckert, p. 122.)
11 *"St Leger's Attack,"* p. 8, cites that the British surrounded the fort from all sides at 3 p.m. on 3 August. DePauw, *Four Traditions*, cites "St. Leger's forces attacked Fort Stanwix on August 3." Ward, Vol. II, p. 483, cites "He [St. Leger] pushed forward a detachment of 30 regulars of the 8th Regiment under Lieutenant Bird and 200 Indians led by Brant. They [Lt. Bird's detachment] reached Stanwix on the 2nd [August], just too late to cut off the convoy of five bateaux and a reinforcement of 200 men. The next day St. Leger and his full force arrived." (In actuality, it was 100 men on 2 August and not 200 as Ward incorrectly cited.) Lossing, Vol. I, p. 242, cites "On the 3d [of August 1777], Colonel St. Leger arrived before the fort with his whole force." (Of interest is that Lossing cites St. Leger's rank was "colonel" when, in actuality, St. Leger carried on his uniform a general's rank.)
12 Downey, *Indian Wars*, p. 15.
13 Willett, *Narrative of the Military Actions of Colonel Willett*, p. 50.
14 DePauw, *Four Traditions*, p. 23, cites that the red material utilized came from a woman's red petticoat. Downey, p. 15, substantiates DePauw's study. According to Lossing, Vol. I, p. 242, "the garrison was without a flag when the enemy appeared. White shirts were cut up to form white stripes, bits of scarlet cloak were used for the red, and the blue ground for the stars was composed of a cloak belonging to Captain Abraham Swartwout." (Captain Swartwout's name has also been spelled as Swartout and Swarthout). Lossing, however, failed to point out that the blue cloak originally belonged to a British officer and was recovered on the field of battle at Peekskill by members of Captain Swartout's company, who that evening gave it to their commanding officer.
15 Willett, p. 42.
16 Some have alleged that at Fort Stanwix, the American flag was flown for the very first time in the face of an enemy. According to Benson J. Lossing,

The Empire State: A Compendious Histroy of the Commonwealth of New York (Hartford, Conn.: American Publishing Co., 1888), p. 271, "It is believed this was the first garrison flag displayed after the passage of the resolution of [Continental] Congress on June 14th, 1777." According to Mark Boatner, "a controversy is raging over whether the first Stars and Stripes to be flown by ground forces in battle was raised over Fort Stanwix or someplace else." (See "Fort Stanwix" in *Landmarks of the American Revolution*), p. 248. Linda DePauw, p. 23, cites the flag appeared on 3 August and "it was reputedly the first American flag ever to fly in the face of the enemy."

A famous painting painted by Edward Buyck titled "The Stars and Stripes Flies Over fort Stanwix, Its First Raising Against an Enemy" depicts a powerful scene with an American flag hanging from the fort. And Lieutenant Colonel Downey, *Indian Wars of the U.S. Army*, p. 15, cites a flag was sewn from an officer's blue cloak, several white shirts, and a woman's red petticoat. Thirteen stars, each depicting a colonial state, were sewn in a circle and the stars were depicted on the flag. According to Downey, "Here at Stanwix, for the first time in the presence of the enemy, the Star-Spangled Banner floated free." Rear Admiral (Ret'd) Rea Furlong, Commodore Byron McCandles (Ret'd), and Harold D. Langley, *So Proudly We Hail. The History of the United States Flag* (Washington, DC: Smithsonian Institution Press, 1981), pp. 102–103, cite such a narrative submitted years later by Colonel Marinus Willett, who was second in command: "The Fort had never been supplied with a Flagg. The importance of having one on Arrival of the Enemy had set our ingenuity to work and a respectable one was formed. The white stripes were cut out of Ammunition Shirts, the blue strips out of the Cloak formerly mentioned taken from the Enemy at Peek-Kill. The red Strips out of different pieces of stuff collected from sundry persons." The authors also cite that evidence indicates, "that the flag flown over Fort Schuyler [Stanwix] was not the stars and stripes but the Continental Union flag." (Ibid., p. 103). Two pieces of evidence that it was the Continental flag are displayed on the powder horns of a William Klein and James Thomson who served during the siege. The Continental flags are engraved onto the powder horns. (In this work, other places are also cited where the American flag was flown in 1777.)

According to Mr. Richard LaCrosse, historian at Fort Ontario, Oswego, NY, "It has never been proven that Stars and Stripes were used [at Fort Stanwix]. It is a legend." (Personal discussion with Mr. LaCrosse.)

In a personal discussion with members of the New York State American Flag Society during the 1999 New York State Fair, its members agreed that the American flag was first flown in combat in the northern theater and in 1777. Although some type of flags were flown on Long Island, in New York City, and other locations in 1775 and 1776, the first official flag depicting the American nation was finally flown in the aftermath of the Continental Congress's official flag decree of 14 June 1777. But where, exactly, the flag was first flown in the northern theater is not known. Some say it was Fort Ticonderoga while others cite Fort Edward. Others claim it was during the Battle of Hubbardton and still others, Fort Stanwix. According to the Society, no one can say with certainty.

In actuality, it does not really matter where the American Stars and Stripes flag was first flown. But everyone agrees that the flag was first flown that summer, and it was flown somewhere during the Wilderness War of 1777.

17 Harold D. Langley, *So Proudly We Hail. The History of the United States Flag* (Washington, DC: Smithsonian Institution Press, 1981), pp. 102–103.

18 Stone, *Siege and Battle,* p. 230.

19 For St. Leger's entire surrender manifesto, see Stone, *Siege and Battle,* pp. 230–231; and Lossing, *Pictorial Field-Book of the American Revolution,* Vol. I, pp. 242–243.

20 Downey, *Indian Wars,* p. 16. According to Hoffman Nickerson, "The sight of the Indians with their feathers, their hideous war paint, tomahawks, and scalping knives, and the sound of their war whoop, showed the garrison vividly enough what would be their fate should their resistance fail and what would happen to the settlements behind them." Cited in Luzader, *Fort Stanwix,* p. 41.

21 Molly Brant's words, doubtless partly conjectural, are cited from Eckert, *The Wilderness War,* pp. 125–126.

22 For a map description of the positions see Eckert, p. 121.

23 Ibid., p. 126. According to Watt and Morrison, "The Operations of the St. Leger Expedition" in *The British Campaign of 1777*, p. 3, "On July 26, on the recommendation of their Oneida friends, the rebels had begun felling trees into and across the twenty-two miles of the creek, creating an incredibly tangled obstruction." Therefore, "general baggage and camp equipage were diverted to a landing at Pine Ridge on Fish Creek. From there, an old military road was reopened through 12 miles of woods so that the expedition's reassembled wagons could be pulled to the encampment sites." (Ibid.)

24 It appears that no Indians were utilized in the construction of the road. The Indians, along with the majority of Sir John Johnson's and Colonel Butler's personnel, remained to continue the siege.

IX

General Herkimer's March to Fort Stanwix

The same morning that St. Leger was aligning his forces around Fort Stanwix and the construction of the road began, General Herkimer's Patriot relief force was marching out of Fort Dayton. Colonel Cox and his regiment were in the lead, followed by the regiments of Colonels Klock, Paris,[1] and Visscher. The baggage trains, pulled by horses and oxen, were inserted immediately to the rear of Paris' regiment. Colonel Visscher, whose regiment fell in behind the baggage, commanded the rearguard. Colonel Samuel Campbell, accompanied by his nephew, Robert, who was a 2nd Lieutenant, would remain close to Herkimer.

Before the sun had even risen on Tuesday, 5 August, Joseph Brant's Indians, along with some of the Loyalists from John Johnson's and Walter Butler's units, were in position before Fort Stanwix. Some had placed themselves behind the newly finished redoubts. Others sought cover behind trees, bushes, and logs, or in depressions. Armed with muskets and rifles, they settled down and peered at the Patriots' defenses. They did not have to wait long. Even before the first light appeared, the first shots were fired. Here and there a fiery arrow streaked through the semi-darkness, shot in hope of starting a rooftop fire.

Knowing that he needed to position his mortars closer to the fort, St. Leger ordered the construction of a trench, approximately five feet in depth and four to five feet in width. The excavated soil and rocks were thrown to the front to provide additional protection. If, for example, the mortar had a range of 500 feet, the trench would be stopped about 450 feet from the fort. Once the trench was finished, the mortar would be moved into place, and its barrel adjusted so that a shell could be dropped directly upon the ramparts and buildings. In siege warfare, the mortar could be a far more effective and devastating weapon than a cannon.

Positioned in a tall tree, Ki sighted a soldier observing through a small porthole. Standing behind the wall in semidarkness, only his face exposed, the soldier believed he was totally safe. But Ki was a skillful shot, and after the crack of his rifle the soldier dropped to the floor, shot through the head. Knowing that his bullet had struck home, Ki unleashed a slight yell. He lowered his rifle on a rope to his assistant who was squatting behind the tree. Once the rifle was reloaded, Ki would hoist it back up. As his assistant reloaded, Ki searched for another target. Soon Ki's skills were noted by both the defenders of the fort and the leaders of the besieging force. Ki was taken to be introduced to St. Leger, accompanied by Joseph Brant, before he set off to continue his sniping. By that point he had eliminated about seven or eight of the fort's defenders.

Arriving at the location from where the road would commence, the work troops immediately began to widen the old trail. They knew that within two or three days, the heavy weapons and baggage would arrive. Then, the fort would surely fall rapidly. Indeed, so confident was St. Leger of victory that he sat down—in a mood of jubilation—and wrote a quick memo to General Burgoyne. Short and to the point, the message informed Burgoyne that Fort Stanwix was under attack, that it would fall shortly, and that "we will speedily meet as victors in Albany." When, in four days at most, Burgoyne received the note, he could assume that St. Leger might have already taken the fort.

That afternoon, General Herkimer arrived near Oriskany Creek.[2] For nearly two full days his men had marched relentlessly, covering about twenty-two miles. Considering that Herkimer's force was accompanied by heavy baggage pulled largely by oxen, they had made good time. Near where Herkimer camped stood the old Fort Schuyler and the settlement of Deerfield, now entirely deserted. Weeks before, its inhabitants—sensing danger and seeking safety—had fled farther eastward and deeper into the Mohawk Valley. General Herkimer was now about eight miles from Fort Stanwix. Nearby was the Oneida Indian village of Oriska, and from there Herkimer received additional support in the early evening hours of 5 August.[3] Sixty Oneida Indians appeared at

Herkimer's camp, among them the scout Thomas Spencer, his brother, Chief Henry Cornelius, and Chief Honyery.[4] The leader of this band, Chief Honyery, was accompanied by his wife, Two Kettles Together. [5]

Spencer briefed General Herkimer and his colonels on the situation at Fort Stanwix. He added that the fort was holding out, but its defenders would need help. Based on Spencer's report, Herkimer began to formulate a more detailed plan. Among the colonels present when Spencer briefed Herkimer was Samuel Campbell. When Campbell and Chief Honyery spotted one another, they immediately embraced as brothers, as they had grown up together. In front of Herkimer and the others, Honyery promised Campbell that he would protect him from all harm. Hearing these words, the officer was tremendously moved.

General Herkimer, however, was facing a difficult dilemma. The Patriot leader had to develop a course of action based on Spencer's information. However, he knew that amongst his senior officers there were those who resented his rank and authority. In addition, the incident with Joseph Brant in Unadilla in late June had tarnished the general's reputation, not only with many in Tryon County but throughout the Mohawk Valley. Some even questioned his military capabilities. The fact that Herkimer's younger brother, Johannes Yost Herkimer, was serving as a Loyalist captain in St. Leger's army[6] did not help the general either. In fact, as General Herkimer was camped near Oriskany, Johannes was assisting the road project. And in that family he was not an exception. Herkimer's nephew, Johannes Hon Yost Schuyler, variously described as dimwitted, or a madman, was also a strong supporter of the Crown.[7]

Back at Fort Stanwix, the defenders had carefully watched Ki's movements, and figured that the sharpshooter tended to remain in the same tree for two shots before moving to a new spot. The fort's defenders were also becoming familiar with the various positions and angles the sniper was using.

A trap was set. The defenders loaded their most powerful cannon with grapeshot, and hoisted it upon the ramparts, carefully keeping it out of sight. A volunteer was asked to walk back and forth behind a rampart as if on guard duty. In the rampart was a sizable opening. The guard would stop, turn, and look out for three seconds—exposed from the waist upwards—before walking on. It was anticipated that after about three such stops, Ki would be ready to fire on the guard. However, by then the man would no longer be the target. After the third pause on his lookout, it would be a straw-filled dummy wearing a uniform and a floppy continental hat that appeared in the opening. If Ki fired, the dummy would be dropped and a cry given out as if someone had been hit. Simultaneously, the cannon, concealed behind the wall, would be swung into action. The cannon crew would also be guided by a spotter armed with strong eyes and a spyglass.

Perched high up in a tree, Ki was observing the fort closely. Suddenly, he spotted the lone sentry on the rampart. Though Ki could only see the upper part of his hat, he was able to follow the sentry's movements. Watching the sizable opening in the ramparts through his rifle sights, he waited for the sentry to reappear. Anticipating another kill, he exhaled half his breath and slowly squeezed the trigger. Ki's rifle barked. A round struck the "sentry," and the dummy collapsed. A loud scream, the cry of death, rang out from behind the rampart. Ki was thrilled! Satisfied, he tied his rifle to the rope and began to lower it down. He didn't see the cannon crew move their gun into position, nor hear the spotter shout to the crew the sniper's location as revealed by the puff of smoke high in the tree. The roar of a massive blast from the cannon sent scores of tiny balls of grapeshot towards Ki. Entire branches, along with Ki, were torn to pieces.

As the Indian tumbled from his perch, cheers from the entire fort heralded far and wide. Standing outside the door of his headquarters building, Colonel Gansevoort saluted the cannon crew. For him, this was indeed a great moment. It was Fort Stanwix's very first cannon shot, and it had been undeniably successful. The sniper duel between the celebrated Indian rifleman Ki and the defenders of Fort Stanwix became one of the most famous events of 1777.

Late that afternoon, Joseph Brant reported to St. Leger the loss of Ki. After conferring with the general, Brant departed, seething with anger. He swore he would kill all of the King's opponents. As for any Indians caught with the white Patriots, particularly Iroquois, he would reserve a special type of treatment for them—and it would not be pretty.

At Herkimer's camp, the men were turning in early, following their commander's orders. Herkimer wanted to approach the fort cautiously, while his colonels, eager for action, wanted to push on with all haste.

Herkimer hoped a good night's sleep would benefit his militiamen and cool the tempers of some of his senior officers. Most of his men were happy to comply, following a long day and a hard march, while others began picket duty. Yet as Herkimer's and St. Leger's respective troops were resting, their commanders were busy formulating plans. Herkimer was working out exactly how to approach Fort Stanwix, while St. Leger was planning how to keep him at bay.

First, Herkimer needed to let Colonel Gansevoort know of his imminent arrival. Shortly before midnight, he personally briefed four volunteers, including Adam Hellmer and John Demuth, both of whom were familiar with this region and its terrain: if anyone could get in, it would be those two. Nevertheless these men faced a difficult and dangerous mission. It would be hard to move quietly and swiftly through at least eight miles of wilderness without being detected. But the worst part would be the last half-mile. Herkimer's messengers would not only have to slip through a circle of enemy personnel ringing the fort, but worse, through the open terrain surrounding it. This terrain was open for only one reason—to be a kill zone. Even if a messenger somehow managed to avoid St. Leger's warriors, there was always a distinct chance that, upon entering the open area, he would be mistaken for a Loyalist and shot by the fort's defenders.

Herkimer emphasized the importance of not only delivering the message, but delivering it accurately—"Human lives, and victory or death!"—hinged on the importance of coordinating the two commands. Once inside the fort, the messengers were to inform Colonel Gansevoort to remain in place. However, Fort Stanwix was to fire three cannon shots with its most powerful cannon to inform Herkimer that his message had been received.[8] Then a group of soldiers were to sally out of the fort to create a diversion. This action would tie down St. Leger's troops and Indians. In the meantime, Herkimer would approach and attack the besieging army from its rear. Once Herkimer engaged with St. Leger's forces, Colonel Gansevoort was to attack from the fort with his remaining troops, and the combined Patriot forces would destroy the enemy.[9] Satisfied that the messengers understood their mission, Herkimer thanked them and wished them Godspeed.[10]

As Hellmer, Demuth, and the two others probed through the wilderness toward Fort Stanwix, in his camp St. Leger was meeting with Joseph Brant, the Butlers, Daniel Claus, and Sir John Johnson. The meeting had been initiated by Brant, following the arrival of Molly Brant's messenger warning of the approaching Patriot column. Realizing that a sizable force would soon be upon them, St. Leger began to question the messenger about what he knew of Herkimer, his militiamen, their strength, and their route. Determined to stop the Patriot relief column, St. Leger decided they would lay an ambush before it could reach the fort. The element of surprise would exert a devastating shock upon the unwary Patriots. Possibly St. Leger believed that the quality of Herkimer's troops was not very high, which would make the ambush even more destructive.

By and large, the region's terrain had been shaped by the ice age, which had carved deep ravines into the land. Brant suggested that one of these, around six miles from Fort Stanwix near the Oneida settlement called Oriska, would be highly suitable for an ambush. It was half a mile long, lying in a northerly to southerly direction after curving from the east, and was exceptionally wide and deep. Although not impossible to negotiate and travel with a team of horses or oxen, a driver had to be especially careful when following the road that traversed the ravine.

Through its center flowed a fairly wide, shallow, year-round stream, bordered by some marshy ground. A bridge, connected by causeways on both sides, spanned this stream and marshy sides. The causeways were constructed from logs, earth, and rocks. The bridge was not large but it was strong, and could easily hold a heavy wagon. Thus far, Herkimer and his force had been using the old Albany–Oswego Road, which eventually led to this deep ravine and its bridge. It seemed likely that Herkimer would continue to follow the road, and once inside the ravine, his force could be trapped and destroyed.

In 1777, the terrain around this ravine was thickly forested and coated with underbrush. It was excellent for cover and concealment. Indeed, so thick was the brush that for those traveling upon the road it could be difficult to see anyone just several yards on either side. Thus, these natural factors compelled Brant to establish an ambush site at this location.

Yet, an ambush, like any military operation, is useless without good troops. Excluding the limited number of British and German soldiers laying siege to Fort Stanwix, most of St. Leger's European soldiers were still detailed on the road project, spread westward along the route, between two and 16 miles away. By the time the work details could be notified, organized, brought in, and dispatched to Oriskany, Herkimer's army would be at the gates of Fort Stanwix. Knowing that he had to act immediately, St. Leger had to rely on his Indian contingent. This was not an illogical choice, because the woodland natives were entirely capable of cross-country movement, as well as concealment, and the concept of ambush suited their traditional style of warfare. Looking up at Brant, St. Leger asked, "Chief Brant, how many men would you need to ambush them?"[11]

"At least 400. Better to have more!"[12]

Knowing that he had to hit the Patriots hard, St. Leger ordered that the majority of the Indians be committed. No fewer than 800 would go. Additionally, he ordered 80 Loyalists to assist. Some would come from Sir John's Royal Greens but most would hail from Butler's Rangers.[13] Colonel John Butler, Captain Walter Butler, Joseph Brant, Major Watts, and John Johnson were to go as well, and St. Leger appointed Johnson to be the top-ranking officer. However, Johnson did not actually participate in the ambush, nor accompany the force, appointing Major Watts to command the Loyalists at the site.[14] In the meantime, the bulk of Johnson's Royal Greens, along with some British and German personnel and the remaining Indians, would continue to besiege Fort Stanwix. Those involved in the road construction project would be left to continue with their task.

The ambushers would be positioned along each side of the ravine. The western and northern perimeters, centered upon a wooded plateau overlooking the depression, would be covered by the Loyalists and some Indians. The southern area would be covered by the Mohawks, Senecas, Cayugas, and the Indians from the various other American and Canadian tribes. Another sizable group of Indians, along with Loyalist soldiers and British military advisors, would be positioned in the forest several hundred yards to the northeast of the ravine. Once the fighting commenced, they would rush in from the northeast to cut the road, secure the terrain adjacent to the road leading into the ravine, and engage the Patriots from behind. Such a move would shatter Herkimer's rearguard and trap his entire force within the ravine in the process.[15]

Proceeding swiftly and quietly toward Oriskany in the early morning hours, the ambushers moved to their positions. Among them was Red Jacket, the reluctant warrior from the Seneca nation.

Notes

1   Paris' assistant was Colonel Bellinger, who also assisted with the baggage train. According to Lossing, Vol. I, p. 245, "The militia regiment of Colonels Cox, Paris, Visscher, and Kloch were quite undisciplined, and their order of march was irregular and without precaution."

2   The present-day village of Whitesboro, located on Route 69, just south of the New York State Thruway. Whitesboro is immediately to the west of Utica. As for the village of Oriskany, it is about 8 miles to the west of Utica, at the junction where Oriskany Creek flows into the Mohawk River. Ward, *The War of the Revolution,* Vol. II, p. 484, cites that Herkimer's force moved 22 miles. Watts and Morrison, "Tryon County Militia Brigade" in *The British Campaign of 1777,* also cite a distance of 22 miles. See also map, "The March of the Tryon County Militia Brigade, August 4, 5 and 6, 1777."

3   "St. Leger's Attack," p. 8; Campbell, *Frontier's Aflame!,* pp. 26, 60.

4   "St. Leger's Attack," p. 8. Honyery's name has also been spelled as Han Yerry.

5   Campbell, p. 26.

6   Eckert, p. 126.

7   Ketchum, *Saratoga,* p. 334. Hon Yost was also a distant cousin of General Schuyler.

8   From where Herkimer was now located, the three cannon shots should easily have been heard. See also Downey, p. 20.

9   According to Downey, p. 20, Herkimer planned to conduct a pincer attack. His plan was such: after approaching and engaging the enemy, Fort Stanwix's garrison would attack out of the fort and, between them and Herkimer, St. Leger's force would be surrounded and destroyed. (This was a much smaller version of what Burgoyne and St. Leger planned to do to General Schuyler's Northern Army. See also Downey, p. 20.)

10 Downey, p. 20, acknowledged that the four runners would have to "creep through the siege lines at night." Although Downey does not directly state that this was a very dangerous and difficult task, in actuality it was.

11 Cited from Eckert, p. 127.

12 Ibid.

13 "St. Leger's Attack," p. 8; Campbell, *Frontier's Aflame!,* p. 25.

14 "St. Leger's Attack," p. 8. Why Johnson did not participate in the ambush has never been explained, but it was common knowledge that although Sir John was an agitator for the British Crown, he was never known to be a courageous leader in battle. Another individual, who for whatever reason did not participate at Oriskany, was Daniel Claus. Joseph Brant commanded the Indians in combat, and Major Watts placed himself under Brant's command.

15 For an excellent, simple portrayal of the ambush site and the placement of the ambushers, see "The Battle of Oriskany" in *The Herald-American,* Sunday, July 4, 1999, p. AA-I.

Brigadier General Barrymore ("Barry") St. Leger, commander of the combined British-Indian-Loyalist thrust eastward from Lake Ontario. *The New York Public Library*

The Mohawk chief Joseph Brant (Thayendanegea), who commanded St. Leger's Indian contingent. Portrait by George Romney in London, 1776. *The Library of Congress*

Loyalist leader Sir John Johnson, who raised the King's Royal Regiment of New York, commonly known as the "Royal Greens."
National Archives of Canada

General Benedict Arnold, before his name became a synonym for traitor, raised the siege of Fort Stanwix in August 1777.
The Library of Congress

General Sir John Burgoyne, who commanded the main British thrust southward toward Albany. Portrait by Joshua Reynolds.
The Library of Congress

The Battle of Oriskany. Early wood engraving which accurately depicts the close-quarters brutality of the fighting. *The Library of Congress*

Colonel Peter Gansevoort, commander at Fort Stanwix. *From B. Lossing's "The Pictorial Field Book of the American Revolution," 1852*

Lt. Colonel Marinus Willett, second-in-command at Fort Stanwix. *From B. Lossing's "The Pictorial Field Book of the American Revolution," 1852*

General Herkimer at the Battle of Oriskany. Painting by Fred C. Yohn. Courtesy of Mr. Frederick T. Proctor and the Utica Public Library.

The Captives
Oil on canvas
© 2008 H. David Wright

The Fort Hunter
Oil on panel
© 2008 H. David Wright

Treed
Oil on panel
© 2010 H. David Wright

Passage To Montreal
Oil on panel
© 2011 H. David Wright

After extensive archaeological research, Fort Stanwix was recreated at Rome, New York in time for America's bicentennial in 1976. It is now the Fort Stanwix National Monument run by the National Park Service. *Author photos*

Open to tourists year-round and just a few miles away from The Battle of Oriskany State Historic Site, today's Fort Stanwix features many details of 18th-century military engineering such as the Chaveaux-de-frise infantry obstacles in the moat pictured above.

Author photos

X

The Battle of Oriskany

By 5 a.m. on Wednesday, 6 August, the ambushing force was in position. As Sir John Johnson was not present, and most of the warriors partaking in the ambush were Joseph Brant's, it appears that Brant was in charge. He was assisted by Colonel Butler, Major Watts, and a host of Indian chiefs.[1]

Following a good night's rest and early breakfast, Herkimer's militiamen prepared to resume their march. For many, this morning meal would be their last. It is difficult to ascertain Herkimer's strength on the morning of 6 August, figures ranging from 800 to 1,000.[2] Herkimer had initially marched out with 800 militiamen from Fort Dayton; however, this strength was soon augmented by the appearance of Chief Honyery with 60 warriors. The column may have absorbed other armed settlers or militiamen en route, while at the same time perhaps losing some ill or stragglers.

General Herkimer was becoming increasingly worried about proceeding farther westward in the manner that he had marched so far. Concerned with what lay ahead, he decided to wait until he heard the cannon blasts which his messengers had requested Fort Stanwix to fire as a signal. He also called a senior officers' meeting at which Colonels Campbell, Cox, Klock, Paris, and Visscher appeared.

Unfortunately for Herkimer, only Colonel Campbell supported Herkimer's decision. A hot argument ensued as to why the militia had to wait. Colonel Campbell—a skilled army officer and soldier who was more knowledgeable of both conventional (British) and unconventional (Indian) warfare and tactics than all of the other colonels put together—strongly advocated a brief halt and cautious approach. Campbell, who at this time was a reserve Continental Army officer serving in the Mohawk Valley, was also one of the few adorned in a full regulation uniform. The other colonels and senior officers were variously dressed, and even Herkimer did not possess an official uniform.

Despite his colonels' disagreement, Herkimer was adamant. They were to stay put. The Indian scout Thomas Spencer was called in, and he voiced the view that Joseph Brant had possibly established an ambush somewhere "along the way to Fort Stanwix."[3] Herkimer proposed to dispatch some scouts to probe toward the fort. After receiving their report, a final determination would be made on whether or not to continue the march.

Herkimer was unable, however, to change the opinions of his colonels, and the tone of the meeting turned ugly. Excluding Colonel Campbell, who maintained a professional stance toward the general, the colonels were neither cordial nor supportive. Colonels Cox and Paris were especially vocal. They accused Herkimer of being a "coward and tory!"[4] Colonels Klock and Visscher also demanded action. All four colonels demanded to push on.

Again, Herkimer tried to explain the importance of waiting—if just for a short while—and urged that scouts be sent out. "I am placed over you as a father and guardian, and shall not lead you into difficulties from which I may not be able to extradite you!"[5] he asserted.

But the rebellious colonels would not give in. Suddenly, Colonel Paris stepped right up to General Herkimer. Starring him directly in the face, he shouted: "Enough! Either lead us now or step down!"[6] Angered and humiliated, Herkimer gave the order to "March On!" in a loud voice.[7]

Thus, with these words, the various regiments assembled and fell into line. After placing the regiments in two columns, Herkimer mounted his white horse. The marching order remained as it had been so far. Cox's regiment was in the lead followed by those of Klock, Paris, the baggage wagons, and Visscher, who still commanded the rearguard. Most of the Oneida warriors were positioned around the main body as flankers, though six were positioned about a half-mile ahead as scouts. Colonel Paris mounted his horse in triumph, bragging to a few of his officers how he had forced Herkimer's hand. Little did the colonel realize that never again would he have a chance to denounce, or even speak to, Herkimer.

Lying low near Fort Stanwix, Adam Hellmer slowly raised his head upward. He sniffed the air and detected no human scent. For nearly the last 1,000 yards, the messenger had been crawling very slowly forward. Several times, he had to stop when he observed enemy personnel not far away. Hellmer was glad that they had no dogs with them. If there was anything that an infiltrator feared most, it was a barking dog.

Parting the brush he looked ahead, and there it was—Fort Stanwix! Observing to his left and right, Hellmer noticed no one. From the other side of the fort, a few shots had been fired, but this was not unusual. For the last several hours Hellmer had noted intermittent gunfire exchanged between the attackers and defenders. Several times he even spotted arrows in the sky flying up toward the fort.

Though he was finally in sight of the fort, the worst part was now approaching. Hellmer knew that once he darted out from the edge of the brush he would be in the open and in the kill zone of both the forrt's defenders and its besiegers. He wished that the sky would just open up and pour like a bucket, or a fog would roll in. But, although the clouds displayed the possibility of some rain, on the whole the weather was very warm. Tempted though he was to wait for darkness, the message was too urgent, and he prepared to make a run for the fort.

Suddenly, he heard the snap of twigs to his rear. Hellmer froze. Then he heard some laughter. It was a small group of Loyalists, just a few yards away. Unfortunately for Hellmer, they positioned themselves alongside the edge of the woodline and brush. One lay not even 30 feet from Hellmer's left side. Noting their crisp, newly tailored greenish uniforms, Hellmer now understood where the term Royal Greens came from. Taking aim, they began to take potshots against the fort.

Hellmer was stuck! From the moment Herkimer had dispatched the messengers, he feared that something like this could happen. Even before he split up with the others, Hellmer warned them about becoming surrounded. And here he was, pinned into hiding by the Loyalists. It was now impossible to make a run for the fort. Out in the open, he stood little chance of success. So until they moved, Hellmer would have to stay put.

Army scout Frederick Sammons did not have to wait long at the Northern Army's main headquarters in Albany, New York. The moment his name was announced, he was immediately ushered into General

Schuyler's office. Schuyler needed information, and the sooner he could get it, the better—his next decisions depended upon it. The general needed to know what was going on west of Albany in the area between Oswego and Fort Dayton, but especially in the area of Fort Stanwix. Schuyler was deeply concerned about whether Fort Stanwix was still holding out, and about General Herkimer's further efforts to stem the British thrust.

As the general spoke, Sammons realized that his one-man mission was of exceptional importance. He estimated it would take him about three days to reach Fort Stanwix, a couple of days to gather up information, and about two or three days to return. To avoid being spotted, he would move solely on foot and undertake the mission by himself. Sammons' mission was dangerous, moving through the wilderness during a vicious conflict with the enemy's Indian scouts flung out in all directions. Sammons knew what every scout knows: that the most dangerous animal lurking in the wilderness was not the one on four legs, but rather the one on two.

By nature, Sammons was a loner. Since youth, he had largely been on his own. Though he occasionally probed deep into the wilderness to trap and hunt with the Iroquois, he was, by and large, a recluse. To be alone with one's own thoughts, fears, and doubts, in heat and cold, in hunger and thirst, in pain and comfort—especially while stalking and fighting—requires a special kind of physical and psychological courage. Alone, the scout "hunts" his prey. Because he is alone, all of his senses must be stronger, sharper, and more finely tuned than that of the average soldier. A scout must learn and respect his enemy. If not, he will err. And in combat, the slightest mistake can easily lose a man his life.

Stepping outside, Sammons noted the two soldiers guarding the main entry into the command building. Other armed guards were positioned around the building. By now, the town of Albany had been transformed into a veritable military base. From where he stood, Sammons could see regular army Continental and militia units heading to the front. Messengers and couriers were coming and going. On Schaik Island, located in the center of the town in the Mohawk River, Continental Army soldiers along with militiamen and civilian volunteers were hastily constructing a fort. Other defense positions were also in the process of being constructed in and around the town.

Sammons saw wagons, loaded with military materiel. Another

wagon, loaded with the wounded—some in bloodstained bandages—was heading to the hospital. Refugees by the hundreds had flocked to Albany, and daily more continued to arrive. To assist the refugees, the Mennonites, along with kind-hearted civilian volunteers, were involved in relief operations. Soup lines, clothing distribution points, and first-aid stations were established throughout Albany. Bread was being baked around the clock. Everything was being done rapidly. Every human, horse, and animal was on a fast trot. The dust rose and obscured vision. On occasion confusion reigned. Yet, amid the tumult, a semblance of order did exist.

Noting the position of the sun, from which he approximated the time, Sammons headed to the southwestern edge of town. His plan was simple: he would move cautiously southwestward, mostly at night to minimize the danger of being observed. Sammons knew about the trails and roads that led westward. But beyond Albany, it would be suicidal to use them. Sammons would only move through the wilderness where he felt truly safe among the trees. He planned to cover the distance as rapidly as possible, yet he would remain constantly on guard. Though time was in short supply, Sammons knew that haste might cost him.

By full daylight, an additional number of Indians, Loyalists, and even some British, German, and Canadian personnel had joined Joseph Brant's ambush position at the ravine. Brant's force was now nearly 1,000 strong and his fighters were placed on both sides of the ravine and road.

When Herkimer's force marched out of camp that morning, most of his newly arrived Oneida Indians were positioned to serve as scouts and flankers. From among those in the vanguard, six were directed to push farther ahead and ordered to immediately warn the main force of any danger they encountered by shot or verbal message. After crossing the bridge and causeway within the ravine, the six Oneida scouts reached the upper western edge of the depression and halted. Sensing that something was not right, they decided to explore further.

Observing the scouts moving cautiously through the ravine, Brant thought that perhaps he would not have to take them out. But when they halted on the upper western crest of the ravine, Brant now knew that he had to move, and signaled to his men. No guns were to be fired; the killing was to be done solely in silence.

Suddenly, a handful of arrows rained upon the scouts. Other warriors, leaping out from cover with their tomahawks, war clubs, and knives in hand, finished them off. In a matter of seconds, the Oneida scouts were all dead. Dragging their bodies deep into the brush, the attackers once again concealed themselves. During this short skirmish, Brant's warriors had remained silent, and moments later the ravine was again quiet and apparently empty, with only the chirping of birds to be heard.

Riding with his force, a worried General Herkimer continued to listen for the cannon blasts from Fort Stanwix. His militiamen were all quiet as they marched, listening attentively as they had been instructed. Among them was 13-year-old Jan Van Eps, who looked up to General Herkimer and was proud to be serving in his militia unit.

After marching about two miles, the Patriot force began to encounter rough terrain that slowed down the baggage and supply units. As it neared the ravine, the formerly compact column had spread out to approximately a mile in length. Colonel Visscher's rearguard behind the wagons was now out of sight of the head of the force.

At approximately 9 a.m.,[8] the leading elements of Colonel Cox's regiment began to descend into the cool depths of the ravine, shaded from the sun by numerous tall trees. Crossing the bridge and causeways, Cox's regiment began to inch its way upward out of the ravine; however the rough western slope slowed their march. As Cox's men struggled up the steep slope, Klock's and Paris's regiments entered the ravine, and the first heavily loaded wagons, pulled by oxen, began struggling cautiously down the eastern slope. The greater portion of Herkimer's force was now inside the ambush area, and his militiamen, oxen, horses, and wagons were bunching up as they covered the difficult terrain. General Herkimer himself was also in the ravine.

Brant's force was not only lurking on both sides of the ravine but also along a good part of the road leading into it. He knew it was time to act. If he waited for the remainder of the slow-moving baggage and rearguard to enter, Herkimer's lead elements and center, along with the general himself, would be outside of the ambush area. And Brant needed to hit them more than the baggage. Many of Brant's warriors were now getting impatient. With their guns and bows raised, they were waiting to fire. The time to kill was now.

Raising his head upward, Brant cupped his hands around the sides of his mouth and yelled one word: "Sa-sa-kwon!" The peaceful tranquility of the ravine was instantly shattered as hundreds of muskets and rifles roared in unison. Bloodthirsty war whoops, accompanied by chants and screams, filled the air. The swishing sounds of hundreds of arrows, many dipped in human or animal waste for additional lethality, flew swiftly toward their targets. Here and there, a warrior emerged suddenly to throw a spear or fling a tomahawk. Reloading as rapidly as possible, the attackers poured firepower into Herkimer's force. And from the cover of trees and brush, some of Brant's first warriors began to run forward. With tomahawks in hand, they rushed the wounded or those too shocked to move.

Tomahawks caved in skulls, broke bones, and shattered lives. But there was no time to scalp—claiming trophies, along with torture, would be saved for later. From high up in the trees, accurate sniper fire raked Herkimer's columns. Struck by several shots, Thomas Spencer collapsed into eternal sleep; within moments, his brother Henry was also killed. Both were among the very first to die. Not far from where Spencer fell, a rapidly flying arrow, its tip drenched in human waste, drove deep into Captain Seeber's upper leg, shattering the bone, and exerting its deadly potency.

The noise was overwhelming; the shouts of orders, the screams of men, and the constant rapid staccato of gunfire, combined with war whoops and screams, filled the ravine and spilled beyond it. Horses galloped past the dead and dying. Some of the oxen, struck by gunfire, arrows, or spears, collapsed. Others, wounded or terrified by the noise, surged forward and—with a number of the wagonmasters dead or wounded—became uncontrollable. As the oxen tried to escape the chaos, their sharp hoofs tore deep into the dead and wounded, while the wagon wheels crushed others.

Struck in the arm, Colonel Paris fell to the ground. Before he could stand up, several warriors leapt upon him. Noting his senior rank, they quickly raised him up and hauled him away.

Surveying the hellish scene, Herkimer began to issue orders. Glancing to his rear, he saw Captain Van Slyck fall. Herkimer knew that he had to bring some firepower to bear upon the attackers. But before he could do anything, his beloved horse was struck. Unable to control his mount, Herkimer remained in the saddle as the animal, screaming in pain, slowly collapsed.

And then, with tremendous force and speed, a musket ball tore deep into Herkimer's left leg just below his knee. The general was hit! Disregarding his wound, Herkimer stood up and and ordered all of those nearby to run up to the top of the ravine, where some militiamen had already sought cover and were holding a position. Noticing that his general required assistance, young Van Eps, along with several others, helped Herkimer to hobble up the steep slope to the top of the ravine. Placed in a sitting position against the base of a large beech tree, Herkimer began to survey the scene. Van Eps raced back down to retrieve the general's saddle.

Within minutes of the commencement of firing, Major John Eisenlord of the Palatine Military District and a secretary to its committee, along with Major Enos Klepsattle of German Flats, and Major Harmanus Van Slyke, also a native of Palatine, lay dead.[9] Colonel Samuel Campbell witnessed his nephew, Lieutenant Robert Campbell, being struck by a bullet which killed him instantly. On that bloody day, Colonel Campbell would be one of many to see a loved one fall.

Spotting General Herkimer sitting at the base of the beech tree and noting his condition, Colonel Cox came running up, ready to assume command.[10] Yet, even as he spoke, one of the ambushing force was sighting in on the colonel. Pulling the trigger, he put a musket ball squarely into Cox's head. Collapsing upon General Herkimer, the colonel's inert form was pulled to the side. Moments later Cox's body was placed upon some of the other corpses to create a "human wall," to provide those still living with some protection from the bullets, musket balls, and arrows.

Returning with Herkimer's saddle, Van Eps placed it underneath the beech tree next to the general. With his back to the tree, the general pulled out a pipe and some tobacco from one of the saddlebag pouches. Filling his pipe and lighting it up, Herkimer calmly began to issue orders. As he smoked, he pointed occasionally with the tip of his pipe in various directions. By remaining calm and poised, Herkimer helped to restore order amidst the chaos, quelling any panic. For personal protection, he drew his sword and placed it across his lap. Someone bandaged Herkimer's leg, while Van Eps remained beside his general. Throughout the entire ordeal he loaded muskets and rifles for those who fought around Herkimer. Van Eps would physically survive the day, but he would never forget his ordeal.

In the rear, Colonel Visscher's regiment collapsed. Although only the leading element of his rearguard came under fire, its effect was devastating. Compounding the situation, some of the baggage personnel, along with some of Colonel Paris' men, directly in front of the baggage unit, began to fall back within minutes of the start of the attack. Dropping their weapons and fleeing in terror, they ran directly into Visscher's regiment. Units became intermingled, and panic set in.

The gap between the rear of the baggage train and the front of Visscher's regiment also worsened the situation. To seal Herkimer's force in its entirety, a number of the Indians and Loyalists, accompanied by some British soldiers, charged the road. As they rushed in, they began to kill those who were falling back from the main column—tomahawks, war clubs, knives, spears, musket butts, and bayonets shattered skulls, bones, and penetrated deep into human bodies. Losing command and control at the start, Visscher was never able to restore it.[11]

Perhaps, had Visscher restored order, he would have been able to circle around and inflict damage upon Brant's ambushing force from behind. But he was unable to exert effective command. A number of Visscher's men, along with those from other units, fled all the way back to Fort Dayton. Later, some of their hacked and scalped bodies were found along the route. The survivors moved farther back into the Mohawk Valley. As they fled, they spread far and wide the horrible news of death and destruction, reports which were further exaggerated and embellished by those who heard them. Needless to say, such misinformation created much fear and anxiety in the Mohawk Valley, and when it reached the headquarters of the Northern Army in Albany, it caused General Schuyler and his staff undue concerns and hardships.

Although the brunt of Visscher's regiment collapsed, two of his companies stood firm.[12] Commanded by Captains Jacob Gardinier, John Davis, and Lieutenant Jacob Sammons, the two companies became surrounded. Spotting one of his militiamen being dragged away by several Loyalists, Captain Gardinier grabbed a spear and charged them. With lightning speed he killed all three, grabbed his trooper, and brought him back. Establishing a defensive perimeter, the officers and their men successfully held the rear.

Farther to the front, near General Herkimer, the battle was raging in full fury. Intoxicated with victory and seeking to finish off Herkimer's force, Brant's Indians and Loyalists surged forward. But as they charged

Map by Shaketa Preal

the Patriots, seeking scalps from their stricken foes, they suddenly encountered stiff resistance.

Charging right into the midst of Herkimer's troops, three of Johnson's Royal Greens sought to kill or capture Captain Andrew Dillenbeck. An officer in the Palatine Military District, Dillenbeck was the son of German immigrants who had settled in the Mohawk Valley and were still residing there. Fluent in English, German, French, and Iroquois, Dillenbeck was an intellectual who had quickly adopted the Revolutionary cause.

Grabbing Dillenbeck's bayonet-tipped musket, a Loyalist attempted to wrestle the weapon out of his hands. Wrestling it free from the Loyalist, Dillenbeck smashed the musket's butt squarely into the face of his opponent. Moving like a cat, he shot the second Loyalist and thrust the musket's bayonet right through the body of the third. Thrusting backward, Dillenbeck pulled out the bloodied bayonet as the dead Loyalist plummeted to the road. But before Dillenbeck could either plunge the bayonet into another opponent or reload the musket, an incoming bullet or musket ball killed him instantly.[13]

Attempting to kill at close range and obtain some scalps, Lieutenant Hare—the Indian leader who had accompanied British Lieutenant Bird to the Lower Landing just several days before—charged forward. Hare, however, never made it. Struck by a volley of gunfire, the Indian lieutenant went down.

Colonel Campbell had been riding in the center of the force near General Herkimer when the attack began. He quickly dismounted and began to command.[14] Organizing a number of militiamen around himself, Campbell was able to mount an effective resistance.

True to his word of the day before, the Oneida chief Honyery protected his colonel. When the first shots were fired, Honyery was within 50 feet of his old friend. Noting the barrel of a musket being lowered in the brush toward the colonel, Honyery quickly raised his rifle, took aim, and fired. A dead Loyalist tumbled out of the brush. Seeking cover with his wife but always remaining close to his colonel, both Honyery and Two Kettles Together extracted a toll from the attackers. According to Jane Cannon Campbell, Colonel Campbell's niece, Honyery shot and killed three Loyalists who attempted to kill her uncle.[15]

By now the battle had become a vicious struggle. Once the shock of surprise had passed, the Patriots grimly fought for their lives, while the attackers suddenly found themselves grappling with a tough and desperate foe. Gunsmoke filled the ravine and drifted upward; blood flowed in rivers, and hand-to-hand combat was the norm. Guns and arrows were fired at point-blank range, while knives, tomahawks, war clubs, bayonets, and spears were used abundantly. Discharged rifles and muskets were swung like clubs. If a weapon struck bone or skull and broke in half, the piece that remained in hand was now utilized as a club. And many an outcome was decided solely with bare hands.

Charging forward to repel a group of Indians and Loyalists, Herkimer's militiamen grabbed an Indian warrior. It was Chief Sanger-achta. Beating and clubbing him, they dragged the semiconscious chief back to the road. As he lay on the ground, a group of men quickly surrounded him. Suddenly, one militiaman squatted down beside the chief and displayed his knife to him. He then informed the chief that they had killed his warriors, and would now kill him. His death was too gruesome to describe.

Just yards away, as a screaming warrior rushed toward him, Colonel Campbell immediately grabbed the hilt of his sword with both hands. As the warrior neared, Campbell raised his sword. Swinging it downward at an angle, and throwing his weight behind it, Campbell struck the warrior in the upper left part of his neck. The sword penetrated deeply—so deeply that it almost severed off the warrior's head. As the warrior fell, Colonel Campbell pulled upward and removed his bloodied sword. Undeterred, he began to issue new orders. Underneath him lay another Indian chief: Gisugwatoh.

Horrified, and shocked at what he was witnessing, the young Seneca Red Jacket dropped his weapons, turned around, and ran. He could take no more. Disgusted with everything, but especially the cursed British with their damn Loyalists, Red Jacket fled westward. He did not stop until he reached the Genesee River, not far from where it empties into Lake Ontario.[16] For Red Jacket the war was over.

Her floppy hat lost, her hair untied and hanging loose, the girl who until now had been posing as a male could no longer hide her identity. But in this hell, it did not matter. What now mattered were her fighting skills. Until now, she had managed to fire and reload five or six times. But as the Indians swarmed in, it was now strictly hand to hand. Seeing a fellow militiaman in need, the girl raised her rifle, charged forward, and swung with her entire strength and fury. As she shattered her opponent's back, she broke her rifle in half.

Until that moment her rifle had been her main weapon. But she still had one more. Slung over her deerskin-fringed jacket was a sizable leather bag. Inside, besides a few personal belongings, she carried another prized weapon: the tomahawk. Reaching for it, she pulled it out and raised it upward. She was back in action.[17]

Under his tree, General Herkimer realised that his militiamen were vulnerable after firing a shot: before they could reload, warriors would often charge forward with a tomahawk, club, knife, or spear in hand, forcing the militiaman into a hand-to-hand battle. To counter this, General Herkimer ordered that his militiamen fight in two-man teams. One would fire and then reload while covered by his partner. If an enemy lunged forward, his teammate would engage the attacker. This change in tactics paid off, and Herkimer's men began to inflict heavy losses upon the attackers. In the meantime, a number of the lightly wounded were designated as reloaders. Muskets and rifles were passed back and forth and reloaded as quickly as possible. Among the reloaders was 13-year-old Van Eps, remaining within several feet of his general.

Honyery, however, did not need a partner as he still had his wife, Two Kettles Together. In his right hand, Honyery held a tomahawk and in his left, he grasped a long knife. Both instruments were covered in blood. Shadowing him was his wife, armed with a rifle and tomahawk, Honyery's brave wife repeatedly fired and reloaded her weapon. So proficient was Two Kettles Together with her rifle that she could reload it while on the run. Charging into two soldiers from behind, Honyery struck one over the head with his tomahawk and drove the knife deep into the lower back of the other. Both collapsed onto the ground. Leaping several yards forward, Honyery turned to see how Colonel Campbell was doing. The moment he did, Honyery's wife came running up.

As for the soldier who was stabbed, he attempted to stand up. Rising to his knees, he touched the gash and felt the warm blood; he knew that it was a serious wound. His entire stomach burned from the deep puncture wound.

His pain, however, did not last long. Suddenly, Honyery's wife moved up. Not wanting to waste a shot, she raised her tomahawk up and drove the weapon's sharp steel blade deep into his head. Plummeting to the ground, blood spilled out in huge red globs from the soldier's shattered skull.

Calm and poised, Nat Foster and his "Dare-Devils"—veterans of Trenton and Princeton—moved among the trees and brush like wildcats. Foster and his men protected one another and inflicted heavy casualties upon their opponents. Virtually every time they aimed and fired, an opponent went down. Spotting a British officer huddled behind a fallen tree over 100 yards away, and viewing the scene through a one-eyed telescope, Foster crawled slightly forward, took aim in a lying position, and drilled a bullet right between his eyes.

Miles away, Adam Hellmer knew that something big was happening. Unfortunately he was still stuck in the bushy woodline outside Fort Stanwix. Hiding next to the same Loyalists who had settled down near him earlier, he was still unable to move. But he was almost certain that the huge rumbling noise he was now hearing in the distance had something to do with General Herkimer. He wondered whether Colonel Gansevoort knew of Herkimer's coming, and he wondered if any of the others had made it in. Since he had not heard the blasts of any cannons, he reasoned that none of the other couriers had made it to Stanwix either. Hellmer toyed with the idea of just making a run for the fort, but he knew the folly of this. He had to remain in place.

As Hellmer waited impatiently, just yards away the defenders of Fort Stanwix were by now fully aware that a battle was underway. From the fort one could not only hear the noise, but from the ramparts everyone could see the huge cloud of smoke and dust above the ravine. Anticipating that wounded personnel would soon be streaming in, Doctor Woodruff, along with his orderlies and eight women, began to prepare the medical area for incoming casualties. Bins of hot water were readied, bandages were laid into place, and tables were set up along with clean sheets, cutting knives, and scissors. In addition, alcohol and chloroform were placed nearby, and the operating tools were brought out. Lives had to be saved.

Doctor Woodruff, however, was not the only one thinking ahead. Inside the safety of the fort, Lieutenant Colonel Willett was considering a sally from the fort. It would be the last thing expected, and perhaps they would even get lucky and capture St. Leger. Approaching Colonel Gansevoort, Willett proposed a raid upon St. Leger's camp. Given the authorization to prepare a striking force, Willett immediately asked for 250 volunteers. Within minutes, he had all the men he needed. Conferring with his officers, Willett began to fine-tune his plan.

By now, the battle in the ravine had reached its climax. Amid the smoke and dust, men fought with a savagery, desperation, and fury never seen previously in upper New York. In the annals of the Revolution, the Battle of Oriskany is regarded as one of the most vicious engagements of the entire war.

The gunfire, the nauseating, thick smoke, the screams and groans of dying men and animals, the high-pitched yells and war whoops, the "swish" of incoming arrows and thrown tomahawks, and the noise of explosions rocked the entire region for many miles around. In the words of Jane Campbell, "The struggle became so murderous that blood flowed down the hill in rivulets."[18] As for the creek that flowed through the ravine, its water was no longer clear; it was now running with a tint of red.

Lying on the ground amid the dead and dying, Honyery pretended to be dead. As the massive battle raged around him, he lay totally still. Even when several individuals stomped on him as they ran by, Honyery remained motionless. Yet, through the narrow slits of his mostly closed eyes, Honyery was carefully observing the Mohawk warrior who was stalking Colonel Campbell.

Campbell was about 50 feet behind Honyery, shouting encouragement and guidance, totally unaware that he was being targeted. Honyery knew that the huge Mohawk shifting his position from the right to the left was targeting the colonel. The warrior was seeking an opening, and once found, the Mohawk would rush in to kill him.

When he fell, Honyery had deliberately placed his right arm about a foot to the front of his head. Such a position would not only conceal his eyes, but also would enable him to raise both his arm and tomahawk rapidly into action. Barely breathing, Honyery just waited. To his immediate front, the battle had suddenly subsided. The group of men fighting directly in front of and around the Oneida chief had shifted themselves farther to the right and left. The Mohawk saw his chance and raced ahead, raising his tomahawk as he approached Campbell, who was still unaware.

Suddenly the Mohawk tripped, stumbled, and fell flat on his face. Before he could stand up, he felt the sharp blow of a tomahawk striking him in the middle of his lower back. His spine was shattered, paralysing him.

Within seconds, Honyery had put his left arm around the Mohawk's neck, jerking him into a sitting position. Honyery raised his right arm, grasping his tomahawk, and readied to strike. Glancing towards Colonel Campbell, Honyery noted the colonel was now looking at him. Momentarily, they stared at one another—but not for long. The colonel nodded his head, and Honyery knew what that meant.

Honyery's tomahawk penetrated deep into the Mohawk's head and tore through his brain. The very last sound the Mohawk heard was Honyery's triumphant scream. Honyery, dripping with blood, released the warrior's body, and raising his bloodied tomahawk up as far as he could, released his scream of victory.

Noting his rising casualties, Joseph Brant began to worry. Though masterfully executed, his ambush had not been a total success. The element of surprise had been expended, and now it was a face-to-face fight between denizens of the wilderness on both sides. Despite Herkimer's losses, the Patriot general was not only holding out, but exacting a grim toll of his attackers. Brant, however, was still convinced that he could achieve a victory. But in order to win, he needed two things: additional time and a strong reinforcement.

As the killing continued, men on both sides continued to stalk each other for open shots and grapple hand to hand. By now, both sides were facing exhaustion; yet, neither would give in. But as often occurs in warfare, nature intervened.

With no warning, the clouds suddenly opened up at around 11 a.m. Caught in the downpour—with the exception of a few who carried on fighting—both sides ceased their struggle. It was, indeed, a true respite.[19] The first phase of the battle was over.

Sensing an opportunity that could be exploited to his advantage, Brant immediately dispatched Major Watts to return to the main camp to bring up reinforcements. Although some of Johnson's Royal Greens had been committed, the greater percentage of his unit was still laying siege to Fort Stanwix. Brant wanted Johnson's entire regiment, along with any additional Indians, British, and German personnel that St. Leger could dispatch. Knowing that the massive storm would soon abate, Brant urged Major Watts to hurry.

Initially, when Brant's ambushers commenced their attack, the brunt of Herkimer's force was caught in the massive ravine. Yet Herkimer and his militiamen had somehow managed to extract themselves from the ravine and secure the western plateau overlooking not only the ravine, but the terrain all around. At the same time, east of the ravine, Herkimer's militiamen also secured some higher ground. Also, as they charged uphill, Herkimer's men slaughtered many of Brant's warriors who had charged into the ravine seeking scalps. Wherever they formed their defensive circles,[20] they not only held the higher ground but terrain that was well protected by numerous trees. Whether Herkimer's men realized it or not, they had not only successfully fought uphill and repulsed their opponents around the ravine, but by their actions had saved their force in the process. It has been argued that had Herkimer and his force instead remained in the ravine, they would have all been wiped out within 45 minutes.[21] Breaking out of the ravine was significant in saving the remainder of the force.[22] The fact that Herkimer's men could assist him in reaching the high ground and even return to recover his saddle and carry it out of the ravine is proof that Herkimer's militiamen had successfully extracted themselves from a precarious situation.

Along with Major Watts, Brant sent back his wounded. Within minutes of Watts' arrival at the main camp, the wounded began to trickle in. Able-bodied individuals under various excuses to avoid further combat begin to appear as well.

St. Leger could not have been pleased to see Major Watts. After all, he had dispatched a sizable force of nearly 1,000 strong, and had been assured by Johnson and Brant that Herkimer's force would be totally wiped out. Instead, St. Leger was now hearing of casualties, watching the wounded enter the camp, and receiving a request for reinforcement.

Sending additional men to Oriskany would reduce the pressure on the Patriot fort, but St. Leger had no choice. Therefore, he issued two orders: the rest of Johnson's Royal Greens, along with some additional British, German, and Indian warriors, were to immediately march to the Oriskany battlefield. In the meantime, half of those involved on the road project were to be recalled. A messenger was immediately dispatched westward to where the project was underway.

Adam Hellmer was still lying still in the woodline at around 1 p.m. when his patience was finally repaid. A Loyalist officer appeared and led off the soldiers. Hellmer knew that it was now or never—Colonel Gansevoort still needed to know of Herkimer's message. Bolting like a rabbit into the open, Hellmer raced for the fort. He began to zigzag.

Initially no one pursued him. But then, he heard shouts behind him followed by a shot. A musket ball whizzed by his ear. As he neared the fort, he noted activity upon the ramparts. Screaming that he was not an enemy, Hellmer raised his musket upwards with both hands as he raced for the fort. The fort's heavy rear gates were opened up just enough for a man to squeeze through. More shots followed, but these came from the ramparts. Good covering fire.

As Hellmer squeezed into the interior of the fort through the narrow opening, the heavy gates were slammed shut. Finally, he was inside! Regaining his breath, he announced to the defenders who he was and his mission. Hellmer was immediately escorted to Colonel Gansevoort. Noting the time, Hellmer hoped that it was not too late.[23]

To support Brant, Sir John dispatched his remaining two Royal Green companies. The 1st Company was commanded by Lieutenant Donald John McDonald, and the 2nd by Captain Angus McDonald.[24] Now, the entire Royal Green Regiment was committed to the Oriskany battle. Additionally, more British, German, and Indian personnel were dispatched. St. Leger may still have been confident that Brant would finish off Herkimer, or he may have begun to have some doubts. Any commander under such circumstances would have had qualms.

As the pitch-black sky rumbled and unleashed a cold rain, the temperature dropped. In central and northern New York, it is not uncommon for the weather to turn very cool, if not cold, during and following rain—even in the summer. As the rain drenched both the attackers and defenders, Brant's Indians began to grumble more and more.

As they had with the ravens at Oswego, the Indians foresaw the cold rain as another sign of doom. With discontent setting in, morale plummeted and the Indians began to seek a way out. Angry and upset about their losses, and realizing that victory would possibly not be theirs, the Indians began to unanimously voice strong resentments, remembering the promises made to them back in Fort Niagara, Irondequoit Bay, and Oswego: "The British will achieve an easy victory. . ."; "there will be plenty of bounty. . ."; "Indian warriors will be kept out of any fighting. . ."; "you will just watch. . ."; ". . . smoke tobacco. . ." But there had been no easy victory, hardly any bounty existed, and very little pipe smoking had taken place. As for the issued tobacco, it was limited and of low grade. What especially infuriated the Indians were the promises that they would be kept out of the fighting. Yet, in actuality, only the opposite had occurred. They had not only been committed into battle, but worse, were thrown into some of the most hazardous and vicious combat. For this, there was a price to pay. From Fort Stanwix to Oriskany, the fields were covered with Indian dead.

Despite the heavy downpour and a halt to the fighting, skirmishes continued. Needing a weapon to replace his privately owned rifle, lost during the fighting, Major Samuel Clyde, a native of Cherry Valley, skirted among the trees and brush in search of a discarded rifle or musket. As he searched, he suddenly came face-to-face with one of Butler's Rangers. A hand-to-hand struggle ensued, the Loyalist gaining the upper hand. He knocked Major Clyde to the ground. Raising up his bayonet-tipped musket to plunge into the major's body, the Loyalist suddenly fell backward as a shot ended his life.

Noting the major crawling away from among his circle of friends, Private John Flock, a native of Johnston, had decided to follow. Suspecting that Major Clyde would need help, Flock monitored his activity from a short distance behind. When the major got involved in a hand-to-hand struggle Flock approached quickly and quietly. Kneeling down, he took careful aim. His well-placed shot saved the major's life. Grabbing the Loyalist's musket, ammunition pouch, gunpowder horn, and canteen, Major Clyde was now ready. Of course, he probably would have preferred a rifle to a musket, but for now, the musket—with its long bayonet and heavy stock—was best suited for close-in fighting. After thanking Flock, the two men dashed back to their position.

On another part of the field, after exhaling half his breath, a militiaman slowly squeezed and fired. Following the shot, he noted his Indian target collapsing to the ground. The militiaman could barely see him, but he knew that the warrior was lying right behind a thick clump of brush. Racing forward with several others, the militiaman quickly reached the spot. Initially his intent was to scalp the warrior, but upon reaching him, they noticed he was a chief.

It was Chief Ghalto. Fortunately for him, the musket ball that had penetrated his body did not tear any critical organs. Semiconscious, the chief could not resist for the moment. Realizing that he might be of more value to the Patriots alive than dead, the militiamen grabbed Ghalto, hauled him back to their defensive circle, and tied him up.

Intermittent gunfire, with individuals making attempts to obtain scalps, characterized the struggle following the immediate heavy downpour. For Herkimer and his militia force, it was a short, but critically needed period of respite for reorganization, checking ammunition, and repositioning. During this lull, Colonel Campbell again played a vital role. After conferring with Herkimer, Campbell immediately moved to his task. During the first hour of the horrific downpour and the second hour of mild rain, Campbell moved among the command, encouraging the men, putting them into good firing positions, and checking on the wounded. He knew that it was not yet over; during this period of respite, the enemy was no doubt renewing their preparations for another attack.

Back at Fort Stanwix, standing upon the ramparts, Lieutenant Colonel Willett scanned the grounds around the fort. It was obvious that the pressure against the fort had subsided. Some of the men on the ramparts had also informed Willett that they had observed soldiers in green-colored uniforms, along with Indians and regulars from the British and German forces, being recalled from the edge of the woodline. Willett was also present when Hellmer briefed Colonel Gansevoort. And when Hellmer stated that he had not been able to come in earlier because he had been stuck in the midst of a bunch of Loyalists, who in time were recalled by one of their officers, Willett began to suspect that perhaps they had been withdrawn to be committed against Herkimer. Peering through his telescope, Willett could not see anything. Other than a rare shot or incoming arrow directed against the fort, it was quiet. The heavy downpour had quieted everything. In fact, the quiet was unusual.

Turning around, Willett looked down into the interior of the fort, still noting the eerie silence. Standing still and awaiting his final decision were the 250 men who had volunteered to follow him in the sally against the enemy. Willett knew that they were the best and bravest he had. To support the raid they even hitched seven wagons to evacuate any wounded personnel or captured enemy materiel. For the time being, the wagons would remain within the fort. Each one had a driver, assistant driver, and about five gunmen. Two to four horses were hitched to each wagon.

Willett could sense that his men were anxious to get started. He could see it; he could feel it, but it was a tremendous risk. Willett knew that if the raid failed, Fort Stanwix would pay a heavy price. Willett also knew that since it was he who had initiated the plan, in the event of failure, he would have to live with it. He had to make a command decision—it was either now or never. Willett decided to conduct the raid.

As the sky cleared and the sun began to emerge, Herkimer's men could hear the sounds of beating drums in the distance. The Royal Greens were on their way to the ravine. Before the regiment reached Herkimer's defensive position, Colonel John Butler made a suggestion to Major Watts. If the men's green jackets were worn inside out, the men of the Royal Greens would look like an American contingent from Stanwix approaching to assist the encircled force, especially as the hats worn by the Royal Greens were similar to those worn by many of Herkimer's militiamen. Heeding Butler's advice, Major Watts ordered the leading ranks of his soldiers to reverse their green jackets.[25]

Spotting the incoming force, Herkimer's men were at first delighted. Lieutenant Jacob Sammons[26] was one of the first to note the incoming infantry. Believing that they were friendly reinforcements, Sammons ran to inform his company commander, Captain Gardinier—"an officer who, during that memorable day, performed prodigies of valor"[27]— that help was coming.

Captain Gardinier, however, was suspicious about these incoming "Patriots." Spotting one of his soldiers running out to greet the newly arriving force, Gardinier tensed for action. The soldier who ran out did so because he spotted a prewar acquaintance. As Gardinier's militiaman jogged up to the Royal Greens' column, he even extended his hand for a friendly handshake. Suddenly, the militiaman was grabbed, but not in a friendly manner. Pulled into the ranks, cries of "prisoner" were heard. Even before he was grabbed, Captain Gardinier had warned Sammons, "Not so! They are enemies! Don't you see their green coats!"[28] Wielding a spontoon, the captain, accompanied by Adam Miller and a small group, charged forward. Once again, Captain Gardinier made a personal effort to assist one of his soldiers in need. A fight ensued, and more blood was spilled. Yet, even now, some of Gardinier's men could still not believe that an enemy force was virtually upon them. "For God's sake, Captain, you are killing your own men!" they screamed.[29]

Suddenly, with fixed bayonets, three of the disguised Royal Greens sprang upon Captain Gardinier. Two bayonet thrusts struck the brave captain in both of his thighs. A third thrust, directed towards his chest, was thwarted by the captain's left hand. His hand, however, sustained a severe cut. Raising his spear-like spontoon upward in a quick motion, Captain Gardinier drove it deep into one of the Royal Greens soldiers, who just seconds before had attempted to kill him.[30] As the soldier collapsed to the ground, he noticed it was Lieutenant Donald John McDonald, a former resident of Tryon County who had adopted the King's cause. On that bloody day of 6 August, during the terrible Wilderness War of 1777, many former friends and neighbors fought one another, even brother fought brother and father fought son.

By now, the entire Royal Greens Regiment had moved up. Other than those in the front rows, most had not reversed their jackets. In precise military fashion, they marched against the defending Americans with bayonet-tipped muskets thrust outward. Supporting the thrust of the Greens were many Indians, members of Butler's Rangers, and some uniformed British and German soldiers.

Captain Gardinier shouted an order to fire. The sudden crack of numerous muskets and rifles again rocked the wilderness. Hearing the gunfire, the defenders of Fort Stanwix knew that the action had resumed. The second phase of the Battle of Oriskany had commenced. Herkimer's militiamen, backed by their remaining Oneida Indians, fired a deadly barrage against the advancing foe. Within seconds, no fewer than 30 of the Royal Greens lay painfully on the ground.[31] Many Indian warriors fell as well.[32]

On the order to charge, the militiamen hurled themselves upon their opponents, springing like wounded bears on an approaching hunter. Instantly, the field adjacent to the woodline was transformed into a massive battleground. Once again, a massive hand-to-hand battle ensued with no quarter given. Because Herkimer's men were running out of powder and ammunition, after the first volley they fought largely with bayonets and hand weapons such as knives and tomahawks.[33]

Shortly after 1.30 p.m., Colonel Gansevoort at the fort gave the order to fire three cannon.[34] It was to no avail. Amid the massive noise of the killing ground, the three blasts were never heard. In the end, despite the best efforts of Hellmer and the others, nothing positive had been gained.

Notes

1   All of the Indian chiefs fell under Brant.

2   Colbrath, p. 29, cites 1,000 militiamen; Lieutenant Colonel Downey, *Indian Wars*, p. 19, cites 800; Lossing, Vol. I, p. 243, cites "more than 800 men, eager to face the enemy"; Eckert, p. 129, cites "800 men" but acknowledged that "60 Oneidas also joined Herkimer's force." (Ibid.). *Syracuse-Herald American*, July 4, 1999, p. AA-4, cites "Herkimer assembled 800 members. . . along the way they camped at the Oneida Village of Oriska and were joined by 60 Oneida warriors." *"St. Leger's Attack,"* pp. 6 and 8, cite 800 also "joined by 60 Oneidas among them whom was Thomas Spencer. . . and Chiefs Cornelius and Honyerry." Dupuy, *Encyclopedia of Military History*, p. 714, cites 800 militiamen but makes no mention of the 60 or so Oneida Indians who joined Herkimer's force. (Dupuy incorrectly stated that the battle was fought on 8 August.)

In a letter written by Ms. Martha G. Hays, a former Historic Site Manager of the Oriskany Battlefield to Mr. Gavin K. Watt, a "Lieutenant" in a re-enactor unit who was residing in King City, Ontario, Canada, Ms. Hayes wrote that regarding Herkimer's troop strength, "Lately, I have never found a record that numbers Herkimer's troops greater than 800, and your figures show this as a minimum." (Letter of April 19, 1977. Ms. Hayes also requested from Mr. Watt that he share any further information with her pertaining to the militia strengths.) In actuality, including the 60 Oneidas, it may be surmised that General Herkimer possessed about 900 men, though his strength may have reached almost 1,000.

3   Eckert, p. 130.

4   Stone, *Siege and Battle*, p. 234; Lossing, Vol. I, p. 243.

5   Lossing, Vol. I, p. 243.

6   Eckert, p. 130. *"St. Leger's Attack,"* p. 8, cites that "Colonel Cox and Paris and various other officers waxed sarcastic as General Herkimer held firmly to his plan for a brief [stay]."

7   Eckert, p. 132; Lossing, Vol. I, p. 244. Regarding this, General Herkimer erred. His initial decision to remain in place until his scouts had ample time to check out the area and those—such as Hellmer—dispatched to the fort enough time to reach it, should have been enforced. A general must always control his commanders. Herkimer should have not only reminded them that he was the senior ranking officer, but also he should have informed the four colonels that they would be relieved of their regiments and duties if their insubordination continued. Herkimer did have a number of other senior and lower ranking commanders available in the event that he would have to relieve the four.

The above view is supported by Lieutenant Colonel Downey when he wrote: "He [Herkimer] ought to have damned them in blistering German for an undisciplined, foolhardy mob. Instead, white-faced with wrath, he waved them forward." (See *Indian Wars*, p. 21).

8   *"St. Leger's Attack,"* p. 8. As for the time, according to Swiggett, *War Out of Niagara*, p. 86, "It was still early morning, six o'clock." Regarding Swiggett's time of 6 a.m., this is incorrect. It is known that Herkimer's force was ambushed at approximately 9 a.m. and not at 6 a.m.

9   Eckert, p. 133, also states that all three were killed at the outset. Eckert, however, spells two of their names as Major Dennis Klepsattle and Major Major Van Slyck.

10 Ibid., p. 133.

11 On 5 August, when Colonel Visscher verbally assailed General Herkimer about some matter, Herkimer retorted that the colonel was big on words but in the event of a battle, his regiment would probably be the least effective. Herkimer's prophecy proved to be correct.

12 *"St. Leger's Attack!"* p. 8.

13 Captain Dillenbeck's body was initially interned in a shallow grave. In the following year the body was exhumed, returned to his family, and buried in a family plot.

14 Some sources have actually identified Colonel Campbell as being the commander during the Battle of Oriskany following the wounding of Herkimer. See Campbell, *Frontier's Aflame!*, p. 25.

15 Ibid., p. 26.

16 Presently located in downtown Rochester, New York. See also Grinde, Jr., *The Iroquois and the American Nation*, p. 87. And Watts and Morrison, "King's Royal Regiment of New York," in *The British Campaign of 1777*, p. 34, acknowledge "the natives [Indians] carried the initial fighting and it was particularly bloody, hand-to-hand combat." According to George Bancroft, *The American Revolution*, Vol. III, p. 379, "There was no chance for tactics in this battle of the wilderness. Parties [of men] fought behind trees or fallen logs; fought close-in with bayonet and hatchet [tomahawk]. Their left hands clenched in each other's hair, their right grasping in a grip of death the knife plunged in each other's bosom."

17 Unfortunately, the girl's name has never been recorded. She probably enlisted under a male alias. At the tender age of 15 or 16, she also perished in the battle. In the aftermath of the Oriskany battle, the valor of an unnamed women warrior was noted in the annals of the Northern Army. For a good account of the fighting as well as the girl's role in it, also see Downey, *Indian Wars*, pp. 22–24.

18 Campbell, *Frontier's Aflame!* p. 26. According to Blacksnake, "Blood Sheds a Stream Running down on Descending ground." See Grinde, Jr., *The Iroquois and the American Nation*, p. 87; and Calloway, *Revolution in Indian Country*, pp. 33–34; and National Park Service, U.S. Department of the Interior pamphlet. According to the National Park Service, ". . . during the Battle of Oriskany on August 6, 1777, neighbor fighting neighbor transformed a quiet ravine into a bloody slaughterhouse." According to Bruce Bliven, *New York. A Bicentennial History* (W.W. Norton and Company, Inc., 1981), pp. 73–74, "The savage six-hour hand-to-hand fight that followed may have

been the bloodiest encounter in proportion to the numbers engaged of the entire war." For a powerful portrayal depicting General Herkimer sitting upon his saddle with a bloodied rag wrapped around his leg and calmly issuing orders as a massive battle is raging all around him see the painting by Fred C. Yohn, "General Hermiker at the Battle of Oriskany." (The painting's scene would also later be utilized by the U.S. Postal Service for a mail stamp). According to Lowenthal, *Marinus Willett*, p. 29, "The battle that became known as Oriskany raged with exceptional fury. Inspired by Herkimer's steadiness, the battered militia held on and began to inflict damage."

19 In a letter to Ms. Martha Hayes, Historic Site Manager of the Oriskany Battlefield, M. Gavin K. Watt wrote: "The gigantic rainstorm comes and calls a halt to the battle." (Letter of April 15, 1977, p. 5, Point 1).

20 Some sources cite that it was Captain Jacob Sieber, an officer in Cox's regiment who initiated the idea of small defensive circles. However, this did not occur immediately and by the time it happened, Herkimer's force had sustained heavy casualties. (Letter to Ms. Hayes on April 15, 1977, p. 5, Point G.)

21 For this view, see *"St. Leger's Attack!"* p. 8 and 10. Lossing, Vol. I, p. 247, cites "The provincials had also made choice of more advantageous ground."

22 See *"St. Leger's Attack!"* p. 10.

23 Lossing, Vol. I, p. 243, says that Herkimer's messenger did not arrive "until near noon." Though various authors have cited different times when Hellmer first arrived to the fort's location (Colbrath, *Days of Siege*, p. 29, cites between 9 a.m. and 10 a.m. in the morning but Willett, *A Narative of the Military Actions of Colonel Willett*, p. 131, cites "about eleven o'clock"), it is known that neither Hellmer, nor any of the others, arrived before noon. Though Hellmer did actually arrive at the vicinity of the fort well before 9 a.m., he was unable to enter. Surviving the war, Hellmer always claimed that although he succeeded in reaching the outskirts of the fort early in the morning, he did not physically enter the fort until 1 p.m. Surely, Hellmer would have known his arrival time. Of the four dispatched runners, Hellmer was the first to enter the fort. Regardless, by then it did not matter. The Battle of Oriskany was well underway.

24 Both were Loyalists who previously had fled to Canada. Old accounts also spell their last name as M'Donald. (These McDonalds should not be confused with John McDonell, or MacDonald, who with a mixed Loyalist–Indian force, was at this very same moment operating farther to the southeast and would fight the Patriots in the Schoharie Valley.)

25 Lossing, Vol. I, p. 247, acknowledges that it was "Colonel Butler [who] instantly conceived a stratagem, and was nearly successful in its execution. He so changed the dress of a detachment of Johnson's Greens, that they appeared like American troops." Lossing also cites Major Watts "came up with a detachment of Johnson's Greens to support them [Brant's ambushing force]." (Ibid.)
      Of interest is that when Johnson's Loyalist troops, along with some

Indians, were pulled out, Fort Stanwix's defenders immediately noted this: "This Morning the Indians were seen going off from around the Garrison towards the Landing." (And from there eastward to Oriskany.) So wrote Colbrath in his journal on 6 August. See *Days of Siege*, p. 29.

26 Sammons' name has been spelled in various ways and his rank is cited as being either a private or lieutenant. According to the Oriskany roster of 1777 (which, incidentally, is not noted for its accuracy), a "Jacob Sammons," also described as a "Mohawk," is cited. But two other Sammons are identified as well: Sampson Sammons and Thomas Sammons. (For the roster of names see Stone, *Siege and Battle*, end of book). As for these two men named Sammons, none are identified in the roster as having the rank of lieutenant. Yet, on p. 238, Jacob Sammons is cited with the rank of lieutenant.

Eckert, p. 136, identifies a Sampson Sammons but only as a private. It is known that Jacob Sammons (and probably two or three other Sammons) did fight at Oriskany on 6 August. Possibly at this time Jacob Sammons was a private, but later on achieved the rank of lieutenant. Regardless of the correct spelling of the person's name and his true rank, it is known that a volunteer by the name of Sammons did spot and report the incoming force, though in error.

27 Stone, *Siege and Battle*, p. 238.

28 Stone, p. 238.

29 Ibid., p. 239.

30 Watts and Morrison, *The British Campaign of 1777*, p. 34, cite that "[Sir] Johnson assembled a 70-man reinforcement composed of his own company and squads from several others. Command was given to Captain-Lieutenant John McDonell (Scotus)." The authors acknowledge that Patriot Captain Jacob Gardinier, who was not fooled by the reversed coat trick, killed McDonell "with a spontoon thrust in the throat." (Ibid.). Watts and Morrison are incorrect that the reinforcement was commanded by "John McDonell (Scotus)." At this time, McDonell (Scotus) was in the vicinity of the Schoharie Valley. As for the commander killed by the thrust of a spear (spontoon), it was actually Donald John McDonald. And it was Captain Jacob Gardinier who struck McDonald.

31 Ibid.

32 Ibid.

33 Lossing, Vol. I, p. 247, cites "It was a terrible struggle. They leaped upon each other with the fierceness of tigers, and fought hand to hand and foot to foot with bayonets and knives." Willett also acknowledged that much of the fighting was hand-to-hand and with tomahawks. "Attacks were made with tomahawks by the militia, as well as by the Indians, and with equal effect." See Willett, *A Narrative of the Military Actions of Colonel Willett*, p. 52.

34 According to Eckert, p. 139, three shots were fired within 15 seconds.

XI

The Patriots Raid St. Leger's Camp

Emerging from Fort Stanwix at around 2 p.m., Lieutenant Colonel Willett's raiders immediately targeted the main enemy camps. Excluding the wagon personnel who remained behind—but were ready to roll on a second's notice—over 200 men sallied out. For extra firepower, they even brought along a 3-pound cannon filled with grapeshot.

By now the majority of the Loyalists, British, and German troops were absent. A sizable number had been committed against Herkimer while others were still miles away working on the wilderness road. Though some of those working on the road had been recalled, they had not yet arrived. Most of the Indian warriors were miles away locked in combat with Herkimer's force.

Willett's raid was well conceived. Up front was an advance party of approximately 50 raiders, including the scouts. The main body, with a strength of over 100, followed close behind. The remainder were organized into a rearguard of 30 personnel who were to be committed wherever they were needed. The raiders, excluding a handful mounted on horses that served as messengers, were on foot. Along with Willett, various other officers participated in the raid—Major Badlam, Captain Allen, Captain Swarthout,[1] and Lieutenant Stockwell were among those who sallied forth.[2]

Dividing his force into two groups, Willett moved quickly against his two primary targets: the camps of General St. Leger and Sir John Johnson. Willett was hoping to kill or capture either one or both of the commanders. And if he got really lucky, maybe capture Joseph Brant or Butler.

Unfortunately for the Patriot raiders, the British general had departed the camp. It is stated that when the raiders struck, St. Leger was actually "on the opposite side of the river."[3] What, exactly, St. Leger was doing there is not known. Possibly, he was en route to Oriskany, but when notified that a raiding force was in action, he ran back to counter the Patriots. Upon returning, St. Leger began to issue orders to resist the raiders. He also dispatched two runners, one to Brant and the other to the road-working party. Moving rapidly toward the Lower Landing, the raiders simultaneously struck John Johnson's Loyalist and Captain Brant's main Indian camp. Approaching Johnson's camp, the raiders captured Lieutenant Warren Singleton, a Loyalist officer, who earlier had been wounded at Oriskany and brought back. Entering Brant's camp, the raiders fell upon three Indians deep in sleep. Never would they see daylight again as raised tomahawks terminated their lives.

Encountering a handful of Indian squaws, warriors, and Loyalists, a gun battle ensued. In their attempt to flee, some of the Indians and Loyalists ran into the river and succeeded in hiding out among the brush and cattails. Still others, near the woodline of the wilderness, fled for the forest. Some made it, but others, pursued by Willett's raiders, were not so fortunate. Rifle bullets and musket balls cut them down; a few more were tomahawked. A body was observed floating slowly downriver.

Unfortunately for the raiders, none of the key leadership was found. Hearing shots and screams, Johnson peered out of his tent and, noting the sizable raiding force charging in, fled as fast as he could for the river bank. Interrupted while taking a nap, Johnson was dressed in no more than a long nightshirt when he fled just moments ahead of the raiders who entered his tent. Lieutenant Bird also barely escaped.

Receiving the order to move forward from a mounted messenger, the seven wagons quickly appeared. Tearing down the tents, the raiders began to quickly grab everything they could. Numerous items were tossed upon the wagons: blankets, clothing, footwear, wampum, food, guns, ammunition, edged weapons, rucksacks, camp equipment, boxes of trinkets, and even unit battle flags were quickly loaded on.[4] Noting a large barking dog tied on a leash to a pole, and suspecting that the animal had been stolen from some farm and was destined to be eaten, a raider quickly cut the rope and threw the dog into one of the wagons.

As soon as a wagon was loaded, it dashed off to the fort. By the time the raid was concluded, 21 wagonloads had been carried off.

Reaching his batteries, St. Leger finally organized a force to counter Willett's raiders. By now, Lieutenant Bird had established contact with St. Leger. The British commander directed him and Captain Eugene Hoyes to advance southward toward Sir Johnson's and Brant's camps where the raiders were congregated. Once Hoyes' force was positioned to the south of Fort Stanwix, it would bar the raiders from re-entering their fort. Trapped on the Mohawk River, the raiders would then either be destroyed or captured on the edge of the river.

Moving toward the raiders, Hoyes encountered them retiring to the fort. But Hoyes was unable to halt their withdrawal. Willett's riflemen, with deadly accuracy, kept the mixed British, German, and Loyalist force at bay; while supporting fire from Fort Stanwix—light cannon fire from the ramparts and fairly accurate long-range rifle fire also targeted those attempting to intercept Willet's raiders. Within minutes, six of Hoyes' soldiers were hit—more casualties that St. Leger could ill afford. Following a brief skirmish, Hoyes was repulsed. St. Leger's attempt to intercept and destroy or capture the raiders had failed.

Retiring victoriously into the fort, Willett and his raiders cheered loudly—the raid had been a total success. Their only casualties were two men slightly wounded. In their final mockery of the British, the flags that had been captured by the raiders were hoisted right underneath the American flag. Because a strong wind had appeared, the flags waved majestically. Gansevoort's defenders also shouted obscenities from the ramparts against St. Leger's forces, and here and there, a captured item was displayed from the ramparts.[5]

To the delight of Colonel Gansevoort, within hours he was provided a letter written to him by a girl he loved and cherished, Catherine (Katie) Van Schaik. The letter had been addressed to him at Fort Stanwix; however its carrier had been caught by Indians. The entire mailbag had been confiscated, ending up in St. Leger's camp, where it was later seen and grabbed by Willett's raiders. Later on that evening, as the bag's contents were examined and the mail finally distributed, a soldier proudly presented the letter to his commanding officer. Noting the perfume emanating from the missive, he humorously asked the colonel, "So, Sir, tell us, any plans on marrying?" Supposedly, Gansevoort's joyful response was, "If you guys can get me through this one, I might be able to do so." And so it would be. On 12 January 1778, in Catherine's home on Van Schaik Island outside of Albany, Colonel Gansevoort married his love.

Notes

1   For his service as an officer in the 3rd New York Continental Regiment, Captain Abraham Swarthout received a grant of approximately 3,000 acres of land in an area designated as Sterling, New York. The property received by Swarthout remained in the family until the 1950s, though the holdings had shrunk in size through the sale of large portions of the land to local farmers, business interests, and mining companies over the years. In June 1967, the house built by Captain Swarthout's son was sold to the parents of the author; in December 2004, though the author sold the house and some of the land around it, the author's family still owns a sizable parcel of the land.

2   Willett cites that such officers participated: Captain Von Benscheten and Lieutenant Stockwell commanded the advance guard. The rear guard, composed of 9th Massachusetts troops, was commanded by Captain Allen and a Lieutenant Deuffendorf. A Captain from the 9th Massachusetts (Willett could not recall his name) along with Ensign Chase, commanded the flank force. In addition, Captains Blacker and Jansen; Lieutenants Comine, Bogardus, McClenner, and Coffraunder, along with Ensigns Begley, Lewis, and Dennison, were in the main body. Captain Swarthout with Ensigns Magee and Ament commanded the field piece. Major Bedlow supervised the force from the rear while Willett, accompanied by Lieutenant Ball, led from up front. (See Willett, *A Narrative of the Military Actions of Colonel Willett*, p. 131.)

3   Stone, *Siege and Battle*, p. 246. Willett also cited the raid was conducted "in order to render Herkimer what service we could in his march." (See Willett, p. 131.)

4   John R. Alden, *A History of the American Revolution*, p. 321. The booty also included Sir Johnson's trunk, which contained his clothing. Johnson's boots, moccasins, hat, jacket, sword, musket, uniform, and various personal items were also removed. But most importantly, Johnson's log or record book, along with personal papers and a number of letters written to him by various high-ranking British officials, were also taken. In the following days, much critical information would be obtained from these captured documents.

    Willett also cited that "50 brass kettles, and more than 100 blankets, (two articles which were much needed), with a quantity of muskets, tomahawks, spears, ammunition, clothing, deerskins, a variety of Indian affairs, and five colours (the whole of which on our return to the fort were displayed on our flag staff under the continental flag)" were also acquired. (See Willett, p. 132).

5   Willett, p. 54. He also wrote: "We totally routed two of the enemy's encamp-
     ments, destroyed all the provisions that were in them." (Ibid., p. 132.)
        Of importance to note is that in the concluding days of the Wilderness
     War of 1777 and after Burgoyne's army surrendered at Saratoga that Octo-
     ber, a British Annual Register for 1777 was also secured by the Patriots in
     Saratoga. In it was a short but important note regarding Willett's raid. Such
     was noted in the register:
        "On the day, and probably during the time of this engagement (that is
     Herkimer's), the garrison, having received intelligence of the approach of
     their friends, endeavored to make a diversion in their favor, by a vigorous
     and well-conducted sally, under the direction of Colonel Willett, their second
     in command. Willett conducted his business with ability and spirit. He did
     considerable mischief in the camp, brought off some trophies, no inconsid-
     erable spoil, some of which, consisted in articles that were greatly wanted,
     a few prisoners, and returned with little or no loss." (For the registry, see
     also Willett, p. 55.)

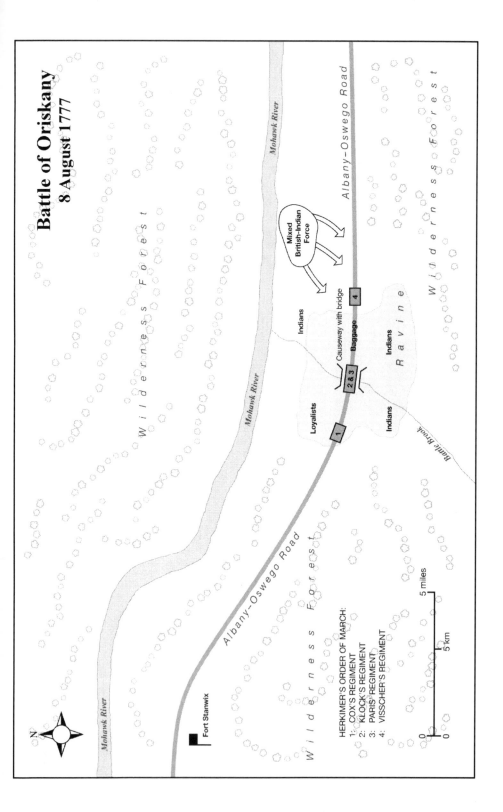

Battle of Oriskany
8 August 1777

N

Mohawk River

Wilderness Forest

Mohawk River

Albany–Oswego Road

Wilderness Forest

Mixed British-Indian Force

Indians

Albany–Oswego Road

Causeway with bridge

Baggage

4

Loyalists

2 & 3

1

Indians

Ravine

Indians

Battle Brook

Wilderness Forest

Fort Stanwix

HERKIMER'S ORDER OF MARCH:
1: COX'S REGIMENT
2: KLOCK'S REGIMENT
3: PARIS' REGIMENT
4: VISSCHER'S REGIMENT

5 miles

5 km

0

0

XII

Retreat from Oriskany

After receiving St. Leger's message to dispatch some warriors and troops immediately back to Fort Stanwix, Brant knew that he could not reinforce St. Leger and continue to battle Herkimer—especially since much of Herkimer's force was still intact.

By now, most of the Indians were willing to call it quits. In fact, individually and in small groups, they were leaving. None of this, of course, went unnoticed among the Loyalist leadership. Desperate to keep the pressure upon Herkimer's militia, the Butlers urged Brant to appeal to the Indians to keep on fighting, but Brant knew that he would not be able to persuade them to continue to fight, especially as some of the Loyalists and European soldiers were themselves easing off. Following the hour-long cloudburst, it appeared that the men could not be persuaded to resume the battle in its former ferocity. By now a number of the Loyalist officers lay dead, wounded, or were missing. Even Major Watts—who had re-entered the battle area—was nowhere in sight, and it was feared that he had been killed. With few leaders around, Joseph Brant was at a loss how to rally his men.

Brant decided to pull out. Cupping his hands around his mouth, he repeatedly shouted one word: "Ooo-nah!" Within moments others repeated the cry. It is likely that Brant was personally relieved to call off the battle. Several times he had come very close to death. He had been shot at, arrows had barely missed him, and a hand-thrown tomahawk missed his head by inches. One Oneida Indian warrior, bent on killing him, had sneaked up so close that only the fact that a handful of warriors were right by Brant at the moment had saved Brant's life.

The order to withdraw echoed through the woods, and the ambushers began to retire. To ensure that the retrograde movement did not turn into a free for all, John Butler quickly gathered up a couple dozen of his rangers and established a makeshift rearguard. Here and there some of the wounded were picked up and carried out. As for those who were left to the elements, most perished. A few, such as Major Watts—despite a severe wound—somehow managed to survive. Awakening from his unconsciousness hours later, Watts crawled to a nearby brook. Though the water revived him; he was still unable to make it back to St. Leger's camp on his own. Found two or three days later by some friendly Indians, Major Watts was finally carried back to the camp. There, he learned that he had been reported as dead.

When Brant's force withdrew from the battle, a number of the warriors did not return to camp. Some of the surviving Indians just headed straight back to their villages. For them, the Wilderness War of 1777 was over. Their defection further depleted St. Leger's strength. John Butler's haphazardly organized rearguard was not very strong, and it was fortunate for the British that there was no real need for a fighting withdrawal. Within minutes of the Indian cries to break off the battle, the forest became very quiet.

Yet, as always is the case, some fanatic will always remain behind to take that last shot. As Herkimer's militiamen began to move around, Captain James Davis was standing behind a tree. Adjacent to him stood Richard Putnam, a militiaman in Davis' company and an assistant to the captain. Noting how peaceful it was, Putnam remarked, "I believe the red devils have pretty much all left us."[1] Captain Davis however responded, "They are not all gone. Some of them are lurking around here yet."[2] Sadly he was right. Scarcely a moment had passed when the crack of a shot shattered the eerie silence and a musket ball tore into the captain's neck, killing him instantly.

Assembling the remainder of his force, General Herkimer ordered the militia survivors to first retire back to their initial rendezvous site of Fort Dayton, and then to the old Fort Schuyler. Herkimer's decision, undoubtedly supported by Colonel Campbell, was correct. Herkimer had no intelligence as to what the enemy was up to, or whether they would return. Though he had managed to preserve a part of his force, Herkimer was in no position to continue his march to Fort Stanwix. He had to retire.

Herkimer's retreat, however, was not one of panic. Strong, all-around security was immediately imposed. Carefully selected frontier militiamen and Oneida Indians served as scouts and flankers. A rearguard, organized and commanded by Colonel Campbell, protected the main body.

Herkimer ordered that none of the wounded were to be left behind. Some of the walking wounded who could still carry a weapon protected those who were seriously injured. For those who could not walk out on their own, makeshift stretchers were constructed. In addition, the few horses and oxen which had not been killed or scattered pulled wagons carrying the wounded. Herkimer insisted that all of the wounded were to be evacuated before him, and so he was the last man to be carried out. Loyal to his men, Herkimer was determined to save as many of them as possible. Assisting Herkimer's stretcher-bearing team was Jan Van Eps. As he helped to carry his commander, Van Eps felt tremendous sorrow for the many who had fallen. Unfortunately for the militia force, Herkimer's chief doctor, Moses Younglove, who hailed from the town of Hudson on the west bank of the Hudson River north of New York City, was not available. He had been spotted rendering aid to the wounded earlier in the day by a Royal Greens sergeant serving in John Johnson's regiment and captured. Along with the other prisoners, the doctor was escorted to St. Leger's camp.

Carried on a stretcher out of the battle area, General Herkimer could not fail to notice the numerous dead lying all around. He hoped that their losses had not been in vain and that their sacrifice would contribute to a Patriot victory in the long run. Herkimer regretted that he could neither remove the dead nor give them a proper burial. There simply was no time for that.

As the militiamen retired, they took one last look at the gruesome field of battle. Among some of the fallen were Lieutenant Petire, Captains John Davis, Andrew Dillenbeck, Samuel Pettingill, Jacob Gardinier, Henry Diefendorf, Robert Crouse, Jacob Bouman, Frederick Helmer, and Graves. Majors John Eisenlord, Van Sluyck, Enos Klepsattle, Lieutenant Colonel Hunt, and Colonels Cox and Paris[3] were just some of the fallen senior officers. Others, such as Colonel Peter Bellinger and Major John Frey, were missing. Estimates for the number of non-officer militiamen who fell tend to vary.

Also within Herkimer's force were some non-militia members. These individuals hailed from the newly created New York State

government. Largely, they came along to raise morale, gather information, and inform both soldiers and civilians about the newly formed
government. Samuel Billington, John Dygert, and Jacob Snell were
several of the non-militiamen who perished at Oriskany.

It may be accurately surmised that in total, no less than one-third of
Herkimer's force had been killed. And if one included the wounded,
missing, and captured, then well over fifty percent of Herkimer's force
should be considered casualties. Some estimates put the survivors at
only 300 of the original 800, with 250 killed, and 250 mortally
wounded, with around 50 captured, whereas others claim 400 Americans were killed and 200 taken prisoner.[4] With such horrendous losses,
it is unsurprising that the battle of Oriskany is seen as one of the most
vicious battles of the entire Amercan Revolution. Without a doubt, 6
August was the bloodiest day in the Wilderness War of 1777.

Herkimer's militia, however, did not just take casualties; amid
the trees of the wilderness, they also inflicted grievous losses on their
attackers.

It seems likely that before the ambush, Brant possessed a strength
of no fewer than 800 well-concealed warriors, Rangers, and soldiers.
This figure would rise because along with the two companies committed, additional Loyalists were also sent in during the second phase of
the battle. Including these, St. Leger must have committed almost 900
personnel at Oriskany.[5]

Sir John Johnson's regiment sustained no less than 33 killed and 41
wounded.[6] To these must be added the missing, captured, and those
who deserted. In all, Johnson lost well over one-third of his Royal
Greens at Oriskany. Butler's Rangers also took a pounding. Neither
Butler nor Sir John would ever fully recover from their 6 August 1777
losses. It is also known that high casualties were incurred among the
committed British, German, and Canadians, though no formal figures
exist.

It is the Indian loss, however, that was most appalling.[7] Decades
later, when Chief Blacksnake was very aged, he was still haunted by the
viciousness of the battle. "There I have Seen the most Dead Bodies all
it over that I never Did see, and never will again. I thought at the time
the Blood Shed a Running Down on the Descending ground During the
afternoon."[8] "Our town [the Indian village]" wrote the captive Mary
Jemison, "exhibited a scene of real sorrow and distress when our

warriors returned and recounted their misfortunes, and stated the real loss they had sustained in the engagement. The mourning was excessive, and was expressed by the most doleful yells, shrieks, and howling, and by inimitable gesticulations."[9]

Colonel Daniel Claus, who was nominally in charge of the Indians, although Joseph Brant was their combat leader, wrote:

> At the first onset the Senecas lost 17 men among whom were several Chiefs and Leaders wch enraged them greatly and altho' the Rebels were put to Flight and left upwards of 500 killed on the Spot yet that was not sufficient satisfaction.[10]

In total, no fewer than 23 chiefs and 68 warriors were killed,[11] while others were captured[12] or missing. Many were wounded, and some later perished of their wounds.[13] And it only got worse—upon arriving back at their siege lines near Fort Stanwix they encountered pillaged camps with additional dead warriors, which further demoralized the Indians.

Much has been written about who actually won the Battle of Oriskany, and various authors and historians have expressed different opinions. In actuality, the battle may be viewed from different angles, and in order to determine who won or benefited most from the battle, it is necessary to examine both the immediate and long-term effects of this engagement.

General Herkimer had two priorities: the first was to protect the Mohawk Valley from a westerly British advance, and the second was to destroy and repulse the enemy in the vicinity of Fort Stanwix. It may be argued that Herkimer accomplished these two objectives.[14]

St. Leger, upon dispatching an ambushing force, ordered that Herkimer's approaching militia be destroyed. In destroying this force, St. Leger hoped to attain a major military, political, and psychological victory. From reading the letter St. Leger dispatched to General Burgoyne on 11 August, one would conclude he attained his victory:

> On the 5th [August] I learned, from discovering parties on the Mohawk river, that a body of one thousand militia were on their march to raise the siege. On the confirmation of this news, I moved a large body of Indians, with some troops, the same night, to lay in ambuscade for them on their march. They fell

into it. The completest victory was obtained. About four hundred lay dead on the field, amongst the number of whom were almost all the principal movers of rebellion in that country.[15]

Yet, despite Brant's best efforts, Herkimer's militia remained on the field and continued to resist despite taking heavy losses. It is impossible to say with certainty that Brant would have finished Herkimer off had he continued to press the battle. Indeed, it may even be argued that had Brant continued to attack, he would not only have suffered additional losses but perhaps suffered defeat.

The main reason that Lieutenant Colonel Willett was able to conduct a successful raid against St. Leger's camps was because right at that moment, Herkimer was successfully fixing in place much of St. Leger's strength farther to the east at Oriskany.[16] The troops, Loyalists, and Indians, critically needed around Fort Stanwix were instead diverted farther to the east to engage Herkimer's force. As a result, Willett's raiders were able to operate with relative ease, destroying and capturing a considerable amount of war materiel badly needed by St. Leger's army.

Unlike Brant's force, which fled in haste, Herkimer's force retired in proper military fashion. True, some panic did occur in the opening stages of the battle, but that is not an unreasonable response to an ambush. Though much of Visscher's rearguard fled in terror, not everyone panicked. Along with the majority of Herkimer's force, a portion of Visscher's force stood firmly in place. Their actions not only solidified Herkimer's rear but also alleviated much of the pressure directed against the main body.

Though a draft proclamation had been imposed by the Patriots, Herkimer's force was almost exclusively volunteers. While a good number had never served previously in any army or militia unit, many others had experience, and his militia also possessed a core of skilled, experienced, and highly dedicated leaders. This explains why when Herkimer's force was initially ambushed, no collapse occurred—despite a breakdown of communications and a period of uncertainty. Because the hardened cadre held, so did the volunteers.

Right from the moment when Herkimer's force came under attack, leaders began to take charge, instill order, control panic and flight, and most importantly, resist effectively. Despite their losses, they not only fought and held out but also succeeded in inflicting heavy casualties upon their opponents. Though they withdrew, they were not defeated.

Willett later described the action: "The general [Herkimer] with a number of brave men, formed themselves in a circle, and defended themselves with great gallantry. Much personal courage was shown. In some cases, attacks were made with tomahawks by the militia, as well as by Indians, and with equal effect."[17]

Colonel Willett, though praising the heroic actions of Herkimer's militiamen, was also critical; though not explicitly criticizing the general, it is apparent that he did fault Herkimer and his senior leadership when he stated: "Had they been sufficiently compact, and under such direction as to have been prepared to support each other, they would have been an overmatch for the enemy. But the loose manner in which they marched, and the want of precaution, produced such sudden confusion as could not be remedied."[18]

Regardless of any later criticism of Herkimer's leadership, it was Brant's force that began to retreat first. In the aftermath of the Battle of Oriskany, Brant and the Butlers would cite that their withdrawal was attributable to Willett's raid and St. Leger's request for reinforcements. To some extent, this is true. But some of Brant's personnel, perhaps sensing defeat, were fleeing from the battlefield even before St. Leger's message arrived. And the Indians were not an exception. Even the Loyalists, British, and Germans were slacking off in their effort to continue the fight.[19]

It must be remembered that St. Leger did not order Brant to disengage and retreat. Rather, he wanted Brant to continue the fight while assisting in the effort to contain or disperse the American raiders who had suddenly appeared out of Fort Stanwix. Brant's retreat was not authorized by St. Leger, but solely undertaken by Brant because he could not defeat Herkimer's force and he was losing command and control.

As for the Patriots who withdrew to Fort Dayton, they never deserted their cause—unlike most of the Indians in Brant's force. Throughout 1777 and the following years, the militiamen who fought with Herkimer organized new militia units or joined some other units within the Northern Army. A number even witnessed Burgoyne's surrender at Saratoga the following October.

On 6 August, both at Oriskany and Fort Stanwix, the British did not just suffer heavy personnel and materiel losses—they also lost spiritually. Morale plummeted, and for the first time even the lowest-ranking soldier began to realize that defeat was possible.

The Battle of Oriskany was not just a serious blow against St. Leger. It also impacted heavily upon the entire British campaign of 1777. General Burgoyne was severely affected by it, as his expected secondary thrust from the west never materialized after meeting such fierce resistance in the wilderness. In the end, the Battle of Oriskany made a significant contribution to the Patriot victory at Saratoga, and for this, General Herkimer and his militia army must be credited. General Washington quickly analyzed that the Battle of Oriskany would tremendously benefit the Patriots, writing:

> It was Herkimer who first reversed the gloomy scene of the Northern campaign. The hero of the Mohawk Valley served from love of Country, not for reward. He did not want a Continental command or money.[20]

Notes

1   *"St. Leger's Attack,"* p. 10.
2   Ibid.
3   Colonel Paris, who was captured, was also a member of the Committee of Safety. Paris was taken to an island in Lake Ontario where he was tortured and killed.
4   Eckert, p. 133, 137; Stone, *Siege and Battle,* p. 241.
5   Compare with Mr. Watt (letter of April 15, 1977) to Ms. Martha Hays (pp. 5–6).
6   Eckert, p. 137. Correctly, Eckert cites that Herkimer's force "had shaken the confidence of his [Sir John Johnson's] troops." (See p. 152).
7   The heavy losses among the Indians was acknowledged by Mary Jemison and Joseph Brant. Years later, Brant would regretfully speak of the heavy losses incurred by "my poor Mohawks in that battle." See Stone, *Siege and Battle*, pp. 243–244; and Eckert, p, 321. Grinde, *The Iroquois and the American Nation,* p. 88, cites that 100 Iroquois died.
8   See Colin G. Calloway. *The Revolution in Indian Country. Crisis and Diversity in Native American Communities* (New York: Press Syndiacte, 1995), pp. 33–34. Blacksnake's remark was largely attributable to the Indian casualties.
9   Stone, p. 244.
10 "Anecdotes of Capt. Jos. Brant," by Col. Dan'l Claus, Superintendent of Indian Affairs. Publications of the Buffalo Historical Society, Vol. IV

(Buffalo: The Peter Paul Book Company, 1896), p. 28.

11   Ibid., p. 137. Eckert also cites the Indians suffered "great losses." See p. 152. Lossing, Vol. I, p. 247, cites "The Indians lost about seventy, among whom were several chiefs." Some of the Indian leaders were also war captains. Tocenando and Asquishahang (known also as "the Axe Carrier") were among the Seneca leaders to perish at Oriskany. According to Watts and Morrison, "The King's Royal Regiment of New York" in *The British Campaign of 1777,* p. 34, "The Indians had borne the brunt of the fighting and taken severe casualties."

Swiggett, p. 87, cites "that the Indians, after appalling losses, fled in confusion." Graymont, p. 138, cites that no fewer than five Seneca chiefs perished at Oriskany: Hasquesahah, Galnahage, Dahwahdeho, Dahgaiownd, and Dahohjoedoh. (Graymont gathered her information from the writings of Mary Jemison.)

12   Eckert, p. 137. Numerous accounts reveal that the first Indian desertions were noted in the aftermath of 6 August.

13   Some of the wounded Indians perished shortly afterwards. The Indian figure of no fewer than 70 killed at Oriskany did not include those who died of wounds later or at the hands of Willett's raiders in the vicinity of Fort Stanwix. It also did not include the missing who had deserted (such as Red Jacket), nor did it include the captured (such as Chief Ghalto). According to George Bancroft, *The American Revolution,* Vol. III, p. 379, just alone "thirty-three or more of the Senecas lay dead [and] about as many more were badly wounded."

14   According to Bruce Bliven, p. 74, "Herkimer's efforts helped Colonel Gansevoort in another way: during the Oriskany battle, when the British camp was nearly empty, Gansevoort's able second-in-command, Lieutenant Colonel Marinus Willet[t], had led a highly successful raid upon it and had made off with twenty-one wagonloads of muskets, ammunition, and assorted supplies." According to Grinde, *The Iroquois and the American Revolution,* pp. 87–88, although 200 to 400 of Herkimer's men were estimated killed and several hundred were wounded, captured, or missing, the Americans (Grinde uses the word "rebels") claimed victory since they were still in possession of the battlefield at the end.

15   Stone, *Siege and Battle,* p. 241, fn. on bottom of page, also Lossing, Vol. I, p. 247.

16   The Loyalist loss was proportionately equal, if not more severe, than that of the Americans. (See Stone, *Siege and Battle,* p. 242). It is known that the Royal Greens and Butler's Rangers also suffered high losses, although no official loss returns are given in any accounts. (Ibid.). And Grinde, p. 88, cites "100 Loyalists lost their lives."

17   Willett, p. 52.

18   Ibid., pp. 52–53.

19   Swiggett, pp. 85–87, accurately describes the march, ambush, and fighting

which took place. Swiggett also cites such: "The Oriskany action was of enormous consequences in the Revolution. It was the first check to the Burgoyne–St. Leger successes, and thereafter every Loyalist invasion ended in rout or retreat. The fighting was of great ferocity and the Palatines held their own." (See p. 85).

20 Bancroft, *The American Revolution,* Vol. III, p. 381. According to Dale Van Every, *A Company of Heroes. The American Frontier, 1775–1783,* p. 104, "What at first had seemed the stunning defeat at Oriskany soon began to appear in its truer aspect."

XIII

The Siege Continues

Upon returning to their camps on 6 August, or what remained of them, the Loyalists and Indians encountered carnage. Ruined tents and destroyed items lay all around. The situation worsened when it began to rain again, and in the evening the temperature fell. As temperatures plummeted, tempers rose. With many of their blankets gone, the Indians became especially vocal. They also began to voice their anger about the situation with Fort Stanwix. After all, they had been repeatedly assured and promised that they would not be committed into any kind of heavy combat. And this had not been the case, as scores of warriors had perished at Oriskany and in the first efforts to take the fort.[1] To calm them, St. Leger issued a rum allotment. The liquor also served to alleviate the suffering of the wounded.

Late that evening, St. Leger met with John Johnson, Joseph Brant, the Butlers, and some of the Indian chiefs. It was not a friendly affair, and there was tension if not outright hostility in the air.

By now, St. Leger had had enough. Disgusted with the events of the day, he had had a few drinks, as he was wont to do in times of stress, and he was rapidly approaching his breaking point.[2] St. Leger was particularly angered by Johnson, who was lamenting the heavy losses his men had taken that day. To rectify the situation, Johnson wanted to immediately attack eastward into the Mohawk Valley to allow the Indians to revenge themselves on the Americans. He thought that otherwise they might desert. He also warned that it was becoming increasingly harder for him to control the Indians.

St. Leger was furious at the complaints; Johnson after all had not led the force to Oriskany as ordered, but had stayed behind, and had been sleeping in his tent while the fighting was raging. Johnson couldn't explain his actions to St. Leger, and from this day on the relationship between the two would only sour. Though angry that he had been verbally assailed in front of the others, Johnson continued to insist that there be an attack down the Mohawk Valley.

St. Leger, however, was adamant that they would stay put. He would not, under any circumstances, split his force and extend it farther to the east, losing control of part of it in the process. Whether Sir John liked it or not, St. Leger would continue with the siege of Fort Stanwix, and he informed the others of this in no uncertain terms. Possibly, in the future, a team might be dispatched deep into the Mohawk Valley to recruit Loyalists, test the sentiment of the valley's inhabitants, and obtain intelligence. But for now, the entire force would stay in place.

Late that evening, Johnson left the meeting in an angry mood. He knew that he had lost his argument with St. Leger. The other leaders were also unhappy with the day's sequence of events.

That night St. Leger issued a series of orders. Fort Stanwix was to be bombarded around the clock with the cannons that had recently been brought up. As for the soldiers and Loyalists who had arrived from the road-building project, excluding a limited number who were to return to the work, the others would be utilized for siege purposes and to construct another trench toward the fort. From now on the priority would be to capture Fort Stanwix.

Through the evening hours, and throughout the night of 6/7 August, the noise of entrenching tools breaking the ground could be heard. With minimal medical care, the seriously wounded brought back to camp from Oriskany began to die. A true humanitarian, Doctor Moses Younglove treated the wounded throughout the long night, with no regard for which side they had fought on.

Hoping to induce the fort into surrendering, St. Leger ordered that the captured officers Colonel Bellinger and Major Frey be brought to him. St. Leger got right to the point. He told the two Patriot officers that they were to immediately write a letter to Colonel Gansevoort. In it the two officers were to report that General Herkimer had been killed, his force had been destroyed, that there would be no further relief, and that the British had captured Albany. Therefore, Fort Stanwix was to surrender immediately. St. Leger threatened that if the two men didn't write out the letter exactly as stipulated, he would turn them over to the Mohawks to do with as they wished.[3] Seeing that the British commander meant business, the two Patriot officers wrote a short message:

Sir,

It is with concern we are to acquaint you that this was the fatal day in which the succours, which were intended for your relief have been attacked and defeated with great loss of numbers killed, wounded, and taken prisoners. Our regard for your safety and lives, and our sincere advice to you is, if you will avoid inevitable ruin and destruction, to surrender the fort you pretend to defend against a formidable body of troops and a good train of artillery, which we are witness of: when at the same time you have no further support or relief to expect. We are sorry to inform you that most of the principal officers are killed, to wit—Gen. Herkimer, Cols. Cox, Seeber, Isaac Paris, Captain Graves, and many others too tedious to mention. The British army from Canada being now perhaps before Albany, the possession of which place of course includes the conquest of the Mohawk River and this fort.

Peter Bellinger, Colonel
Major John Frey,
Tryon County[4]

The moment the letter was prepared, St. Leger ordered Major Wesley Ancrom and Colonel John Butler to deliver it to the fort. Because it was nearing midnight, there was danger in approaching the walls. But the two officers did as requested.

Ancrom and Butler, however, were not gone very long. An hour or so later they returned, with the same message. It is not even known if they actually met with Colonel Gansevoort.[5] After submitting their report, the two departed. Taking the message, St. Leger added such words to the back of the letter:

Gen. St. Leger, on the day of the date of this letter, made a verbal summons of the fort by his Adjutant General and Colonel Butler, and who then handed this letter; when Colonel Gansevoort refused any answer to a verbal summons, unless made by Gen. St. Leger himself, but at the mouth of his cannon.[6]

The following day, Thursday, 7 August, Northern Army scout Frederick Sammons was standing upon some high terrain east of Oriskany, when he saw large numbers of ravens, crows, and turkey vultures flying high overhead. Amid the hovering birds, one or two would suddenly drop down rapidly. Cautious from the moment he first stepped into the wilderness, Sammons knew the birds were devouring something.

While Sammons had previously witnessed birds of prey hovering high over the carcass of an animal or human, he had never seen so many before. Suspecting that something very tragic had occurred in the vicinity, Sammons decided to investigate, proceeding cautiously.

As he moved forward, he paused. His nose, trained through years in the wilderness to pick up the slightest scent, noted an unusual smell. As he neared, it became obvious that it was the smell of something that had died. Combined with the clutter and noise of the birds, Sammons' curiosity rose. Approaching closer, the stench was more powerful, and he could now identify that the dead was human, and not just one, but many.

Finally, Sammons came across a body. Clothed in buckskin, the blouse was marred by a large dried bloodstain. Lying barefoot behind a log, the victim appeared to be in his forties. Apart from his footwear, his possessions were untouched and his rifle lay next to him. Beside the body lay a powder horn, a box of primers, and a small pouch of bullets. A hunting knife in its bearskin sheath hung from his belt. Sammons also noted the steel-edged tomahawk that lay adjacent to the body. Clearly, it was positioned for close-in combat if the need arose. It appeared to Sammons as if this man had attempted to run away, but unable to flee had made a one-man stand. The deceased had not been scalped, stripped, or robbed—rare in the wilderness. Evidently he had died unnoticed, succumbing gradually to his wound.

Proceeding slowly forward, he spotted another body. Unlike the first, this one was bloated and had been torn apart by some wild animal. Moving on, he continued to see more corpses. But as he approached the vicinity of the road that ran through the ravine, he came across a sight that totally horrified him.

Dead whites, Indians, and here and there a corpse clad in a British or German uniform lay all around, scores upon scores of them. Sammons immediately noted the bashed-in heads. Spears and arrows were still protruding from a number of the bodies, while bayonet-tipped muskets protruded from others. From what he could see, Sammons concluded that the brunt of the fighting had been close-in and vicious. Within several days, Sammons would report in Albany:

> I befell the most shocking sight I had ever witnessed. The Indians and white men were mingled with one another, just as they had been left when death had first completed his work. Many bodies had also been torn to pieces by wild beasts.[7]

Sammons knew that he had to move. Besides the two-legged threat that could suddenly appear from out of nowhere, there now existed danger from numerous wolves, black bears, and other wild animals. And the last thing Sammons wanted to do was to tangle with a powerful black bear seeking more human flesh.

Sammons, however, knew that it would be suicidal to follow the road directly westward. He also reasoned that if he attempted to approach Fort Stanwix from the north the chance of him encountering enemy personnel was great, since St. Leger had most likely moved against Fort Stanwix from the northwest. Thus, he decided to first proceed in a southwesterly direction and afterward head directly toward the fort from the south. Once in its vicinity, he would carefully scout out what was going on before heading back to Albany. Sammons knew that time was of essence. General Schuyler was waiting.

Notes

1   Eckert, p. 116. Alden, *A History of the American Revolution*, p. 321, cites that "the Indians sustained perhaps 150 casualties."

According to Mary Jemison, in 1777, when the Seneca warriors drifted back to their tribes, they were very critical of the British. The warriors stated that the British had promised much, but actually delivered very little. According to Jemison, the Indians were deceived into the campaign. (Stone, *Siege and Battle*, p. 243–4.) According to *"St. Leger's Attack,"* pp. 10–11, "instead of supporting the whites, they [the Indians] were being asked to take the brunt of every engagement. . . The Indians had been disgruntled ever since their losses in killed and injured at Oriskany and in property before Fort Stanwix."

2   Watt and Morrison, p.26, footnote 1, cite St. Leger did have a strong craving for alcohol and under moments of stress it was his solace.

3   Eckert, p. 142.

4   Stone, *Siege and Battle*, pp. 249–250. For the entire letter see appendix sec-

tion, pp. xxxiv–xxxv. As also acknowledged by the authors, the letter was written under duress.

5   No records exist on this.

6   Although the old English style of writing still existed, a simple review reveals that St. Leger's words are not clearly written. Tired, angry, possibly the worse for wear after a drink to calm the nerves, St. Leger was no longer thinking clearly. The events of 6 August had not only exhausted him, but actually had turned the tide against him. After 6 August, St. Leger stood no chance of succeeding in his campaign unless, somehow, he could receive a massive reinforcement of troops backed with heavy weapons.

7   Stone, *Siege and Battle*, p. 243.

XIV

General Herkimer Returns to the Mohawk Valley

At the very moment the scout Sammons was cautiously probing toward Fort Stanwix, the remains of General Herkimer's battered force, among them Honyery and his wife, were cautiously retreating eastward. The very same route taken previously from Fort Dayton was now again being utilized to return.[1] There were around 150 able-bodied survivors, and an unknown number of wounded and injured, some of whom walked, with assistance, while others were carried in litters.[2] Despite his wound General Herkimer remained in command, though Colonel Campbell assisted in the retreat. Of Herkimer's initial strength of nearly 900, no fewer than 400 and as many as 700 had been killed, wounded, captured, or scattered.

En route, his force rested for a short while near the ruins of the old Fort Schuyler. Along the way, some of the more seriously wounded had died. Unlike the dead left behind at Oriskany, these men were buried, albeit quickly and in shallow graves. No markers were placed upon the graves, and leaves, grass, and branches were strewn over the fresh soil to conceal the sites. This was done to prevent any pursuing enemy personnel from digging up the bodies and mutilating or scalping them.

During the march there was an ugly incident which, had it not been controlled, could have devastated Herkimer's survivors. As they marched, some of Herkimer's men were guarding the prisoners captured at Oriskany, including the Indian Chief Ghalto. For some reason, several militiamen suddenly surrounded Ghalto. Readying their knives and tomahawks, they screamed curses and death threats, demanding that the guards hand him over. Others joined in, and soon an entire mob of angry, threatening militiamen swirled around the chief, his guards, and the other prisoners. Noting the tumult, Colonel Campbell rushed forward. In an authoritative manner, he informed the men that Ghalto would not be killed under any circumstances. The chief, insisted Campbell, was more valuable alive than dead. Vital information could yet be obtained from him. The colonel also reminded the militiamen that murder would not be tolerated, discipline would be maintained, and—despite the enemy's cruelty—the Patriots would act honorably and with civility.

The angry militiamen backed off. Colonel Campbell was, after all, a highly respected officer. His valor, calmness, and quick thinking in combat had been proven. Chief Ghalto's life was spared.[3]

Finally, in the dark evening hours of 7 August, Herkimer's force reached Fort Dayton. There the main task was to assist the wounded. Since Herkimer had lost his chief medical officer, no competent doctor was available. Throughout the night, on makeshift litters and tables, efforts were made to assist the injured but it was no easy matter. Soon, more of Herkimer's men entered their eternal sleep. While the wounded were treated to the extent that was possible, Colonel Campbell's rearguard maintained their careful vigilance over the remainder of the Patriot force.

Placed on a table made from a door removed from its hinges, Captain Seeber was told the grim news that his leg could not be saved. Gangrene and blood poisoning had set in. In order to save the captain's life, the limb would have to be amputated. The captain was given a strong dose of alcohol and then a stick wrapped in cloth was inserted between his teeth. Then the leg was sawed off. Herkimer's wound remained untreated.

Although the retreating force had reached Fort Dayton without further incident, General Herkimer knew that he had to move farther away from the battle area. He was, after all, still too close to the British besieging Fort Stanwix, and he wanted to move his wounded and injured personnel as soon as possible to their homes.

Throughout Friday, 8 August, the wounded were placed on boats and floated eastward down the Mohawk River. Along the way they were dropped off at various locations. In the following days, they were taken to their respective homes, and by and large were afforded care by their families. The remaining non-wounded militiamen were disbanded at Fort Dayton to return home for the time being. Although Herkimer's force was dispersed and was never again reconstituted in 1777, many of his militiamen continued to serve in the Northern Army until October–November that year. In the following weeks, many of them would join the various militia units engaging Burgoyne at Saratoga. Among them were men who previously had been lightly wounded at Oriskany. A small number also entered Washington's main Continental Army. Others served as cadre personnel and instructors in newly formed militia units. And some served that same year in the vicinity of West Point against British General Sir Henry Clinton.

Unable to recover from the amputation of his leg, Captain Seeber passed away before reaching his home. General Herkimer, following a journey of at least thirty-five miles by stretcher and wagon, finally arrived home.

Despite daily ministrations, Herkimer's leg became gangrenous. Based on the medical opinion of Doctor Louis Chambreau, he agreed to have his leg amputated. A native of France, Doctor Chambreau had immigrated to the colonies prior to the war. Enlisting in the Northern Army, the doctor was one of General Benedict Arnold's medical officers. In 1777, the Mohawk Valley lacked doctors, and the Northern Army dispatched Chambreau to attend the valley's militia and army personnel, and also treat to any civilians requiring medical attention.

Chambreau undertook the amputation on Friday, 15 August; however, he was not a highly skilled surgeon. Despite his best efforts, he performed a poor amputation and was unable to stem the flow of blood.

General Herkimer began to weaken, but regardless of his deteriorating condition he maintained a high spirit. Shortly after the operation, he was visited by his close friend, Lieutenant Colonel Willett. Smoking his pipe, Herkimer joked with his companion. But Willett knew that Herkimer was only putting on a brave face, and guessed that the general's end was near. Willett informed Herkimer that he, Colonel Gansevoort, and the defenders of Fort Stanwix held Herkimer and his militia in high esteem. General Arnold was another visitor to the general's bedside. He expressed how grateful General Schuyler and the entire Northern Army were for the efforts undertaken by Tryon County's militia. The German community residing at German Flats was also praised.

The following day, Herkimer assembled his family and loyal servants around him, and opened his family bible—brought over from Germany by his ancestors—to the 38th Psalm. He began reading the verses in German, but his voice faded and he never finished. As he lapsed into eternal rest, he passed into history.

Notes

1   *"St. Leger's Attack,"* p. 10.
2   According to Stone, *Siege and Battle,* p. 241, "Between forty and fifty of these crude liters were constructed." Swiggett, p. 87, cites "Herkimer fell back toward the river eastward, probably with less than 400 men on their feet."
3   Chief Ghalto survived. In the aftermath of the Revolutionary War he lived for a number of years and tremendously regretted that he ever took up arms against the Patriots. The chief also always held Colonel Campbell in high esteem.

XV

Continuing Actions
at Fort Stanwix

Swinging wide from the southwest, scout Frederick Sammons circled the fort. Though he had no intention of entering or even coming close to it, he did manage to catch a glimpse of its embattered walls in the late evening hours.

The siege of Fort Stanwix was now fully underway. Cannons roared both day and night. Heavy rifle and musket fire riddled the fort, while fire arrows rained down. After a day or so, two firefighting teams were created by the Patriots to address the danger posed by the fire arrows. Operating twenty-four hours a day, each team undertaking a twelve-hour shift, their mission was to extinguish flames and ensure that the fort was not burned.

Trenching operations to bring the British mortars within range of the fort's ramparts and its interior continued non-stop. The heavy pressure began to take its toll. More and more of the defenders were killed or wounded. An incoming cannonball, bursting within the compound, sent pieces of shrapnel flying in every direction. Caught out in the open, a piece of shrapnel tore deep into the thigh of one of Fort Stanwix's female defenders.

The massive flashes constantly bursting high over the fort, combined with the steady cannonading, told Sammons that it was still holding out. He now knew everything that he needed. The fort was still resisting. The British force was largely an Indian/Loyalist army augmented with British and German personnel. Though the white presence was not huge, Sammons calculated their strength ranged from about 400 to 600 soldiers. Herkimer's force had been ambushed but, in turn, had inflicted heavy losses upon its attackers. A road was being constructed from Lake Oneida eastward toward the fort. Trenches were also being dug toward the fort, and Sammons calculated by the firing that the British had between six and eight pieces of light and medium cannon. As for their mortars, Sammons noted that these pieces had not yet been positioned. But once the trenching operations concluded, this would change.

Sammons was now ready to head back. Setting off directly eastward, he reasoned that in about three days of fast travel, he would re-emerge from the wilderness in Albany.

By Saturday, 9 August, the fort had been subjected to two and a half days of continuous bombardment. Intermittent gunfire and cannonading continued through the early evening hours of 9 August and into the morning. War whoops and shouts thundered from the forests ringing the fort. A fire arrow came streaking in on occasion. General St. Leger decided to once again approach the defenders of the fort with a surrender proposal. Perhaps, they would finally come to reason.

Hostile activity against the fort ceased, and three officers approached its walls under a large white flag of truce. The three men, all in uniform, were Colonel John Butler, Major Ancrom, and an unidentified army surgeon.[1] Approaching the main gate, the three halted and requested permission to enter.

The main gates opened just a crack, and four regular army Continental officers squeezed out, all attired in uniforms of blue coats and white pants. Lieutenant Colonel Willett stood among the four.

Speaking politely, Major Ancrom introduced himself and his companions, then requested to see the commander of the fort, Colonel Gansevoort.

Willett agreed. Provided, of course, that the three had no objections about being blindfolded in order to enter. Voicing no objections, the three officers were blindfolded and quickly escorted into a room within the fort. To ensure secrecy, its windows were shut and sealed. A number of candles were lit for illumination.

Colonel Butler, Major Ancrom, and the medical officer sat at one end of the table inside the room. On the other end sat Colonel Gansevoort and Lieutenant Colonels Willett and Mellon. Extra chairs were also placed around the table, which seated some of the other officers. In addition, still more officers sat on chairs farther away from the table or stood against the walls. Colonel Gansevoort wanted to have as many of his officers as possible to witness this soon-to-be historic event. To ensure accuracy, a young Continental Army officer sat not far from the table with paper and pens ready to record the discussion.

To show the visiting enemy officers Patriot hospitality, a tablecloth was set and a couple of dishes of crackers and cheese were laid out. Wine bottles were produced and toast glasses were provided. Though simple, such a gracious welcome demonstrated that some civility did exist within the terrible Wilderness War of 1777, and that the Patriot defenders were honorable men. After filling their glasses, each side toasted the other for continuous health, and compliments were passed around.

Then, everyone got down to business, and the friendly atmosphere turned rather cool when Major Ancrom began to speak. He stated:

I am directed by Colonel St. Leger, the officer who commands the army now investing the garrison, to inform the commandant, that the colonel has, with much difficulty, prevailed on the Indians to agree, that if the garrison, without further resistance, shall be delivered up, with the public stores belonging to it, to the investing army, the officers and soldiers shall have all their baggage and private property secured to them. And in order that the garrison may have a sufficient pledge to this effect, Colonel Butler accompanies me to assure them, that not a hair on the head of any one of them shall be hurt. I am likewise directed to remind the commandant, that the defeat of General Herkimer must deprive the garrison of all hopes of relief, especially as General Burgoyne is now in Albany; so that, sooner or later, the fort must fall into our hands. Colonel St. Leger, from an earnest desire to prevent further bloodshed, hopes these terms will not be refused; as in this case, it will be out of his power to make them again. It was with great difficulty the Indians consented to the present arrangement, as it will deprive them of that plunder which they always calculate upon, on similar occasions. Should, then, the present terms be rejected, it will be out of the power of the colonel to restrain the Indians, who are very numerous, and much exasperated, not only from plundering the property, but destroying the lives of, probably, the greater part of the garrison. Indeed the Indians are so exceed-ingly provoked, and mortified by the losses they have sustained, in the late actions, having had several of their favourite chiefs killed, that they threaten,—and the Colonel, if the present arrangements should not be entered into, will not be able to prevent them from executing their threats,—to march down the country, and destroy the settlement, with its inhabitants. In this case, not only men, but women and children, will experience the sad effects of their vengeance. These considerations, it is ardently hoped, will produce a proper effect, and induce the commandant, by complying with the terms now offered, to save himself from future regret, when it will be too late.[2]

It is interesting that Major Ancrom mentioned that the Indians were "mortified by the losses they have sustained, in the late actions," and that "several of their favourite chiefs" had been killed.[3] Perhaps, it would have been best had the major not stated this as he was revealing to the enemy that the Indians had suffered heavy losses. Although the major did not officially describe the status of the rest of St. Leger's force, it would have been natural for the Patriot officers to begin to wonder about their condition, if the Indians had suffered so grievously.

Upon the conclusion of this rather threatening speech, total silence reigned in the room. Then, after momentarily staring at Colonel Gansevoort and the other Patriot officers, Lieutenant Colonel Willett began to speak, getting right to the point:

Do I understand you, Sir? I think you say, that you come from a British colonel, who is commander of the army that invests this fort; and by your uniform, you appear to be an officer in the British service. You have made a long speech on the occasion of your visit, which, strript of all its superfluities, amounts to this, that you come from a British colonel, to the commandant of this garrison, to tell him, that if he does not deliver up the garrison into the hands of your Colonel, he will send his Indians to murder our women and children. You will please to reflect, Sir, that their blood will be on your head, not on ours. We are doing our duty: this garrison is committed to our charge, and we will take care of it. After you get out of it, you may turn round and look at its outside, but never expect to come in again, unless you come a prisoner. I consider the message you have brought, a degrading one for a British officer to send, and by no means reputable for a British officer to carry. For my part, I declare, before I would consent to deliver this garrison to such a murdering set as your army, by your own account, consists of, I would suffer my body to be filled with splinters, and set on fire, as you know has at times been practiced, by such hordes of women and children killers, as belong to your army.[4]

Before Major Ancrom could respond, Willett's officers gave a loud round of applause. Colonel Gansevoort immediately added that he had no intention of surrendering. Ancrom and his companions must have felt very uncomfortable, if not fearful, surrounded by cheering, armed Patriot officers.

It was now obvious to Ancrom that the Americans were obstinate, and so instead he proposed an armistice for three days, to commence immediately after midnight on 10 August. When informed of this, Colonel Gansevoort agreed. No official reason was cited as to why the Patriot commander consented, but a three-day truce was a great way of buying critical time, saving ammunition and powder, shoring up the defenses, and resting the garrison. Major Ancrom also requested that the British surgeon be allowed to inspect any wounded British personnel captured during Willett's raid. His request was honored and, accompanied by Dr. Woodruff, the surgeon was taken to inspect the prisoners.

Prior to their departure, Colonel Gansevoort wrote a short note directed to Barry St. Leger. He wrote:

Fort Schuyler [Stanwix], Aug. 9th, 1777.

Sir,

Your letter of this day's date I have received, in answer to which I say, that it is my determined resolution, with the forces under my command, to defend this fort to the last extremity, in behalf of the United States, who have placed me here to defend it against all their enemies.

I have the honor to be, Sir,
Your most ob't. humble serv't.,

Peter Gansevoort,
Col. commanding Fort Schuyler
[To] Gen. Barry St. Leger.[6]

The message was clear—the Americans were not going to surrender. Angered by Gansevoort's reply, St. Leger ordered his forces to resume the bombardment of Fort Stanwix. The cease-fire was off. Within minutes, the sound of gunfire and the booming of cannons cracked through the countryside as the first rounds were fired against the fort.

Four or five days after the Battle of Oriskany, St. Leger revisited his decision not to attack into the Mohawk Valley. He concluded that perhaps it would not be a bad idea to dispatch a small force throughout the nearby settlements. Such a raid would demonstrate British strengths, raise morale amongst the pro-British element, would possibly induce many of the neutrals into supporting the Crown, and obtain vital information.[6] Captain Walter Butler was selected to lead this group and, accompanied by a small number of Loyalists and a handful of Indians,[7] he set off down the Mohawk Valley. His mission was to commence in the vicinity of Fort Dayton.

Walter Butler was not the only one slipping into the valley seeking allies. Late that evening on 10 August, at around 10 p.m.—in a howling and raging storm and in total darkness—Lieutenant Colonel Willett, accompanied by Lieutenant George Stockwell, slipped out of Fort Stanwix through a sally port and raced into a marsh.[8]

Prior to the war, Lieutenant Stockwell had been a professional hunter. A first-rate woodsman, he knew the entire north country and could move swiftly through the wilderness. Also an ardent Patriot, he was one of the first to join the Northern Army.

Willett's mission was to inform Northern Army headquarters that Fort Stanwix was still holding out, to bring information to the residents of the Mohawk Valley on what was occurring, and obtain additional support and reinforcements for the garrison. To move rapidly, each man was armed with only a short spear and tomahawk. Each also carried a bag on his shoulder containing a small number of crackers, some dried beef jerky, and pieces of cheese. In addition, a canteen of "spirits" was carried by each man.

Once inside the marsh, the two succeeded in crossing a stream, then entered a swampy forest. It was so dark that it was virtually impossible to see one's own hand within this morass of trees and tangled vines. Suddenly, a dog began to bark. Fearing that it was on the prowl for them, Willett and Stockwell froze in place and immediately leaned against a huge tree for additional cover and camouflage. They remained in that position for several hours.

In time, the barking ceased and the weather cleared a bit. Some stars became visible, and from these Stockwell set a course. His plan was to head north and, after a short distance, proceed eastward and then southeastward. Stockwell wanted to get to Fort Dayton.

The men moved rapidly, as they had much ground to cover. To evade any pursuing party, they occasionally hopped and skipped over the ground, crossed and recrossed streams, moved through water, and utilized swamps.

The two halted to rest and sleep during the night of 12 August. Because it was a cold night and their clothes were damp, they laid back to back to stay warm. At the crack of dawn, they resumed their efforts. They were refreshed after coming across a "forest of ripe raspberries and blackberries." Later that day, after a trek of approximately fifty miles through unexplored wilderness and swamps, they finally arrived at Fort Dayton.

It is of interest that Willett's feat was later honored by the British:

> Colonel Willett afterwards undertook, in company with another officer, a much more perilous expedition. They passed by night through the besieger's works, and in contempt of the danger and cruelty of the savages, made their way for fifty miles through pathless woods and unexplored morasses, in order to raise the country and bring relief to the fort. Such an action demands the praise even of an enemy.[9]

Notes

1   According to Eckert, p. 144, on 9 August "two British officers approached the main gate of Fort Stanwix under the flag of truce. . . .."

Yet, Willett wrote in his narrative, "Colonel Butler, who commanded the Indians, with two other officers [requested] to enter the fort, with a message to the commanding officer." (See Willett, p. 55). And on page 56, Willett also cites three officers approached when he wrote: "Colonel Butler and the two other officers who had come with him."

Stone, *Siege and Battle*, p. 250, cite "On the following day [9 August

1777] a white flag approached the garrison, with a request that Colonel Butler, and two other officers, might be admitted into the fort as bearers of a
message to the commanding officer."

Lossing, Vol. I, p. 248, cites "Colonel Butler and two other officers
approached the fort with a white flag. . . ." All sources reveal that a total of
three officers appeared before Fort Stanwix. Elizabeth Eggleston Seelye,
"Brant and Red Jacket" in *Hudson, Mohawk, Schoharie. History From
America's Most Famous Valleys and the Border Wars* (New York: Doss,
Mead and Company, Publishers, 1879), Chapter 30, cites that Colonel Butler, Major Ancrom, and a third unidentified officer (possibly the British doctor) entered the fort to negotiate with the Patriots. (Hereafter cited as *Border
Wars.*)

2   Stone, *Siege and Battle,* pp. 250–251; and Willett, pp. 56–57. In Eckert, *The
Wilderness War,* pp. 144–145, Eckert's version of what was said is quite
close. But the meaning is the same.

3   By "late actions" Major Ancrom meant the losses incurred at both Oriskany
and during the siege of Fort Stanwix. In actuality, Major Ancrom made a
horrendous mistake in revealing the loss of the Indians. Indirectly, if not
directly, he also acknowledged that along with the Indian losses, the Loyalists also took a pounding.

4   See Willett, pp. 57–58; Stone, *Siege and Battle,* pp. 251–252; and Ward, Vol.
II, p. 489.

5   Stone, pp. 252–253.

6   According to Lossing, Vol. I, p. 250, Butler also delivered an address to the
people of Tryon County signed by Johnson, Claus, and Colonel Butler. The
address, however, was not without a warning. The address stated that if the
residents would not submit and cooperate, they would experience Indian
cruelties.

7   Exactly how many personnel accompanied Walter Butler into the Mohawk
Valley is unknown. It is clear, however, that his force consisted of both Loyalists and Indians.

8   According to Willett's personal narrative, p. 59, he and Lieutenant George
Stockwell slipped out of the fort at 10 p.m. (Stockwell's rank has also been
cited at this time as that of "Major" but although he ended the Revolutionary War as a major, in the summer of 1777, he was a lieutenant.) According
to Watt and Morrison, *The British Campaign of 1777,* p. 4, "Colonel Gansevoort was also worried that St. Leger was spreading rumors in the
[Mohawk] Valley below. He had his deputy commander Willett slip through
the siege lines to encourage another relief effort and to inform Major General
Philip Schuyler, the Northern Army commander, that all was well inside the
fortress." According to Bancroft, Vol. III, p. 380, Willett and Stockwell were
"both good woodsmen."

9   *The British Annual Register of 1777* (published in 1778), see also Willett,
A Narrative of the Military Actions of Colonel Willett, p. 61.

XVI

Loyalist Raids and Probes into the Mohawk Valley

On 15 August, over 100 Loyalist volunteers, commanded by Captain Jacob Miller, arrived to join General St. Leger. Little is known about them, except that this reinforcement was the only one that St. Leger received. Most of Miller's men went into the Royal Greens Regiment, although others were dispersed among the Indians for support or to serve as advisors.

Yet little became of this Loyalist effort. In the upcoming days, some deserted. A fear of the Indians, the desire to return home, disillusionment with the way St. Leger was handling his irregulars, coupled with fears that the British would soon be defeated, compelled a number to flee.

In mid-August, angered by his losses at Oriskany and seeking revenge, Joseph Brant began to conduct raids on various Indian villages sympathizing with—or suspected of doing so—the Patriot cause. Brant had encouraged Loyalists and Indians to support the King, yet despite his best efforts had failed.[1] He wanted to not only punish the Indians who had failed to support the Crown, but also terrorize others into submission. Several Oneida villages were especially targeted. For the Iroquois Confederacy, the 6 August 1777 Battle of Oriskany is cited as the date when a brutal civil war commenced among its constituent tribes.[2] One targeted village lay just a few miles to the south of Oriskany. With a strength of about fifty warriors[3] and a handful of Butler's Rangers, Brant struck the village in the early dawn hours. Thoroughly meticulous, the raiders showed no mercy.

Each longhouse was torched, and every man, woman, and child

that could be found was shot, clubbed, tomahawked, or knifed. Some of the women ran out of the flaming longhouses clutching babies in their hands. Struck by a tomahawk or club, the women and their infants were picked up and thrown back into the red-hot, all-consuming flames. Immobile wounded villagers were also thrown into the fires. Amid the crackle of the flames were heard the ugly screams of the dying. Several men were bound but for now, they were spared—though not for long. By the end of the day, deep in some wilderness campsite, they would undergo a cruel fate known only to those who ever had the misfortune of being selected for torture. Gathering up scalps, weapons, booty, and their prisoners, the raiders withdrew deep into the wilderness. Soon, other villages would be targeted. Within weeks, Brant earned a nickname that would be attached to his name forever: "Monster Brant."

Sent into the Mohawk Valley by St. Leger, Walter Butler lost no time in trying to win over neutrals to their cause. In the late hours of 17 August, thirteen men gathered at Shoemaker's Tavern.[4] Owned and operated by Mr. Hector Shoemaker, the tavern was located in Andrustown, a small village located in the German Flats about two miles to the north of Fort Dayton in the Mohawk Valley.[5]

In the aftermath of what Walter Butler perceived as General Herkimer's defeat, he concluded that now was the perfect time to recruit additional manpower for the British.[6] Butler had selected Shoemaker's Tavern because its proprietor was a prominent person in the area and a loyal follower of the British Crown. He reasoned that Shoemaker would exert a positive influence upon the locals.

Unknown to Butler, however, Shoemaker had shifted his allegiance in recent months. In addition to holding pro-Patriot sentiments, Shoemaker was also spying for the Americans. Information loosely expressed in his tavern—especially by those under the influence of "spirits"—found its way to the Patriots. When informed by a Loyalist that Walter Butler would be holding a meeting at his tavern in the evening hours of 17 August, Shoemaker had immediately passed the information on to Lieutenant Colonel James Wesson,[7] commander of the 9th Massachusetts Continentals who was in charge at Fort Dayton.

That evening Walter Butler arrived, accompanied by a dozen Loyalist and Indian followers. Attired in uniform, he looked like a true British officer. On his chest, he wore the gorget of the King's Royal

Green Regiment. Beautifully designed, the gorget displayed a powerful white horse with the Latin motto, *Nec Aspera Terrent* (Fear No Difficulties). Delighted that a large crowd had gathered, Butler began to speak. As they listened to his words, some of the attendees were seen to be nodding their heads in agreement. Standing alongside Butler was Peter Ten Broeck, a Loyalist lieutenant fluent in both Dutch and German. Ten Broeck had accompanied Butler from Fort Stanwix in order to translate his words for the inhabitants of the Mohawk Valley who couldn't speak English.

As Butler spoke and Ten Broeck translated, against the rear wall stood a handful of Cayuga and Seneca Indians. Armed, stripped to their waists and adorned with war paint, these warriors were present to demonstrate the power of St. Leger's force. Also present was Hon Yost Schuyler, who was generally considered to be simple-minded or mentally ill.[8] Approximately twenty years of age, this sympathizer of George III resided with his mother and younger brother in the nearby hamlet of Little Falls.

As Butler continued to speak, it became increasingly apparent that many not only resented his words, but indeed his very presence. Sensing a volatile situation, he tried to assure everyone that the British wanted to restore law and justice to the area, and only required their cooperation.

Suddenly, German words boomed through the room. Looking to Ten Broeck, Butler quietly asked his lieutenant what had been said. But before Ten Broeck could even respond, a local loudly translated for Butler that the first speaker's son had been killed at Oriskany.

Butler calmly asked for order. He attempted to speak. Raising his arms to settle the crowd, he acknowledged that many good men had perished on both sides. But it was to no avail. Many in the crowd began to push forward. The other Loyalists and Indians who had accompanied Butler felt the threat as well.

Suddenly, through the main door, a group of Continental soldiers led by Lieutenant Colonel Wesson poured in. Outside, militiamen surrounded the building. In a loud voice Wesson announced that he was arresting Butler as a spy and traitor on the authority of the Congress of the United Colonies and the Committee of Safety of Tryon County.

Butler protested that he was not a traitor but on the King's business, however Wesson proceeded and Butler was tied up and taken outside.

Amid the crowds and scuffling, several of the Loyalists succeeded in slipping out and avoiding arrest. Hon Yost was less lucky—Lieutenant Colonel Wesson was tired of Hon Yost's constant activities for the King and had him arrested as well.

Butler's next stop was a local jail cell, soon followed by a prison cell in Albany where he was slated for execution. Butler remained a prisoner in Albany during the winter of 1777–78, but the following April he managed to escape. From Albany, he fled northward via Lake Champlain and the St. Lawrence River back to Quebec, Canada. In time, he returned to Fort Niagara and from that location he continued to direct raids into the Mohawk and Schoharie Valleys.[9]

Notes

1   Graymont, p. 115.

2   Ibid, p. 142; Calhoon, *The Loyalists in Revolutionary America*, p. 428.

3   Eckert, p. 152; Calhoon, p. 428, cites "Sir Johnson . . . burned a neutral Oneida settlement." Graymont, p. 142, cites "So resentful were the British Indian allies of the Oneidas who fought against them there [Oriskany and Fort Stanwix] that a band of warriors later invaded the Oriska settlement, burned it to the ground, destroyed the crops, and drove away the cattle."

4   17 August 1777, and thirteen men, are both cited by Eckert, p. 147. "The notorious Walter Butler was captured here in 1777 while holding a midnight meeting to spark a Loyalist uprising to support St. Leger's siege of Fort Stanwix." (See Boatner, p. 306.)

5   Swiggett, *War Out of Niagara*, p. 136, cites that Walter Butler was captured in Andrustown, located in the German Flats. Eckert, p. 147, and Stone, *Siege and Battle*, p. 255, cite "about two miles above Ft. Dayton." Presently known as the Shoemaker House, the tavern still stands, located in the town of Mohawk on West Main Street, New York State Route 5S. See also "Shoemaker House" in Boatner, *Landmarks of the American Revolution*, pp. 306–307.

6   According to Stone, *Siege and Battle*, pp. 255–256, "Walter N. Butler, from St. Leger's army, who, with fourteen white soldiers and the same number of Indians, had visited the German Flatts secretly, with the appeal of Sir John Johnson, Claus, and the elder [John] Butler, for the purpose of persuading the timid and disaffected inhabitants to abandon the Provincial cause, and enroll themselves with the King's army before Fort Schuyler [Stanwix]."

7   Wesson's name has also been spelled as Weston. His rank has also been cited as "colonel," but in the summer of 1777, his rank was actually that of lieutenant colonel.

8   It is not certain if Hon Yost Schuyler was, indeed, a distant relative of Gen-

eral Philip Schuyler. Eckert, p. 452, fn. 138, cites that Hon Yost was not related to the Northern Army general.

9   One of his most vicious raids was upon Cherry Valley. Despite the warning by friendly Oneidas on 8 November 1778 that an attack was imminent, it was disregarded. Three days later, on 11 November, Walter struck. His mixed Loyalist–Indian force decimated much of the valley and many innocent people were killed. Indeed, so horrible was the massacre that in its aftermath, Walter's father, Colonel John Butler, was known to exclaim, "Had I been there, I would have killed my own son!"

On 30 October 1781, near the current town of Poland where the Black River empties into West Canada Creek, a heavy skirmish was fought between the remnants of Walter Butler's force and pursuing Patriot militia. Among the pursuers was the half-breed Indian "Colonel" Louis who was determined to kill Walter once and for all. The skirmish, which actually developed into a sizable battle, was also fought in a ferocious snowstorm.

Unable to disengage from his opponents, Butler was forced to make a stand. Shot by "Colonel" Louis, who for years had wanted to kill Walter, he lay wounded on the ground; within moments, Louis was upon him. Noting Louis' tomahawk, Walter begged to be spared. But it was to no avail. Shouting—"this is for Cherry Valley!" Louis drove his instrument of death deep into Walter's head. For Louis, it was also a moment of justice because when Walter had struck Cherry Valley in 1778, one of his victims was a young black girl who Louis had loved and planned to marry. Despite the heavy snowfall coming down, Louis still scalped the young Butler. His scalp and rifle were taken to Albany and sold there. The spot where Walter was killed is presently under water, covered by the Hinckley Reservoir. According to Lowenthal, *Marinus Willett*, p. 67, "No one can be sure of the exact site of the clash in which Walter Butler was killed, but this spot on West Canada Creek is probably close." (See photo of creek.) Needless to say, word of Butler's death spread quickly "and the settlers rejoiced at the news of his death" and "[though] word of the climatic victory at Yorktown reached the area at nearly the same time, the inhabitants of the Mohawk [Valley] took more pleasure in the death of the young Butler." (Ibid. pp. 67–68)

XVII

Cushetunk's Resistance

While St. Leger was besieging Fort Stanwix, General Schuyler was rushing troops and materiel westward, Walter Butler was being arrested, and Burgoyne was advancing southward to Albany, other critical events were also underway. Though smaller in scope, these events played an instrumental role in achieving a major victory for the Patriots during the Wilderness War of 1777.

In preparation for St. Leger's expedition in 1777, Joseph Brant had established his headquarters in the vicinity of Oquaga.[1] An Indian settlement along the Susequehanna River, Oquaga was located in a wilderness region in lower New York State adjacent to Pennsylvania. In June and July of 1777, Brant departed Oquaga with a number of Indians to Oswego, where he and his men were incorporated into St. Leger's army. It was also in Oquaga in the spring of 1777 that Loyalist leader McDonell (Scotus) was given the mission of creating a fourth thrust toward Albany.

In and around Oquaga resided some settlers who harbored pro-British sentiments. Organizing themselves, they began to conduct raids into neighboring and distant regions. They reasoned that their actions would benefit the British campaign of 1777. Some raiders however, were only criminally motivated. Pretending to be loyal to the British Crown, they attacked those with pro-Patriot sentiment solely to benefit themselves.

At first, the raids struck lone farms and tiny hamlets. But as they fanned further out from Oquaga, the attacks increased in both size and scope. Soon, the sizable settlement of Cushetunk, currently known as Cochecton,[2] was targeted.

Cushetunk was located on the upper northern (or eastern) bank of the Delaware River in New York State's present-day Sullivan County, nearly 30 miles directly southeast of Oquaga. Immediately across the Delaware lies the state of Pennsylvania, which in fact can be seen from Cushetunk. Approximately five miles down the Delaware from Cushetunk, outside the present-day town of Narrowsburg, stood Fort Delaware. From there just a short distance farther downriver, lies present-day Port Jervis and the town of Matamoras. Here, the Delaware River veers sharply to the southwest; likewise, the borders of New York, New Jersey, and Pennsylvania come together at this location.[3] Overlooking the bend from the northwestern tip of New Jersey is High Point. At 1,803 ft, it is the highest point in the state of New Jersey.

Fort Delaware was constructed in 1755. It arose when the so-called "Connecticut Yankees," recent inhabitants of Connecticut, began to enter the region seeking land. Trappers and early settlers knew that the fertile lands found in the valleys near and adjacent to the Delaware and Susquehanna Rivers could support agricultural production and animal livestock. Additionally, much lumber could be obtained from the rich forests.

As oftentimes happened in pre-Revolutionary America, tragic conflicts arose between regional natives and incoming settlers. By the conclusion of the French and Indian War of 1754–1763, the regional Lenape Indians were no longer a power. Many had departed the area. Dissatisfaction with Pennsylvania's government, especially with its attempts to enforce rules and regulations upon a region regarded by Cushetunk's inhabitants as non-Pennsylvanian territory, encouraged the Connecticut residents who had settled in the region to turn to their former Colony's government for assistance. Successfully, they convinced Connecticut to claim the region under its own title.[4] Under this title, Connecticut's argument of rightfully possessing territories farther to the west of where its western border actually stood was only further intensified.[5] With the eruption of the Revolutionary War in 1775, the issue was still unresolved. But it did not matter. In 1777, far more pressing and critical issues were at stake.

Although some Loyalists resided in the region, by and large Cushetunk's inhabitants regarded themselves as Patriots. This was attributable to the fact that Connecticut itself was largely a Patriot stronghold. As its inhabitants pushed westward, they brought into the wilderness a pro-Patriot sentiment and laid the seeds of rebellion.[6] This explains why during the Revolutionary War many of Cushetunk's Patriots joined the regular army and served in the various New York, New Jersey, and Pennsylvania Continental forces, while others served either as militiamen or scouts.[7]

For the British a firm control of Cushetunk, along with the southern wilderness region of present-day New York State, would have tremendous advantages. Another vital river network, rich agricultural valleys, and the wealth of the immense forest would tremendously benefit the Crown while denying these resources to the Patriots. Politically, the Patriots of lower New York, Pennsylvania, and New Jersey would find it almost impossible to operate if a strong British bastion existed among them. Therefore, in late 1776 and early 1777, British officials advocated a series of Loyalist and Indian attacks against Cushetunk. These commenced with ferocity in 1777 and lasted in some form or another until 1783.[8]

Yet, despite the best efforts of the Loyalists to suppress Cushetunk's populace by terror, by the conclusion of 1777 Cushetunk's Patriots had not only succeeded in holding their own, but most importantly they maintained the region for the newly established nation.

In the aftermath of St. Leger's retreat and Burgoyne's surrender at Saratoga in October 1777, Oquaga was still utilized, along with nearby Unadilla, as bases by both Loyalist and pro-British Indians to stage raids into various parts of New York State, western New Jersey, and Pennsylvania. In 1779, Patriot Generals Sullivan and Clinton, in an attempt to destroy the Loyalist–Indian threat, targeted Oquaga and Unadilla. Yet, despite the destruction of most of the pro-British element, raids continued to be launched from these centers until the end of the war, with hostilities continuing to simmer even afterward.

As historian James Burbank wrote, "As in all Wars the mothers, wives and daughters experienced their full share of trouble and suffering. Such was the case in Cushetunk as well as elsewhere. The stories of horrors, trials and atrocities which befell the women of Cushetunk would fill a book."

Notes

1   Now known as Ouaquaga. It is located in Broome County, 12 miles directly east of the city of Binghamton on Route 79. A state park, known as the Oquaga Creek State Park, exists in the vicinity. Ouaquaga lies just to the

south of the Susquehanna River on a river that connects into the Susque-hanna River's southern bank. Approximately 3 miles directly to its south lies the town of Windsor and Route 17. (Hereafter, for simplicity, Ouaquaga will be spelled solely as Oquaga.)

Prior to 1775, approximately 750 Indians resided at Oquaga and it served as a fur-trading post. Most were Mohawks, although the remnants of a small tribe known as the Esopus, which initially had hailed from the eastern portion of the Royal Colony of New York but had been forced out of their (now Kingston) area, resided in Oquaga as well. (For further information on this region see Boatner, *Landmarks of the American Revolution*, pp. 289–290).

2   In addition to Cocheton, there is also a Cocheton Center. The name Cushetunk, which also depicts a region, has many spelling variations—i.e. Cashiehtunk, Casheitung, Cashethon, etc.—but, likewise, many different explanations for how the name arose and what it actually means. Perhaps Mr. Charles A. Philhower, formerly from Westfield, New Jersey, and an eminent authority on the local Lenape language, provides the best answer. Kach or kash means red stone; Te or Tet stands for stone or stone hill; Ung, Unk, or Tunk designates a location, site, spot, or place. Since many red stones abound in the region, perhaps the Lenapes were the ones who coined the phrase. (Hereafter, Cushetunk only will be used).

The Lenapes were divided into three groups: Turkey, Turtle, and Wolf. They resided in the lands that now encompass Sullivan County and some adjacent territory.

3   Pennsylvania is across the Delaware River. Pennsylvania shares a water border with southeastern New York State and the entire state of New Jersey.

4   James W. Burbank, *Cushetunk, 1754–1784. The First White Settlement in the Upper Delaware River Valley* (New York: Printed by Sullivan County Democrat), p. 10. For a short but concise history of this region, its first settlers and its politics see pp. 1–23. (Hereafter referred to as *Cushetunk, 1754–1784.*)

5   Some even claimed Connecticut's border stretched to the Pacific Ocean. "From Sea to Sea" was the motto.

6   Although some Loyalists were also found in Connecticut, by and large the support for England and George III there was minimal.

7   James W. Burbank, *Cushetunk, 1754–1784*, p. 26. Ibid. In the National Archives in Washington, DC, the names of many soldiers from Cushetunk who served in the Continental Army are recorded.

8   Ibid., p. 25.

XVIII

The Battle for the
Schoharie Valley

The partisan fighting in Cushetunk was by no means an exception during that year. Farther to the north, across the hills and valleys of the wilderness, other critical events also took place. Combined with the defeat of the Crown's primary thrusts, these events played a vital role in achieving a victory for the Patriots during the Wilderness War of 1777.

To the west and southwest of Albany lies the Schoharie Valley, through which flows the Schoharie River. The river flows in a northerly direction where, in the vicinity of Fort Hunter, it empties into the Mohawk. The very first settlers of what is now Schoharie County arrived from Livingston Manor, farther to the south in the Catskill Mountain region. In 1713, these settlers purchased land from the local Indians and began to establish villages. By 1777, seven of them stood between Central Bridge and Wysertown and toward Fort Defiance (later Middle Fort, and presently known as Middleburg). Initially, the first settlers were German Palatines, followed soon by Dutch and other ethnic groups. As more settlers arrived, other villages appeared such as Harpersfield and Duansborough.

Prior to the eruption of the Revolutionary War, peace had reigned in the Schoharie Valley. But as the war intensified and spread, its inhabitants—largely pro-American—began to make preparations. In late 1776 and early 1777, the "Schoharie Military District"[1] arose. This military district spanned to the west and east of Harpersfield[2] and north to Duansborough (now known as Duansberg), about 37 miles away.[3]

In 1777, war came to the Schoharie Valley, raging in and around its settlements, villages, and towns.[4] Economically, the valley's rich grain and animal livestock would benefit the Crown and deny critical food items to the Patriots. And outside the sizable town of Schoharie, sulfur deposits were discovered. High in grade, these deposits could be utilized in the production of gunpowder.[5]

In military terms, a successful attack into the Schoharie Valley would create a tremendous disruption in the rear of General Schuyler's Northern Army, which was engaging Burgoyne's army advancing southward from Canada toward Albany. It would also unhinge the Patriot defense system at West Point and cut the critical roads and communication lines leading from Albany to the west and south. The Patriots were utilizing these roads for communication and also to move troops, equipment, supplies, and materiel to the various fronts during the Wilderness War of 1777. It would become very difficult—if not impossible—to reinforce and resupply Fort Stanwix if Schoharie County were controlled by a pro-British element. Likewise, to counter any British successes, it would force the Northern Army to shift soldiers and materiel into the Schoharie sector, and in the process the Northern Army would weaken its main effort.

Anticipating danger, four militia companies, the 1st, 2nd, 3rd, and 4th, were organized within the Schoharie Military District. These companies were subordinated to the 15th Regiment[6] and, in turn, this regiment was placed under the Northern Army's high command in Albany.[7] The 1st, 2nd, and 3rd Companies were initially raised in 1775, with the 4th being added in 1777.[8] This 4th Company was raised from the town of Cobbleskill.[9] In the aftermath of the Wilderness War of 1777, a 5th Company was also assembled.[10] A review of the Militia Roster reveals that all five of the companies were in full (if not actually above) strength.[11]

Weapons were largely a personal responsibility. Each militiaman was armed with either a musket or rifle. Those who had muskets were required to obtain a bayonet. A number of the officers carried swords. Ammunition, accoutrements, knives, and other necessities were largely procured by the individual militiaman. At home, he was required to maintain no less than one pound of gunpowder and three pounds of bullets or musket balls.[12] Amongst Schoharie's militiamen, the toma-hawk was a prized weapon.[13]

Colonel Peter Vrooman, a long-time resident and well-established gentleman farmer, was appointed as commanding officer, with Lieu-tenant Colonel Peter U. Ziele serving as his assistant commander. Two majors, Thomas Eckerson, Jr. and Joseph Becker, were included. Lawrence Schoolcraft served as adjutant and Peter Ball was the unit's quartermaster. Ball also held another important job: he supervised the transportation of wheat, meat, and other food products raised in the Schoharie Valley to Albany. Once in Albany, the food supplies went directly to the Continental Army's supply depots.

Most of the inhabitants of Schoharie Valley were sympathetic and supportive of the Patriot rebellion. But, as in other places, there were those who either did not care or who remained loyal to the British Crown. Among those residing in Schoharie who harbored strong loyalties to the King were Captain George Mann, John McDonell,[14] and the three Crysler brothers, led by the oldest brother, Adam.[15] Captain Mann was actually a Patriot militia captain in the Schoharie Valley in charge of a company until 1777.

It is important to emphasize that the events that occurred in Schoharie in the summer of 1777—especially in the month of August—are not fully known. Although much occurred, unfortunately little was ever properly recorded;[16] however, from the bits and pieces of information that are available, a somewhat accurate account may be surmised.

In early 1777, Schoharie County's Loyalist leader McDonell was in Oquaga. There, he was given the mission of creating a fourth thrust toward Albany, approaching from the southwest.[17]

A part of McDonell's force was initially assembled in Fort Niagara. From there, it moved in a southeasterly direction through the wilderness to Oquaga. Once there, additional Loyalists and Indians strengthened the force. After building up his force, McDonell first repositioned it to the Susquehanna River and its valley directly to the east of the present day city of Binghamton. From there, he moved up the Susquehanna Valley, and into the southern part of the Schoharie Valley, where he linked up with Schoharie's Loyalists, who had been told to await his arrival. McDonell's strengthened force was to continue to advance in a northeasterly direction all the way to where presently lies the city of Schenectady on the Mohawk River, where he was to link up with St. Leger's army advancing east. McDonell was to place his entire force under St. Leger's command, and the united units were to converge upon Albany to link up with General Burgoyne.

McDonell's mission, however, was not just to rendezvous with St. Leger. En route to the Mohawk, he was to recruit additional Loyalists, incorporate existing Loyalist units into his force, spread pro-British propaganda, and destroy the farms, food production sites, and settlements known or suspected to be supporting the Patriot cause. McDonell's actions would fit well into the overall British strategy of defeating the rebellious colonists of the northeast in the year 1777.

McDonell commanded a mixed force composed of Loyalists and Indians. Its strength hovered at 300[18] but it was also bolstered with British advisors, officers who dressed as Loyalists to conceal their identities. It is important to note that some of McDonell's "volunteers" were actually recruited through a combination of fear, uncertainty, and intimidation.[19]

Prior to 1777, some efforts had been made to construct a couple of forts within the Schoharie Valley, but nothing had come of this. By the summer of 1777, not one fort formally existed; however, some strong stone and wooden structures had been temporarily converted into forts.[20] Farthest to the south, and on the highest terrain, was the Upper Fort, which lay on the west side of the river and guarded entry into the Valley.[21] In the middle of the valley was established Fort Defiance, the largest and first completed of the three.[22] At the northern point of the valley was established the Lower Fort. Initially constructed as a church in 1773, it was enclosed and built up into a fort in 1777–78. This Lower Fort was also known as the Old Stone Fort because the church was constructed with Schoharie limestone.[23] This Lower or Stone Fort protected a large area to include the settlements of Cobus Kill and Turlo.

In addition to the three temporary positions, Schoharie Valley's residents also established various other defensive measures. For example, a 24-hour vigilance was created; four nightwatch patrols, led by an officer, and each operating from a different center, were put into motion.[24] Along with the watch centers, some houses and strong barns were also converted into mini-fortifications. Defensive measures were also coordinated with the nearby Ulster County Militia commanded by Colonel Harper. It was very fortunate that Schoharie's inhabitants undertook such measures, because it would not be long before they would be embroiled in the events of the Wilderness War of 1777.

It is not known exactly when McDonell and his men entered the Schoharie Valley, but they were definitely in the area by Friday, 8

August. After penetrating into the military district, his force concealed themselves in various predesignated locations. One of the sites selected was the farm of Adam Crysler. In the aftermath of the conflict, Crysler acknowledged that he "was maintaining 25 Indians and 70 [loyalist] men for the British government."[25] In fact, as early as 1 June 1777, Crysler had been notified via a letter from Joseph Brant "to remain in Schoharie in readiness."[26]

The attack into the Schoharie Valley and Albany County in August 1777 was, in fact, a very serious matter. By now, five counties were under British occupation and three other counties suffered from disunion. Tryon County, though not overrun, was requesting immediate help. The militia in Westchester County was fighting its own defense, and in other nearby counties few able-bodied men remained behind to work the crops. Therefore, it was imperative that both the Schoharie Valley and Albany County remained in Patriot hands.[27]

On Saturday, 9 August, Mr. John Barclay, a resident of the Schoharie Valley, dispatched a message to Albany to warn the Northern Army's high command that a mixed force of Loyalists and Indians had penetrated into the Schoharie Military District:

> A Capt. Mann of the Militia of Schoharry [sic] has collected a number of Indians and Tories, declares himself a Friend to King George, and threatens destruction to all who do not lay down their Arms, or take protection from our Enemies. In order to support our Friends in that Quarter a force should be sent to them.[26]

On the very same day that Barclay was dispatching his letter to Albany, Adam Crysler's men attacked Colonel Peter Vrooman's farm. Prior to 1775, Crysler had been a neighbor and close friend of Vrooman.[28] He targeted Vrooman's place to unnerve the colonel, terrorize him into resigning his position, and force him to cease his support of the Patriots. Perhaps, Crysler was hoping that the colonel would just gather up his family and flee from the valley. With Vrooman out of the picture, it would be much easier to secure the valley. By then the Loyalists also knew that Fort Ticonderoga had fallen and that the Northern Army was in retreat. They also began to hear word of General Herkimer's bloody clash with Joseph Brant. With the Patriots repulsed at Fort Ticonderoga and Oriskany, now was the time to exploit these victories to their advantage.

Colonel Vrooman's farm, located to the east of the Middle Fort on a stretch of territory known as Vrooman's Land, was decimated. Vrooman's house and buildings were torched, all his animals slaughtered (excluding eight live head of cattle and twenty killed sheep and hogs that were carted off), and 600 skipples of grain, along with ten loads of hay and much flax and hemp, were burned.[29] The colonel's favorite dog was shot, ripped open with a knife, and thrown into a well next to his burning home.

Unfortunately for the residents of Schoharie Valley, many of its militiamen were absent when McDonell and Crysler struck. A number were still serving with Herkimer, while others were serving within the various Continental and militia units of the Northern Army. Those who had survived the 6 August Battle of Oriskany were only now beginning to return home.

On Sunday, 10 August, the day after torching Colonel Vrooman's estate, McDonell moved his force through the valley adjacent to the Schoharie River and halted to the north of the Village of Breakabeen.[30] Here, he rendezvoused with Crysler, who was accompanied by his Indians and Loyalists. For the people of the Schoharie Valley, especially its German and Dutch inhabitants, Sunday was normally a day of rest, prayer, and peace; but not this Sunday.

After combining their forces, McDonald and Crysler struck. Prior to attacking, the raiders had a good knowledge of who was pro-Patriot or pro-Loyalist. The raiders targeted the homes and farms of those who presently were serving in militia or Continental Army units. Breakabeen, Fultonham, Watsonville, Middleburgh (Middle Fort), and Schoharie were just some of the settlements struck. Wyserstown, a village with an exceptionally strong pro-Patriot sentiment, was burned totally to the ground. Never rebuilt, to this day only its stone ruins exist amid overgrown trees and brush. Wyserstown typified the savagery of the Loyalist raiders. Colonel Vrooman commented: "This valuable settlement lyes in ruin and desolation. Our houses plundered, our cattle destroyd."[31]

Here and there along the way the raiders left a home or farm intact if they knew its owners professed loyalty to the Crown or if, at the last moment, its owners swore allegiance to the British and provided the raiders some food or other items. But this was the exception as the raiders had made a thorough study of the entire Schoharie Valley and they were not going to spare any of the Patriots or their families. One of their first victims was Colonel Vrooman's brother. He died defending his land. And so it went on. From the 10th to the 13th of August, the Schoharie Valley was one huge battleground, and a true nightmare for its residents.

News of the raid into Schoharie quickly reached New York's Patriotic leadership in New Windsor and Albany. From New Windsor on 11 August, Governor George Clinton urged "an expedition against the Schoharie Tories." Clinton also identified "Captain Man [Mann] of the Schoharie Militia a Dangerous Man."[32]

In a letter to the President of the Council of Safety dated 11 August 1777, Mr. John Barclay cited some critical issues facing New York State and added, "The People from Schoharie have informed us, they will be obliged to lay down their Arms."[33] Why Mr. Barclay wrote this is unknown because most of Schoharie's inhabitants had no desire to capitulate. In fact, at the very moment when Barclay was writing his words, Schoharie's inhabitants were not only furiously resisting but were actually turning the tide against McDonell's and Crysler's raiders. Possibly, Barclay wrote such in order to obtain a quick reinforcement for the valley's Patriots.

Homes, farms, mills, along with entire fields of crops, were burned. Cattle, goats, sheep, hogs, poultry, and other farm animals were slaughtered. Even family dogs were not spared. Since the Indians regarded any animal with a bell suspended around its neck as a demon, these animals were especially targeted. Any livestock not secured by the raiders was shot, tomahawked, killed with a spear, or burned alive in barns. Men, women, and children were slaughtered, and more often than not were scalped.

Yet, by no means was the raid into the Schoharie Valley an easy affair for the raiders. Word quickly reached one and all that the valley was under attack. Gunfire, screams and shouts, or the sight of smoke or flames, alerted residents that they were in imminent danger. They then had a choice to make.

Some of Schoharie's inhabitants gathered up their weapons, children, a few animals, and a handful of possessions and fled into the larger, more strongly built stone houses. Reinforced with militiamen, these armed citizens successfully fought off the attackers. Fort Defiance, built around Mr. Johannes Becker's house, was one such site. Barricading the windows and doors and placing sharpshooters on its upper stories and roof, the defenders held off the attackers.

Others, however, refused to leave their farms and offered resistance from their homesteads. Neighbors, either on foot or horseback, rushed from one place to another to assist those in need. Most of Schoharie's citizens were armed, and some were crack shots. Many of the women knew how to handle a gun. Vicious skirmishes were fought around farms and barricaded stone houses. Amid the carnage, Loyalists, Indians, and their attached British advisors began to perish. Any captured pro-British personnel were immediately hanged from the nearest tree or shot on sight, even if they were wounded.

Despite his personal loss and the murder of his brother, Colonel Vrooman remained calm and poised, establishing his headquarters at Fort Defiance. Militia companies, reinforced with armed citizens, fell in. From out of the blue, Captain Jacob Hager suddenly appeared with his entire 2nd Militia Company. Hager and his men were returning home from the Northern Army, where just several days before they had been resisting Burgoyne and had distinguished themselves by transporting some cannons to Fort Edward.[34] After conferring with Colonel Vrooman, the entire company began to pursue and search the countryside for the raiders.[35]

Two men, identified as a Vrooman and a Swart,[36] were dispatched to Albany to seek assistance. Simultaneously, a Mr. John Harper proceeded on horseback to Kingston on the Hudson to seek help from there.[37] En route to Kingston, Harper was pursued by several Indians, but he managed to outrun them.

On 13 August, Colonel Harper, who commanded the Ulster County militia, reported to Fort Defiance, accompanied by John Harper.[38] Reinforcing the colonel was a mounted cavalry company from the Northern Army, commanded by a Captain Degolier and Lieutenant David Wirt.[39] Another unit, an independent French-speaking outfit with mounted soldiers, also appeared.[40] Colonel Harper and Colonel Vrooman conferred, and concluded that the key to victory lay with the destruction of the McDonell–Crysler raiding party, because if the two leaders could be killed or captured and their force shattered, the battle would cease.

By now, McDonell and Crysler were feeling the impact of the resistance bolstered by sizable Patriot reinforcements.[41] Deciding to retreat, Crysler ordered the survivors to his farm, located on a stream a short distance to the southwest of Fort Defiance and to the north of Breakabeen. But when he arrived at his farm, Crysler saw that it no longer stood. While Crysler had been burning other people's homes, Schoharie's Patriots had burned his house and outbuildings. Other than charred and smoldering wood, nothing remained.

An inspection of their force revealed to Crysler and McDonell that it was now significantly reduced. A number had been killed, among whom were Crysler's two brothers. Others were wounded and some, such as Captain Mann, were missing.[42] Lieutenant Christian Stubrach assumed command of the remains of Captain Mann's company.[43]

Realizing that he needed time to rest and reorganize his exhausted and battered force, Crysler proposed to remain at their present location for the time being. McDonell agreed. To protect the survivors, Crysler dispatched 35 Loyalist fighters to Breakabeen to intercept any Patriots approaching from the south. It was, however, to no avail.

Colonel Harper, reinforced with Schoharie's militiamen, the cavalry company, the French soldiers, and armed citizens, moved directly against the remnants of McDonell's and Crysler's force. Although Harper's exact personnel strength is unknown, it was in the hundreds.[44] After crossing the Schoharie River, Harper's force went through Vrooman's Land and entered the Flat Lands, which by 1777 were referred to as the "Flockey, " where Crysler's farm lay in ashes.[45] Encountering the Loyalists and Indians, Harper ordered the militiamen and cavalry to attack.[46]

The Loyalists attempted to hold, firing a quick volley. But they could not stand long against the charging Patriots. With a "terrifying blast of the trumpet, the mounted troops dashed impetuously amongst the Indians and tories."[47] Supported by hundreds of charging militiamen, the Patriots tore the Loyalists apart. Surrounded by cavalry troopers, David Ogeyonda, described as a "notorious offender," was repeatedly struck with swords and killed.[48] Although he had stayed loyal to the British crown, none of his three sons had taken their father's stance. In fact, on that very same day, his sons were fighting against the McDonell–Crysler raiders. Shattered and unable to hold, the surviving raiders fled into nearby woods. With darkness setting in, the Patriots had to abandon their pursuit. According to Watts and Morrison, this short but sharp clash "became known as the 'battle of the Flockey' and is believed to have been the first pitched battle between the U.S. Cavalry and Indians."[49]

In the late evening hours of 13 August, McDonell and Crysler retreated out of the Shoharie Valley and its adjacent lands and fled westward to Fort Niagara.[50] Burgoyne would soon learn of the Loyalist defeat at Schoharie from George Chilsholm, a Loyalist raider who served with John McDonell.[51] The Loyalist defeat at Schoharie helped seal Burgoyne's fate. In its own way, the Patriot victory achieved in Schoharie in mid-August proved to be a significant factor in the collapse of the entire British military effort in 1777.[52]

On Thursday, 28 August, Colonel John Harper wrote to Governor Clinton and the Council of Safety to report on events in the Schoharie Valley. Harper emphasized that "we put Capt. McDonald [McDonell] and army to flight." Colonel Harper added how he and "some volunteers proceeded to Harpersfield, where we met many that had been forced by McDonald, and some of them much abused." Colonel Harper also wrote how many of McDonell's men "were in the woods" [hiding] but "I gave orders to all to make their appearance."[53] Colonel Harper's letter marked the end of the Schoharie Valley's nightmare. But nightmare it had indeed been, as evidenced by the letter from Mr. William Harper and Frederick Fischer written to Governor Clinton, also on 28 August:

> That the late Incursions of the Enemy & their Savages into the said county, & upon a part of the county of Albany have reduced the Inhabitants to the utmost distress. The Harvests not yet gathered in are rotting upon the ground. The Grass uncut. The fallow Grounds not yet ploughed. The Cattle in a great measure destroyed.[54]

But the inhabitants of the valley recovered quickly. Assisting one another, they rebuilt their damaged and destroyed farms, settlements, and villages. In September and October of 1777, a sizable number of its militiamen volunteered to serve in the Northern Army, now successfully engaging Burgoyne's army at Saratoga. That fall, the valley was able to deliver some grain, corn, and dried smoked meat to the Continental Army.[55]

Cushetunk and Schoharie were not exceptions. By mid-August 1777, all of the regions within and around the wilderness were afflicted by vicious raids. Raiding and skirmishing was rampant throughout the Mohawk and Hudson Valleys from New York City and West Point to around Albany and beyond. It even spilled into Vermont, western Connecticut, and Massachusetts.

Notes

1   In 1777, the present-day County of Schoharie did not exist; however, a district named as Schoharie did exist within Albany County, one of sixteen such districts that made up the county. And within Schoharie District a village by the name of Schoharie existed in 1777 (as well as to this day.)

   In 1777, Tryon County bordered on Albany County's western Schoharie District. In the aftermath of the Revolutionary War, the Schoharie District was separated from Albany County and redesigned into a separate county. As well, about one-third of eastern Tryon County was included into the new Schoharie County. Some of the fighting which took place in 1777 within the Schoharie Valley actually took place in eastern Tryon County. (See Edward A. Hagan, *War In Schohary, 1773–1783*, The Middleburgh News Press, 1980, Introduction Section, p. VIII. Hereafter referred to as *War In Schohary.*) In the aftermath of the Revolutionary War, Tryon County was renamed Montgomery County, in honor of Richard Montgomery, the Patriot general who died at Quebec.

2   The village of Harpersfield is located on Route 23. To its west is the city of Oneonta and State Highway 88. East of Harpersfield on the intersection of County Routes 23 and 10 is the village of Stamford, and approximately 5 miles farther to the east lies the Schoharie Reservation.

3   Duanesburg lies on Route 20, immediately to the north of Route 88. Twenty miles to the northeast of Duanesburg lies the city of Albany. Presently, the villages and towns of North Harpersfield, Jefferson, North Blenheim, Breakabeen, Fultonham, Middleburgh, Watsonville, Cobbleskill, Schoharie, Quaker Street, and Duanesburg are located between Harpersfield and Duanesburg. Though most of these towns were not incorporated until well after 1777, a sizable number of inhabitants did reside in this region where these towns now exist.

   Excluding Duanesburg, which lies to the north of Route 88, most of the events that occurred in Schoharie County in 1777 took place on the south side of Route 88.

4   Edward A. Hagan, *War In Schohary*, introduction Section, p. VII.

5   On 26 June 1777, Mr. William Harper, a resident of Harpersfield, submitted a report to the newly forming New York State Government regarding these sulfur sites. Mr. Harper (no relation to Colonel John Harper or Captain Alexander Harper) was a New York State Commissioner tasked to locate

WITH MUSKET AND TOMAHAWK II

lead and sulfur sites and to establish projects for extracting and manufacturing the lead and sulfur. He cited that following ten days of exploring the sulfur sites and mines at Schohary, studies revealed the sulfur to be of a very high grade. See Hagan, *War In Schohary*, p. 81.

6   Hagan, p. 2. Watt and Morrison, "The Schoharie Uprising" in *The British Campaign of 1777*, Vol. I, Chapter 4, p. 200, cite the 15th was an Albany County Militia Regiment.

7   Hagan, p. 65.

8   Ibid.

9   Ibid.

10 Ibid.

11 In 1777, the first four militia companies registered such strengths: 1st Company, commanded by Captain Christian Stubrach registered a strength of 108; 2nd Company, commanded by Captain Jacob Hager, registered a strength of 84 (at this time, Hager and his company were away serving with the Northern Army); 3rd Company, commanded by Captain George Richtmyer, registered a strength of 87; and the 4th Company, commanded by Captain Christian Brown, registered 55.

At this time, a typical infantry or militia line company contained a strength of 50–60 soldiers or militiamen. So all four of the companies were over strength. A review of the names reveals a heavy German and Dutch presence. However, Irish, Scottish, and English names are also listed on the company rosters.

12 Hagan, p. 2.

13 Hagan, p. 2, states that each militiaman "was required to furnish himself with a gun, bayonet, sword, or tomahawk."

14 Simms, *History of Schoharie County,* p. 237. Hagan, Introduction Section, p. VII, cites the name as McDonald.

John McDonell's true family surname was MacDonald, sometimes also spelled as McDonald. "McDonell" was an alias, as was "John Scotus." Because various authors have used the name McDonell, from here forward McDonell will solely be utilized.

McDonell was not a native of the Schoharie Valley. He hailed from Sir William Johnson's Charlotte River Patent. For a list of the names of the other Loyalists participating in the Schoharie attack, see Watt and Morrison "The Schoharie Uprising" in *The British Campaign of 1777*, Vol. I, Chapter IV, pp. 202–204.

Watt and Morrison also cite that John McDonell (Scotus) had emigrated to the colonies in 1773. He was a former lieutenant in the Irish Brigade of the Spanish Army. (Hence his nickname, "Spanish John.") Later, he was employed as a guard officer for Prince Charles Edward's treasury. On 25 July 1777, "Spanish John" met Sir John Johnson in Oswego. Here, Sir John ordered McDonell to return home to prepare an expedition to rendezvous with Adam Crysler in Schoharie. After suppressing the Patriots, Sir John expected McDonell, Crysler, and the Indians and Loyalists to link up with him and St. Leger somewhere in the Mohawk Valley. (See Watt and Morrison, "The Schoharie Uprising" in *The British Campaign of 1777*, p. 200.)

15 Adam Crysler's surname was originally spelled as Creislaer.

16 This fact has also been acknowledged by Hagan. See Introduction, p. ix.

17 Jeptha R. Simms, *History of Schoharie County and Border Wars of New York* (Albany, New York: Musell and Tanner, 1845), p. 237. (Hereafter cited as *History of Schoharie County*.) According to Hagan, Introduction Section, p. VII, "The plan was to dismember the New York Province and split the colonies in two brought the realities of war to the Schoharie Valley in the summer of 1777. The British General William Howe, at New York City, was to move up the Hudson. General Burgoyne, in Canada, was to come down the Champlain Valley and St. Leger's route was from Montreal to Oswego and the Mohawk Valley. McDonald [McDonell] coming from Niagara and up the Susquehanna was to enter the Schoharie Valley, move north recruiting Tories and meet St. Leger at the Mohawk River. All were to converge on Albany."

In a personal discussion with Mr. William Sawyer, curator and historian at Fort Stanwix, he acknowledged that the Loyalist–Indian military force sponsored and organized by the British with the mission to proceed through the Schoharie Valley was established to play an important role in the British campaign of 1777.

18 Simms, *History of Schoharie County*, p. 237. Personal discussion with Mr. Sawyer revealed that at least 300 were to be utilized; however, as also acknowledged by Mr. Sawyer, the raiders were to recruit additional Loyalists within the valley.

19 Simms, p. 237. As for their movement, en route to their destination from Oquaga, the McDonell force moved in and around the present-day towns of East Windsor, Doraville, Sanford, Trout Creek, Masonville, Bennesttsville, Northfield, Sidney Center, East Sidney, Franklin, Treadwell, North Franklin, Oneonta, Meridale, Bloomville, South Kortright, Hobart, East Meredith and the townships of Davenport. The Mountain of Utsayantha, 3,214 feet high, might have also been utilized as a lookout point prior to attacking Harpersfield. These mentioned places lie between the Susquehanna and the West Branch Rivers.

20 Hagan, *War In Schoharie*, p. 2.

21 Hagan, p. 7.

22 It was constructed around Mr. Johannes Becker's two-story stone house. Before it took the name of Middle Fort in August 1778, it was known as Fort Defiance. Centrally located in the Schoharie Valley, in 1777 it became the headquarters of the Military District of Schoharie. (Hagan, p. 7–8.) Presently, the town of Middleburgh is at its location.

23 When the church was built, parishioners hauled limestone blocks from as far away as 15 miles on oxcarts and wagons to the construction site. (Boat-

ner, p. 304.) Hence, the church was also referred to as the "Old Stone" church. In the fall of 1777 and throughout 1778, the church became enclosed by a stockade. Two blockhouses mounting small cannons were also established at this time. The church's steeple, topped by a graceful belfry and spire, was removed and transformed into a square tower. In the event of an attack, sharpshooters would man the tower.

After 1777, the Schoharie Valley was still targeted for raids by Loyalist forces operating out of Canada and Fort Niagara. Therefore, the "Old Stone" or Lower Fort was used (along with the other two forts) for regional defense.

The church still stands and is a historic site. To this day a sign in the church points to a hole in the roof made by a small cannonball in 1780 when the fort was attacked that year by Loyalists. Outside and in front of the church is the grave of Mr. David Williams, one of the three men who came upon and captured the famous British spy Major John Andre at Tarrytown. Inside the church the names of those who helped to construct it in 1772 are preserved, carved into the face stones. The names of those who helped to erect the church, but then sided with the British during the Revolutionary War, were etched out by the Patriots in the aftermath of the war. (Boatner, pp. 304–305.)

For further information on the three forts see Boatner, *Landmarks of the American Revolution*, pp. 304–305; Hagan, *War In Schohary*, pp. 6–8; and Simms, "History of Schoharie County" in *Schoharie County and Border Wars of New York*, Chapter VIII, pp. 237–271.

24　Hagan, p. 2.The 1st Watch operated from the home of Captain George Mann with eight militiamen; the 2nd Watch, commanded by Captain George Rechtmyer with six militiamen, was established in Mr. Hendrick P. Becker's home; the 3rd Watch, also with a strength of six militiamen, was commanded by Lieutenant Martynus Van Slyck from the home of Mr. Johannes Feck; and the 4th Watch, commanded by Captain Jacob Hager with six men, operated out of Mr. Hager's home. (See Hagan, p. 2). Throughout the night, these militia watchmen conducted foot and horse patrols in two- or three-man teams.

25　Hagan, p. 2.

26　Cited from Hagan, p. 2.

26　Ibid.

27　George Bancroft, *The American Revolution*, Vol. III, p. 374.

28　Born 20 June 1735 on the place known as "Vrooman's Land"—which, in time, he would inherit—Peter Vrooman was of Dutch descent. Vrooman began his military career when Royal Governor James DeLancey administered the British Province of New York. In 1754, Vrooman was commissioned a lieutenant and in 1759, a captain. In 1770, he rose to the rank of Major. He also fought with the British during the French and Indian War.

When the Revolutionary War broke out in April 1775 Vrooman, a reserve officer in the British military, immediately favored the Patriot cause. On 20 October 1775, the Provincial Congress of New York commissioned him a colonel of militia. Vrooman also commanded the Schoharie Military District and served as the Secretary of the Committee of Safety. Colonel Vrooman also had the distinction of being a member of the Continental Congress. In 1777, he was elected to be a member of the newly formed Assembly of New York. Re-elected in 1779, he also served in the assembly in 1786 and 1787.

Following the burning of his home, Colonel Vrooman relocated himself and his family to Becker's Stone house, now referred to as Fort Defiance. From here, Vrooman directed Schoharie's defense. After the war, he purchased the Eckerson Mill located on Fox Creek. Erecting a new home near the mill, Colonel Vrooman resided there until his death on 29 December 1793. He was buried in the Old Stone Fort Cemetery. (See also Hagan, p. 61.)

Despite the destruction of his home and the murder of his brother, he and his family refused to flee. Before the end of the war in 1783, he would experience the loss of several family members. John Vrooman (also spelled as Vroman) was killed and Lieutenant Ephraim Vroman, along with Bartholomew Jr., another John Vrooman, and Simon Vroman were captured. Simon died in captivity.

29 Hagan, p. 2.

30 Simms, *History of Schoharie County*, spells Breakabeen as Brakabeen on various pages (e.g., p. 237).

31 Hagan, p. 1.

32 George Clinton, *The Public Papers of George Clinton* (Albany, New York: New York State Publication, 1904),Vol. II, pp. 207–208. (Hereafter cited as *The Public Papers of George Clinton*.)

33 Ibid., p. 210.

34 According to Simms, pp. 237–238, Mr. Henry Hager suddenly appeared at the Becker Stone House to warn the Patriots that on 10 August, McDonald (McDonell) and his party had reached the river above Breakabeen. There, also at the Stone House, he jubilantly met his son, Captain Jacob Hager. It is not known if Mr. Hager's warning was issued on 10 August. It appears that the date of his warning was either 11 or 12 August 1777.

35 Simms, pp. 237–238; Hagan, p. 3.

36 Either Peter or Peter Powlus Swart. It is not certain which Vrooman went with Swart. Colonel Vrooman definitely remained behind to control the battle. Simms, p. 239, acknowledged that a "Vrooman and Swart" were dispatched to Albany for assistance, but does not cite any first names.

37 Some have alleged that John Harper also went to Albany. In future years, Reverend Mr. Fenn, who resided in Harpersfield, cited this as well. (See Hagan, p. 3.) Yet, in a letter written 30 March 1791, John Harper stated that he went to Kingstown (and not Albany) to inform the convention of the situation at Schoharie. (Hagan, p. 3.) Harper, who years after the Rev-

olutionary War would attain the rank of Colonel, also stated that upon his return, with militia and cavalry support, he participated in the fighting and "defeated McDonald and the Indians at Schoharey." (Hagan, p. 3.) Harper also claimed that he dispatched two quick letters on 20 August 1777 from "Schoharey, Fort Defyance [sic]."

38   It is not known if Colonel Harper was related to Mr. John Harper.

39   The strength of this company has been cited between 28 and 200. (See Simms, *History of Schoharie County*, footnote on p. 243.) According to Watt and Morrison, p. 200, Harper was given two units: the 2nd Troop of the 2nd Continental Dragoons commanded by Captain Jean-Louis de Vernejoux with a strength of 41; and the Ulster County Light Horse under Captain Sylvester Salisbury with a strength of 29 (p. 200). A number of "footloose Frenchmen were also hired" (pp. 200–201).

40   Simms was unable to identify the commander's name. But Schoharie's senior citizens informed Simms that the commander was a Frenchman who "spoke imperfect English." (Ibid.)

41   While reinforcements were en route to the Schoharie Valley, Governor George Clinton—who on 11 August had written to a Colonel Pawling on the importance of "destroying Man [Mann] and his party by a sudden Exertion with a Detachment of the Militia under an active officer"—wrote to Pierre Cortlandt, the President of the Council of Safety on 12 August:
      "I dare not however at present Venture to take any of the Continental troops from the Garrison in the Highlands for this [Schoharie] Business." (See *The Public Papers of George Clinton*, Vol. II, p. 214). Clinton emphasized "the Designs of the Enemy under Genl. Howe are yet uncertain, the Garrison [in the Highlands] not over strong, and should any unlucky Accident happen in that Quarter in the Absence of such troops as might be drawn from thence for this Expedition, I should be greatly and perhaps deservedly censured. If Militia are to be employed they can be much easier and more expeditiously had in the neighbourhood of Kingston and Marble Town than by marching them up from the Fort." (Ibid.). Governor Clinton also wrote that, "Major Rawling was charged with my Letter to the Council on this Subject who left my House this Morning for Kingston." (Ibid., pp. 214-214). Clinton added that, "Major Rawling expressed a strong desire to Command the Party to which I consented provided a Party proper for him to Command should be ordered out on this Occasion." (Ibid., p. 215).
      Even as Pierre Cortlandt received Clinton's letter, militia and Continentals from Kingston were en route to assist the defenders of Schoharie. (For the entire letter see Vol. II, pp. 214–215) Clinton was correct that Kingston would be able to assist Schoharie.

42   Some of the missing had been captured, but these few were very lucky as not many prisoners were taken in the fighting in the Schoharie Valley.
      According to Simms, pp. 249–250, Captain Mann, after spending a cold, wet, and miserable night hiding out proceeded to Kneiskern's Dorf,

where he had close friends. He remained there, concealed by them, until the fall. Surrendering to military authorities, he was soon transferred to Albany for trial and imprisonment. Released after the Revolutionary War, Captain Mann returned to the Schoharie Valley. He applied for parole and it was granted. His property was also returned to him. Although he was never bothered, until the end of his life he was always regarded as a traitor within the Schoharie community. Few had any dealings with him, and he lived his life in total seclusion on a small farm.

43　Simms, p. 251.

44　In future years, Crysler described it as a "small army, numbered at 400." See Hagan, pp. 3–5.

45　Early German settler referred to these lands as Die Flache (The Flats). In time, the word "Flockey," a corruption from "Flache," came into existence.

46　In the Wilderness War of 1777, cavalry charges were rare. This one was unique because the cavalry charge at Flockey was the very first one ever undertaken by a U.S. army.

47　So recorded Simms, a survivor of the "Battle of the Flockey." See also Hagan, p. 5.

48　According to Simms, p. 247, Ogeyonda was not "inhumanly hacked to pieces by the cavalry" as alleged by some. Rather, he was killed later when he attempted to escape. But Simm's version was based on someone's verbal account, which, in turn, was inherited from someone else. It appears that Ogeyonda was killed from a series of saber blows during the cavalry charge. This explains why some sources reveal that Ogeyonda was "hacked to pieces."

49　Two cavalry troopers were killed, Lieutenant David Wirt and a private by the name of Rose. Rose succumbed to his wounds several days later on 16 August 1777. It is not known how many of the enemy were killed. See also Hagan, p. 5. Watt and Morrison, p. 201, cite "One [patriot] man was killed and another was mortally wounded."

50　According to Watt and Morrison, "The Schoharie Uprising" in *The British Campaign of 1777*, p. 201, "John McDonell and 44 men traveled to Oswego. There, they joined the shattered King's Royal Regiment, which fell back to Oswego as well following St. Leger's defeat. Within days, they all fell back to Canada." For the entire section on "The Schoharie Uprising" see pp. 198–216.

51　Following McDonell's defeat, George Chisholm did not flee to Oswego. Instead, he worked his way northward to Burgoyne. In Burgoyne's army, he served as a carpenter/artificer. Captured in 1777, he escaped in 1778 and made his way to New York City. There, he joined a "Highlander" Loyalist unit commanded by a Captain Normand Tolmie. Chisholm also became a minor merchant in the city. In 1783, along with many other Loyalists, he departed the city. He ended up in Nova Scotia, Canada, and remained there for the rest of his life.

52 Personal discussion with Mr. William Sawyer. Mr. Sawyer acknowledged that until recent years, few people actually knew what had occurred in Schoharie. Yet, the battle that took place in Schoharie in 1777 played a major role in defeating the British campaign of 1777. Had the enemy been successful in Schoharie, even with St. Leger's defeat, a very serious situation would still have remained. Schoharie, not far from Albany, would have been utilized as a base to cut Patriot communications, harass Patriot forces, and strike Albany proper. A sizable Loyalist–British force within the Schoharie region would have also denied the Patriots a critical food base. And it would have been much more difficult for the Northern Army to operate both in the vicinity of Saratoga and in the Highlands with a British threat hovering on their western flank and almost centered in their midst.

53 For the entire letter of 28 August, see the congratulatory letter of 1 September 1777 in response. (See Simms, pp. 251–253.)

54 *Public Papers of George Clinton*, Volume 2. In the aftermath of the Revolutionary War, Crysler was unable to return to his farm, which had now been confiscated by the Patriots. Settling in Canada, he petitioned the British government for the monetary sum of £13814.4 (nearly 70,000 U.S. dollars) for such loss: a 70 acre farm in Vrooman's Patent, 89 acres in Bouch's Patent, 80 acres on the Charlotte River, one Gist Mill, and one-quarter of a sawmill. (See Swiggett, *War Out of Niagara*, p. 142. See also *The Loyalist Papers* [New York: New York Public Library], Vol. XXX, p. 227). Crysler also emphasized that his two brothers died for the Crown. It is not known, however, if he ever received the payment he sought.

55 One convoy alone, consisting of 17 wagons of flour and foodstuffs, was soon dispatched in the fall to General Gates' Northern Army. (See Hagan, p. 5.)

XIX

Patriot Plans to
Relieve Fort Stanwix

On Wednesday, 13 August, the Patriot scout Frederick Sammons reached Albany and reported to Northern Army headquarters. There he came before General Schuyler and his staff and provided them with the information he had risked life and limb to obtain. Based on the information Sammons provided, Schuyler concluded that St. Leger's effort was part of a major British plan directed against the northeastern colonies.

Schuyler was determined to defend the critical Mohawk Valley and halt St. Leger's thrust. He concluded that if the British in that quarter could be repulsed, it would not only safeguard a portion of New York's population but weaken General Burgoyne's main effort and help to shatter the entire British offensive.

To counter the British thrust, General Schuyler ordered that a Massachusetts Continental Brigade, commanded by Brigadier General Ebenezer Learned, be deployed to Fort Stanwix. Learned's unit was a crack outfit. Schuyler also dispatched orders to various Mohawk Valley militia commanders to assist Ebenezer with men and materiel. Schuyler then asked his assembled commanders for a volunteer to accompany General Learned into the wilderness. The first to speak up was Major General Benedict Arnold, Assistant Commander of the Northern Army.

Though Benedict Arnold was Schuyler's right arm, the general was more than willing to let Arnold accompany Learned and serve as the senior ranking commander on the expedition, because Schuyler knew that if anyone could resolve the situation in the wilderness, it was Arnold. General Arnold was, after all, a highly aggressive combat officer with an exceptional talent for motivating men.

A week later, on Wednesday, 20 August, Arnold rode into Fort Dayton.[1] He was accompanied by General Learned and his 950 Continental soldiers.[2] At the fort, the Continentals were reinforced with about 100 militiamen, who mostly hailed from Tryon County.[3] Among them was Nat Foster, who just a few weeks before with his veteran "Dare-Devils," had been serving with Herkimer. En route to Saratoga to join the Northern Army, they encountered one of General Arnold's leading detachments and immediately attached themselves to this Patriot force. Within days, they would be traversing the same ground that they had fought over on August 6 with such bloody results.

Further militiamen continued to arrive, and Arnold's force grew in strength by the hour. Some of the militiamen were responding to an appeal issued by the Governor of New York State, George Clinton. Clinton had written the memo from his headquarters in Half Moon to his commanding officers in Tryon and the neighboring counties. In it the governor praised the actions of General Herkimer and the men of his militia, and asked his commanders to:

> . . . join the army under general Arnold, and thereby enabling him to finish the war in that quarter by raising the siege at Fort Stanwix and destroying the enemy's army in that quarter, and restoring peace and safety to the inhabitants of Tryon County.[4]
>
> Governor Clinton made it clear that the volunteers would only serve for a brief period of time and "as soon as the service will admit [end], General Arnold will dismiss you."[5]

Governor Clinton was not the only one dispatching messages. General Arnold issued a decree on 20 August from Fort Dayton:

> By the Hon. Benedict Arnold, Esq. Major-general and Commander-in-Chief of the army of the United States of America on the Mohawk River.
>
> Whereas a certain Barry St. Leger, a Brigadier-general in the service of George of Great Britain, at the head of a banditti of robbers, murderers, and traitors, composed of savages of America, and more savage Britons, (among whom is the noted Sir John Johnson, John Butler, and Daniel Claus), have threatened

ruin and destruction to all the inhabitants of the United States. They have also, by artifice and misrepresentation, induced many of the ignorant and unwary subjects of these States to forfeit their allegiance to the same, and join with them in their atrocious crimes, and parties of treachery and parricide.

Humanity to these poor deluded wretches, who are hastening blindfold to destruction, induces me to offer them, and all others concerned, (whether Savages, Germans, Americans, or Britons) PARDON, provided they do, within ten days from the date hereof, come in and lay down their arms, sue for protection, and swear allegiance to the United States of America.

But if, still blind to their interest and safety, they obstinately persist in their wicked courses, determined to draw on themselves the just vengeance of heaven and of this exasperated country, they must expect no mercy from either.

       B. Arnold. M.G.

       Given under my hand, Headquarters, German Flatts,
       20th August, 1777.[6]

As General Arnold was issuing his decree and more Continental and militia troops were arriving at Fort Dayton, Molly Brant was sending another warrior through the wilderness to warn her brother of Arnold's sizable, and growing, force.

On 20 August, a court-martial was held for Butler's Loyalists who had been arrested at Shoemaker's Tavern. General Arnold was one of the presiding judges and president of the court-martial board. Lieutenant Colonel Willett was one of the presiding officers. Ten of the soldiers and three of the Mohawk warriors were sentenced to "an indefinite term of imprisonment."[7] They would be transported to a jail in Albany.[8] Walter Butler, Shoemaker, and eleven other Loyalists[9] were to be transported to Albany, but these thirteen were destined to be executed by firing squad.[10] One of the thirteen sentenced to be executed in Albany was Hon Yost.[11] General Arnold himself pronounced the court's ruling upon the sentenced.

Major General Benedict Arnold was a no-nonsense leader, always straight to the point. Born 14 January 1741, in New Haven, Connecticut, Arnold had lived quite an exciting life prior to the American Revolution.

In the latter years of the French and Indian War, he had soldiered in the British Army. An educated man, he traveled widely. He once operated a pharmaceutical shop, was a book dealer, traveled to England for business, and was a livestock and timber businessmen. He did, however, falter in business on several occasions. At the age of 25, he married Margaret Mansfield. He dueled honorably but never killed anyone. And he lived under the Latin motto *Sibi Totijue*—For Himself and For All. But his positive attibutes were tempered by other, less charming character traits: opposing his sister's marriage, he almost killed the man who had courted her; he deserted the British Army; it was rumored that Arnold was behind the theft of a sizable amount of British currency; and he was also wanted by British authorities for smuggling stolen contraband. It seemed that Arnold's biggest vice was greed; he was always in need of a large sum of money. In fact, the more he had, the more he needed. In the end, his greed would bring him down.

With the eruption of the American Revolution, Arnold was one of the first to side with the Patriots. In 1775 and 1776, he served with much bravery and distinction. He began by helping Ethan Allen to capture Fort Ticonderoga. (Here, also, was an immense British army pay chest that, after the fall of Fort Ticonderoga, disappeared.) He then led a column to invade Canada, making a torturous march through the wilderness. During the cold winter months in Canada, Arnold never faltered. He was so determined to capture the city of Quebec that, despite a serious wound, he continued to press the attack. Though brave, his efforts were still fruitless.

After retreating to Crown Point in early 1776, Arnold created a makeshift navy and fought the British on Lake Champlain. Though he was again defeated, the fierce Patriot resistance at the Battle of Valcour Island forced the British to withdraw to Canada. For the moment, New England was saved and a critical water route was denied to the British.

In April 1777, Arnold played an instrumental role in repulsing a British attack into Connecticut, his birth state. That same year, he again volunteered to serve in the Northern Army, in a theater of operations well known to him. Second-in-command to General Schuyler, Arnold demonstrated competency and loyalty to his superior and subordinates. Just as before, he again proved to be an aggressive commander. He was also one of America's youngest generals, at just 36 years of age.

Learning that her son was to be transported to Albany to be

executed, Hon Yost's mother appeared at Fort Dayton late on 20 August, accompanied by her younger boy, Nicholas. She appealed directly to General Arnold, begging that her son not be sent to Albany to be executed.

Hon Yost was afflicted with mental health problems; some regarded him as a lunatic.[12] Residing in Little Falls, on the edge of the wilderness, Hon Yost had had frequent contact with the Indians, among whom mental defects were regarded as something highly exotic and out of the ordinary;[13] therefore, Hon Yost was held in high esteem by them. Some Indians even believed that he possessed some kind of supernatural powers.

Hon Yost's mother pleaded that her son's intellect was such that he was unable to judge right from wrong. As for his pro-British sentiment, the woman claimed he had been simply steered into that direction by some Loyalists without understanding what he was doing.

Fortunately for Hon Yost, Lieutenant Colonel John Brooks happened to be present as his mother pleaded his cause. Brooks proposed to General Arnold that Hon Yost be utilized to the Patriots' advantage. Knowing that his simple-mindedness prompted superstitious sentiment among the Indians, Brooks suggested that the young man be released to spread a wave of terror amongst St. Leger's warriors. If successful, his actions would also unnerve the Loyalists, and even the regulars serving within St. Leger's force. After conferring with Brooks, General Arnold discussed the matter with Lieutenant Colonel Willett and several other officers. Arnold also sought the advice of several Oneidas, such as Chief Honyery. All agreed that Hon Yost should be utilized.

Arnold met with Hon Yost, and informed the lad what his mission was to be. He was to infiltrate the British camp and approach the Indians. Once there, he was to inform them of a huge Patriot force on the way. He would also tell them a tale of horror and brutality and urge the warriors to escape, to avoid the death that would otherwise be their reward. To support his tales, Hon Yost's oversized coat was taken off and "shot." Also, a couple of friendly Oneida Indian warriors would accompany him almost to the Indian camps. Hon Yost would go on ahead, but then shortly after, the Oneidas would appear to support, and elaborate on, his story.

Hon Yost was to go immediately. If everything went as planned, he would be in the Indian camp on the following day, sometime in the late evening hours. The dark night in itself would provide extra sensation-alism. If Hon Yost succeeded, his life would be spared. By simply being in the right place at the right time, in his own way, Hon Yost could dra-matically alter a major event for the Patriots in the western theater of the Wilderness War. Whether the Patriots realized it or not, this was psychological warfare at its best.

With his mother standing beside him, urging him to comply, Hon Yost agreed to the plan. But as he prepared to leave, General Arnold suddenly grabbed his brother, Nicholas, declaring that he would hold the younger boy hostage. If Hon Yost failed, or betrayed the plan to the British, the fifteen-year-old would be shot. So powerful were Arnold's threats that Hon Yost's mother began to weep in terror. Arnold warned the mother to remain silent about the matter and sent her home. Nicholas was placed in a prison cell under guard.

It had been a long day for Arnold; he had not rested since his arrival at Fort Dayton, but he had much more to do. Having laid the ground-work for his advance on Fort Stanwix, the Patriot general began to formulate his next course of action.

Notes

1 Ward, Vol. II, p. 470.
2 Ibid.
3 Ward, Vol. II, p. 490. Eckert, cites "just over a hundred militiamen." Alden, p. 321, cites that General Arnold's 950 volunteers were "soon joined by 100 militia." All sources reveal that these militiamen joined General Arnold's force at Fort Dayton.
4 For the entire short but very moving text with an appeal to continue the resistance, see Eckert, pp. 149–150.
5 Ibid., p. 150.
6 Stone, *Siege and Battle,* Appendix No. VIII, p. xxxviii.
7 Eckert, p. 151.
8 Ibid.
9 Ibid.
10 Ibid.
11 Ibid. Stone, *Siege and Battle,* p. 258; Ward, Vol. II, p. 490; and personal dis-cussion with Reverend George Reed.
12 Stone, *Siege and Battle,* p. 258, describes him as such: "Hon-Yost Schuyler was one of the coarsest and most ignorant men in the [Mohawk] Valley, appearing scarce half removed from idiocy; and yet there was no small share of shrewdness in his character."
13 Ibid., p. 258.

XX

The British Abandon the Siege

Miles away from Arnold, surrounded by the sounds of the siege of Fort Stanwix—screams of orders, the occasional war whoop, the blast of a cannon, and the staccato of rifle and musket shots—General St. Leger was also thinking.

Like Arnold, St. Leger was tired. He was also angry with Joseph Brant. On more than one occasion, St. Leger had directed Brant and the others not to reveal to anyone the contents of any message brought in by a courier until he had seen it. Yet, once again, Brant had violated St. Leger's order. When the messenger dispatched by his sister Molly reported, Brant had spoken to him first instead of taking him directly to St. Leger. Overheard by Loyalists and warriors close by, the contents of the conversation quickly made the rounds of the camp: General Arnold was en route with a large force.

St. Leger also knew that this information, and the rumors and exaggerations that would inevitably follow, could prove to be very detrimental, especially as over the last few days, more desertions had been noted. In singles, twos, and threes, the Indians were leaving. Even several Loyalists had fled. St. Leger could sense an air of defeat setting in.

Despite his losses and the warnings about another sizable Patriot force approaching, St. Leger was still determined to take the fort. North of it where one of the first batteries had been erected, a second trench had also been started. Initially, it was dug straight toward the fort, but once within the range of Fort Stanwix's guns, the trench zigzagged to protect those inside from any small arms and cannon fire directed against them. The excavated soil and rocks were piled on the side of the trench closest to the fort, and in addition to this, large logs were placed on the trench edge. From behind these logs, St. Leger's sharpshooters fired on the defenders.

The trenching operation was a 24-hour affair. Despite the best efforts of the fort's defenders, it was anticipated that in several more days, the head of the trench would be close enough to lob mortar rounds into the fort. Alternatively the besiegers could continue to dig, taking the trench right up to the wall. This would be no easy task. But if supported with heavy fire directed against the fort to keep the defenders pinned down, the diggers could burrow right up to the wall, enabling explosives to be placed against its base and detonated. Once a sizable hole was created, St. Leger's regulars, Loyalists, and Indians could rush in through this opening to capture the fort.

The defenders aimed to interdict the trenching operation with small arms wielded by sharpshooters and cannon fire. With cannonballs and grapeshot exploding all around, and sharpshooters taking effective shots, such efforts could slow a work project. Grapeshot was particularly lethal against compacted groups of soldiers digging in the trenches.[1] What further complicated matters for the defenders was that two such trenches were now being dug.[2]

One of the defenders of Fort Stanwix was a private by the name of Colbrath, who in his diary described the action around the construction of the trench. Colbrath wrote:

> The enemy threw shells at us near noon. They were busy at their trench all day. At night they struck their trench towards the point of our northwest bastion and by day light he got within 150 yards of the ditch. We fired some grapeshot at them now and then all night. At every shot we fired they threw shells at us but did no damage.[3]

Colbrath noted in his diary on the following day:

> The enemy could work but little on their trench, it being so nigh that our small arms, as well as our cannon shot, was too hot for them. In the evening they began their trench again and worked all night on it, under fire of our cannon and small arms but did not approach any nearer.[4]

In an effort to take the fort, St. Leger's troops even stopped the flow of a stream that ran into it. To counter this, Colonel Gansevoort ordered that two wells be dug. By the time the siege was lifted, one of the digging crews had struck water.

In addition to the constant small arms and cannon fire directed against the defenders, small groups of Indians lay in wait, especially at night, hoping to catch anyone attempting to sneak into or out of the fort.

By now, the continuous heavy pressure against Fort Stanwix was taking its toll. The battle damage was becoming more and more visible, and incoming shells continued to kill or wound defenders.

St. Leger, however, did not just bombard the fort with guns and arrows. For several days prior to 21 August, a massive campaign of false propaganda was constantly being directed against the fort, with messages such as: "Burgoyne is in Albany. . ."; "General Herkimer is Dead. His force was wiped out. . ."; "The Mohawk Valley is in our hands. . ."; "You are alone and no help is on the way. . ."; "Surrender. And spare your lives. . ."

Though the bulk of the defenders of Fort Stanwix remained strong, a handful did succumb to the propaganda. Unsure of the situation and fearing defeat and death, within the 24-hour period of 21–22 August, a total of five soldiers, a corporal, and four privates deserted.[5] Though seemingly unimportant, desertion is a very serious matter, for if a deserter falls into enemy hands, a tremendous amount of valuable information may be obtained from him. Even the lowest-ranking deserter can harbor a wealth of information. To counter the enemy propaganda Colonel Gansevoort repeatedly assured his soldiers that help was on the way. Willett's raid was also cited to raise morale, as such measures kept desertion to a minimum.

Braving the enemy bombardment, and the concealed warriors lying in wait, a detachment of soldiers left the safety of the fort in the early hours of Friday 22 August to gather wood. Gathering up as much as possible, they raced back to the safety of the fort without suffering any casualties.

Throughout the day, St. Leger's army continued to bombard the fort, and work continued on the two trenches. Sometime in the day, Colbrath recorded in his diary, "Our guard kept a constant fire at those working in the trench. In the evening 12 of our best marksman were picked out to harass them at work in the night. . ."[6] During the day, two soldiers previously injured succumbed to their wounds and Sergeant Major Robert Welding, Fort Stanwix's highest ranking enlisted soldier, was wounded.[7]

That evening, inside his headquarters, Colonel Gansevoort was contemplating the situation; he knew that the fort could not hold out forever. Gansevoort was also upset by the desertions. Though he was positive that the intent of the five deserters had been simply to flee rather than to join the enemy, he could never be certain. He was heartened that nothing had been heard about them from the enemy, and he hoped that none of the five had been caught. Yet, he knew that if not controlled, the desertion rate could increase or possibly even lead to a mutiny. So far, however, Gansevoort did not think either likely. No suicides had been reported and morale seemed to be good. But he knew that from now on, he had to be careful.

That evening, Barry St. Leger was alone in his tent, writing a letter to General Burgoyne when he was interrupted by a commotion outside. Folding up the letter and putting it in his uniform pocket, he stepped outside and came face to face with John Johnson, Colonel Butler, Daniel Claus, Joseph Brant, and some Indian chiefs. Standing among them was a foolish-looking young man. Hon Yost had reached the British camp.

Following his release by Arnold, Hon Yost had headed northwestward toward Fort Stanwix. Not far behind him followed the two Oneida warriors. In the event he decided to change his mind or attempt to flee, the warriors had been given orders to kill him.

En route to St. Leger's camp, Hon Yost came across a couple of Brant's Indians. The conversation was not recorded, but he seems to have convinced them of the approaching danger. When the two Oneidas approached, they not only verified Hon Yost's story but for extra sensationalism added that Burgoyne's army had been cut to pieces. Moving on with Hon Yost, they noted the two warriors turning around and fleeing rapidly westward. Soon, these two would be in St. Leger's camp.

Appearing alone at the camp in the late evening hours, Hon Yost began to speak. As his words came out he appeared to be trembling with fear. Opening his coat, he showed the assembled Indian crowd the bullet holes. He told them that Walter Butler and his men had been captured and sentenced, some to death. He told them Burgoyne had been defeated and was in full retreat, and he told them Benedict Arnold was only hours behind him, marching on Fort Stanwix with a huge force. When asked how many men Arnold had, Hon Yost pointed to a nearby tree, proclaiming that there were more soldiers than the tree had leaves. Turning, he began to shuffle away, explaining he must leave to save himself. As quickly as he appeared, he disappeared into the darkness. Within minutes of his departure the two Oneidas appeared and further exacerbated the fear.

The Indians believed him. Unhappy with their role in St. Leger's army, angry that the defenders of Fort Stanwix had not yet succumbed, disgusted with their heavy losses, and informed that a massive force was now coming their way, the Indians, individually, in pairs, and in small groups, began to flee.

St. Leger attempted to hold the remainder but to no avail. Sir Johnson, Brant, Claus, and Butler did not care to support St. Leger in his attempts. Desperate to hold his warriors, St. Leger ordered that the rum barrels be opened, reasoning that after drinking and sleeping it off, he would be able to deal with them.

St. Leger's gambit, however, turned the situation even more ugly. With alcohol flowing in their veins, the intoxicated Indians began to vent their anger. They began to assault the Loyalists, British, and Germans. Knives and tomahawks intended for us against the Patriots were now instead raised against their allies. The slain were immediately robbed, and some were even scalped.

Calling Brant to his side, St. Leger demanded that he put an immediate end to the killing. Brant was unable to do so, and the two commanders, both furious and upset by events, began to argue. In warfare, commanders must always maintain strong command and control. If not, collapse will only ensue. In St. Leger's case the authority upon which he relied was fast slipping away.

Hon Yost and the two Oneidas were continuing to spread alarm and panic in the camp.[8] At least 200 of the Indians had already fled, and others were leaving by the minute. The Canadians were also packing up. Realizing that he would not be able to stop his warriors from fleeing, St. Leger agreed to an organized retreat. He began to issue orders. All of the heavy weapons, artillery, baggage, and equipment were to be taken along.

As the siege began to be dismantled, intoxicated Indians began to loot. They tore into the supplies along with the deserting Canadians. Even some of the Loyalists joined in. Ammunition, blankets, food, liquor, and various other items were stolen. After the pillage ceased, chests and gunpowder barrels were torched. When a British supply officer attempted to stop them, he was killed by a tomahawk-wielding warrior.

Terrified that his pay chest would be broken into, St. Leger placed around it a guard of soldiers from his trustworthy 34th Foot Regiment, armed with fixed bayonets. Orders were issued that anyone attempting to break into it was to be shot on sight. After retrieving some personal items from his tent, St. Leger headed for Wood Creek with a small entourage, including the pay chest and its guards. From there, they would board bateaux to head back to Oswego via Wood Creek, Oneida Lake, and the river system.

Shortly after midnight on Saturday, 23 August, Colonel Gansevoort and his men were standing on the ramparts of the fort, puzzled as to what was happening in St. Leger's camp. They knew it was something very big, but they could not figure it out. A little earlier the small arms and cannon fire directed against the fort had suddenly ceased. Then came much shooting and shouting from the woods. Some men were spotted running in various directions, and sporadically they could see flames rising from a torched tent or wagon. As the flames and sparks flickered upward, the eerie sights only magnified the uncontrollable chaos within the camps, which by now had devolved into a raging madness.

As St. Leger hurried toward Wood Creek, he cursed those who had ever formulated this plan, but especially those who got him personally involved. St. Leger knew the severe consequences of his failure. To begin with, his career was ruined; never would he formally make general. He would face investigations, criticism, and possible charges. He might even be dismissed from the army altogether. Turning around, he saw the fort he was unable to take. Lit up by the moonlight, the walls stood with continued defiance in the distance.

By daybreak, the defenders of Fort Stanwix were fully aware that something out of the ordinary had occurred. The only movement outside the fort was the occasional wisp of smoke rising from a smoldering wagon or tent. An eerie silence hovered across the landscape.

By now, the terrain around Fort Stanwix resembled a shattered lunar surface. No grass or flowers remained in the open ground that ringed the fort, and it was edged by piled dirt, and shattered tree stumps. The two trenches zig-zagging towards the fort further ripped the terrain apart. Guns, bows and arrows, spears, tomahawks, pieces of clothing, along with other equipment, lay scattered around the fort. Here and there amongst the debris lay a decomposing body.

Standing on the ramparts among his troops, Colonel Gansevoort scanned the grounds. It seemed that the siege was over, but he was still wary in case it was a trick. After consulting with his staff operations officer, Colonel Gansevoort decided to heed his advice to dispatch a handful of scouts into the outer area.

Notes

1   A cannonball was one solid projectile composed of metal. It could, upon impact, break into smaller pieces known as shrapnel. Flying with tremendous force and speed, shrapnel can kill or seriously wound anyone on impact. Cannon balls came in various sizes, shapes, designs, and weights.

     Grapeshot balls were stored in a canister. As with cannonballs, they came in different sizes, shapes, designs, and weights. The difference, however, was that when fired, the canister would tear apart in flight and a number of small balls were discharged. In effect, it was as if a giant shotgun was fired. These balls would kill or wound anyone struck. Grapeshot balls did not fly as far as a cannon ball or shell. But at close to medium ranges, grapeshot was much more lethal, especially against compact groups of soldiers.

2   *"St. Leger's Attack,"* p. 10.

3   Ibid.

4   Ibid.

5   Ibid.

6   Ibid.

7   Welding's last name has also been spelled as Weldon. On 11 December 1779, he passed away. He was still in the service and with the rank of Sergeant Major. It is not known if he was replaced when wounded. If so, possibly Quartermaster Sergeant Francis Jackson, who served on the 3rd New York Continental Regiment's Regimental Staff, assumed Sergeant Major Welding's position.

8   In Chapter Thirty, "How A Simpleton Raised the Siege," in Elizabeth Eggleston Seelye, *Hudson, Mohawk, Schoharie. History From America's Most Famous Valleys and the Border Wars* (New York: Dodd, Mead and Company Publishers, 1879) largely credits Hon Yost for spreading fear and uncertainty amongst the Indians besieging Fort Stanwix. (Hereafter cited as *Border Wars.*) Alden, *A History of the American Revolution,* p. 321, credits

in addition to Hon Yost an Oneida warrior who not only accompanied him, but likewise helped to terrorize St. Leger's Indians. And *Excelsior Studies in American History* (New York: William H. Sadlier, 1921), p. 193, cites "A half witted tory boy prisoner [Hon Yost] was promised his freedom if he would spread the report that a large body of Americans was at hand. The boy ran breathless into the camp of the besiegers, describing his narrow escape from the enemy. Asked their number, he mysteriously pointed upward to the leaves on the trees. The Indians and British were so frightened that they fled leaving their tents and artillery behind them. Thus was Burgoyne deprived of the help expected from this expedition."

XXI

The End of St. Leger's Army

General Benedict Arnold set forth from Fort Dayton early on the afternoon of 23 August. Fully conscious of the dangers of an ambush, he positioned his forward scouts miles ahead. These leading scouts were actually put out almost two full days before the main force, in the late evening hours of 21 August. Other men were operating between the advance scouts and Arnold's main force. Flankers, along with a strong rearguard, protected his flanks and rear.

About ten miles to the west of Fort Dayton, General Arnold learned that his ruse had worked. St. Leger's army, or what remained of it, was in full retreat. As Arnold's scouts probed forward, they encountered an Indian warrior fleeing eastward. Hearing from him a story that seemed to be unbelievable, the scouts immediately passed the warrior directly on to the general. Needless to say, Arnold was delighted with this news. Still, he continued to maintain his strong security vigilance all the way up to Fort Stanwix.

Unlike General Arnold's force, marching in unison and in proper military fashion, St. Leger's force was fleeing as an unorganized mob through the wet and thickly vegetated wilderness. Amid the fleeing mass remained Hon Yost working to maintain the feeling of panic and pressure with cries of "The Americans are coming!"[1] Hon Yost followed the fleeing army up to Wood Creek. Along with the two Oneidas who remained in the rear screaming like demons and firing their muskets for extra effect, and occasionally sniping on those fleeing, Hon Yost continued to spread fear and panic. Near where Wood Creek flows into Lake Oneida, he finally called it quits and disappeared into the woods. He had more than performed his task.

Stumbling frantically through the brush, the Indians, Loyalists, and regulars began to discard their equipment and rucksacks to aid their flight. Some even threw aside their weapons. All of the cannons and wagons were left behind. Likewise, the horses that pulled them were released. No effort was made to destroy the remaining ammunition or gunpowder barrels. The looting, however, did not cease. In fact, it only intensified.

Those attempting to retire back to Oswego, and eventually Canada, faced a brutal ordeal. Night and day, mosquitoes and black flies swarmed and hunger was a constant companion. Cold evening rains soaked the ragged remains of what had once been a proud army. Wild animals roved in packs as the men trudged back to the safety of Lake Ontario, and at night the howls of wolves and coyotes reminded the survivors that they were now being hunted. There also existed the two-legged threat, for until St. Leger reached Oswego, the British, Germans, and Loyalists were being stalked in the forests and killed. Stragglers, whether wounded or just exhausted, were robbed, beaten, and shot. Cries of mercy fell on deaf ears as blood-stained tomahawks were raised to shatter lives.[2] The bodies of those robbed and killed were never buried, instead being left to the wolves, bears, coyotes, ravens, and crows.

Divided along tribal lines, the Indians began to disappear. Angry and mourning their losses, and disgusted with failed promises, St. Leger's "Indian allies departed in anger to their homes to mourn over their many slaughtered brethren. . . having vented their wrath by plundering the boats and murdering the straggling soldiers of King George."[3] By the time St. Leger reached Oswego, he was accompanied by solely British and German survivors. Few Indians were with him.

With many of his Rangers dead, missing, or captured, Colonel John Butler had separated himself from St. Leger. Even his own son was missing. Disappearing into the wilderness with his survivors, Colonel Butler headed for Fort Niagara. Sir John Johnson's Royal Greens regiment had taken such heavy casualties it barely existed. Tumbling through thickets, St. Leger suddenly encountered Johnson. After a furious exchange of words, both men drew their swords. For several moments both men stood poised with blades directed against one another.[4] However, after a final exchange of curses, they just parted.

Reaching Wood Creek, St. Leger's surviving soldiers rowed out in their boats. The Indians who had not yet fled on foot piled into their canoes and boats, but first they "plundered several of the boats and robbed the officers of whatsoever they liked."[5]

Within several hours of the Patriot scouts being dispatched from Fort Stanwix, two returned to provide Gansevoort an initial report. They said that the enemy left "awful fast." The scouts stated that no enemy personnel were around and most of the baggage, cannons, mortars, wagons, and heavy equipment had been left behind. As for those who had been killed, none had been buried. The scouts also reported that chests were torn open and thoroughly ransacked. Some of the contents of the chests lay scattered. A number of weapons were also found.

What really puzzled Colonel Gansevoort were the reports that amid the debris lay dead British and German troops, some Loyalists, and even a few Indian warriors. All had been tomahawked, knifed, bayoneted, or shot at point-blank range. It was obvious that a sizable and violent struggle had been waged within the besieging force. Indeed, the scouts' report left many bewildered. Assembling his troops, Gansevoort announced to them that the enemy had been repulsed and he thanked his garrison for their efforts. The Patriot commander also stated that for the time being, the garrison would stay in place. Loud cheers rose in unison at the conclusion of his speech.

From 2 August until 22 August 1777,[6] Fort Stanwix had stood firm and defiant. For 21 continuous days, its brave defenders had held their own.

Colonel Gansevoort, however, did not remain idle. On 23 August, he dispatched messengers to General Arnold and the Northern Army headquarters to inform Arnold and Schuyler on what had transpired.[7] Seeking more information on the state of the retreating enemy, Gansevoort dispatched scouts and patrols to pursue St. Leger. Throughout 23 August and well into the following days, Gansevoort's scouts and patrols roamed deep into the wilderness in pursuit.

Upon receiving a report that 17 intoxicated Indians were in the vicinity of Wood Creek where it flows into Lake Oneida, and that some British personnel were also in that vicinity, Colonel Gansevoort dispatched a sizable party commanded by Major Cochran to intercept any personnel attempting to flee. According to Colbrath's journal "[Major Cochran] returned with prisoners and four cohorns and some baggage. He also reported there were 17 bateaux [boats] lying there."[8]

Major Cochran's force was not the only one patrolling outside the fort. Another party, dispatched to the enemy's north camp, brought back ammunition, camp equipment, and entrenching tools.[9] But the biggest haul was found to the southwest of the fort. The party dispatched to that site returned with 15 wagons and a 3-pound field cannon with all of its apparatus.[10] Although most of the wagon wheels had been cut to pieces, it would not take much to repair them. A long-range patrol dispatched northwestward to Canada Creek found a carriage for a 6-pound cannon and 3 boxes of ammunition. All of these items were brought back to the fort.[11]

One three-man scout team returned with a German prisoner. Interrogated by Von Benscheten, the man revealed that about ten miles from the fort, probably in the vicinity of Wood Creek and Lake Oneida, the Indians fell on the "scattering tories, took their arms from them, and stabbed them with their own bayonets."[13] Fearing the Indians, he and nine other Germans "took to the woods."[14] There, they became scattered and lost contact with one another. Fearing for his life, the German prisoner also revealed how it was rumored that the Americans would not be taking any prisoners and "when orders were given to retreat, those [from St. Leger's army] who fell into our [Patriot] hands would be hanged immediately."[15] Clearly, Hon Yost and the Oneida Indians had done a superb job in terrorizing St. Leger's personnel.

As Colonel Gansevoort's scouts and patrols were searching the countryside and bringing in prisoners and discarded military materiel, General Arnold was rapidly marching to Fort Stanwix. En route, he conferred with the messengers dispatched earlier in the day by Gansevoort. Now, it was official. In turn, General Arnold dispatched a quick letter to the Northern Army which, as of 19 August, was commanded by General Horatio Gates. Arnold wrote:

> . . . This morning I marched from G. Flatts for this place. I met an express from Col. Gansevoort acquainting me the enemy had yesterday retired from Fort Schuyler [Stanwix] with great precipitation. I am at a loss to judge their real intentions, whether they have returned home, or retired with a view of engaging us on the road. I am inclined to think the former from the account of the deserters and from their leaving their tents and considerable baggage which our people have procured.

I shall immediately detach about nine hundred men and make a forced march to the fort in hopes of coming up with their rear and securing their cannon and heavy baggage.

My artillery, tents, etc., etc., I shall leave here, the bateaux with provisions follow me. As soon as the security of the post will permit, I will return with as many men as can be spared.[16]

On Sunday, 24 August, as General Arnold approached Fort Stanwix, and the fort's scouts and patrols were bringing in prisoners and discarded materiel, a baby girl was born in the fort. Delivered with the assistance of Doctor Woodruff, the new baby instilled some hope in those defending Fort Stanwix on the very day that the 46 gallant heroes who had perished defending the fort were finally laid to rest, with a musket salute fired by a delegation of their fellow soldiers.[17]

Hungry, tired, and with no place to go, Hon Yost arrived back at Fort Stanwix weaving a tale of intrigue revolving around a special mission he had undertaken for General Arnold to create the panic that had led to St. Leger's flight. He even claimed that he had spoken with St. Leger. Colonel Gansevoort did not know what to make of him and his story, so the youth was put in a prison cell and provided with a hot bath, fresh clothes, and food and drink.

In the early evening of 24 August, General Arnold arrived at Fort Stanwix.[18] He immediately dispatched a sizable party westward in an attempt to capture any remaining personnel from St. Leger's force. Moving swiftly through the wilderness, the pursuers halted upon reaching the mouth of Wood Creek where it empties into Lake Oneida. From the shoreline they spotted what appeared to be a few boats far out in the lake heading westward. This was the tail end of St. Leger's once-formidable army.

General Arnold did not intend to stay at Fort Stanwix long, as he knew that he had to return as soon as possible to the main Northern Army. He did, however, verify who Hon Yost was, what his mission had been, and the role of the Oneida Indians accompanying him.[19] Arnold also rested his troops and gathered as much information as he could for the Northern Army's high command.

Late in the afternoon of Monday, 25 August, St. Leger arrived at Oswego Falls. On the way, he passed the ruins of the old Fort Brewerton, journeyed through the site of the Three Rivers, and rowed up the

Oswego River. Here at the falls, a Loyalist messenger from General Burgoyne caught up with him. Burgoyne wanted St. Leger to launch an attack into the Mohawk Valley as soon as possible. Near where the waters of the Oswego River tumble downward, St. Leger stayed overnight. The defeated commander instructed Burgoyne's messenger to remain with him because very soon he would be responding.

Sometime on 26 August, St. Leger arrived back at Oswego.[20] Neither Joseph Brant nor Colonel Butler were with him. Though Sir John Johnson and Daniel Claus remained with the British commander, no one was on speaking terms. If a roll call of the survivors was ever taken it no longer exists, but it is known that St. Leger had lost well over 70 percent of his force. Needless to say, this was a shocking figure and the entire British campaign of 1777 suffered a massive blow as a result of St. Leger's failure.[21]

At Oswego, St. Leger reached into his pocket and pulled out the unfinished letter that he had begun to write to Burgoyne just moments before Hon Yost appeared before him. Finished in Oswego, the letter reveals not only anger but also what St. Leger perceived as treachery:

> That [General] Arnold was advancing, by rapid marches, with 3,000 men. It was at this moment I began to suspect cowardice in some and treason in others. . . I learned that 200 Indians were already decamped. . . . In about an hour they insisted that I should retreat, or they would be obliged to abandon me. . . by night, they [the Indians] grew furious and abandoned; seized upon the officers' liquors and cloaths, in spite of the efforts of their servants; and became more formidable than the enemy we had to expect.[22]

St. Leger was not the only one writing a negative report. At Oswego, he encountered a senior-ranking German officer, Lieutenant Colonel Karl Von Kreutzbourg, who just days earlier had been dispatched from Montreal by the German army high command in Canada because they were concerned about the fate of the German personnel under St. Leger. Initially, Von Kreutzbourg was meant to link up with St. Leger in the Mohawk Valley. But he never traveled any farther than Oswego because almost the moment the German officer set foot on the shoreline, he encountered the first stragglers drifting into Oswego.

At Oswego, Von Kreutzbourg interviewed a number of the German and other personnel for several days. The Lt. Colonel found St. Leger to be arrogant, unprofessional, and ineffective. Because St. Leger was drinking heavily, it was even difficult to speak with him; therefore, at this time, Von Kreutzbourg placed the surviving German personnel solely under his command. It appears that St. Leger made no objections to this. On 27 August, Von Kreutzbourg and the German contingent pulled out, heading directly to Montreal.[23]

What also unnerved St. Leger was that upon his arrival at Oswego he was met by the Loyalist commander, John McDonell. Accompanied by only 44 survivors—some of whom were suffering from battle wounds and injuries—McDonell had just retreated to Oswego in the aftermath of the Loyalist defeat in the Schoharie Valley. From McDonell, St. Leger learned that the Patriot resistance had been far tougher and better organized than anyone had expected. McDonell's defeat undoubtedly further dampened the spirits of those accompanying St. Leger.

Loading his remaining personnel aboard a sloop named *Snow* and a handful of bateaux, St. Leger proceeded back to Lachine on 27 August. Other than their personal weapons, a few meager possessions, and the chest full of gold and silver, nothing else was taken. Sir John and the survivors of his Royal Greens headed for Oswegatchie.[24] Neither Johnson, Butler, nor Claus would ever again soldier with St. Leger. In fact, until the end of their lives, they would despise one another. Most of the Indians who drifted back to Oswego retired to Fort Niagara. From there, they returned to their respective tribes. Needless to say, upon returning to their villages, they brought back a strong condemnation of Claus, St. Leger, the British, and the Butlers.[25]

On 27 August, General Arnold, accompanied by his force, returned to Fort Dayton. From 28 August, he was busy making arrangements to transport 1,200 soldiers by bateaux back to Albany. Through the remaining days of late August and early September, many soldiers and militiamen headed back eastward via the Mohawk River and adjacent roads.

On Thursday, 28 August, another prisoner was secured. Exhausted, starved, and covered with mosquito and black fly bites, the British soldier was more than happy to enter captivity. His ordeal had started five days earlier when he had been unable to get on a boat after reaching the mouth of Wood Creek. Stuck on the shoreline and fearing for his life amid the panic, chaos, and rampaging Indians, he fled. He had roamed aimlessly in the woods and swamps, until, spotting a Patriot patrol, the soldier called out to them and walked over. After being fed on the spot, he was taken to Fort Stanwix. He was, in fact, truly lucky. As Gansevoort's scouts and patrols probed far and wide, they came across murdered soldiers and Loyalists. All they had to do was watch the sky, as hovering vultures and birds of prey led the Patriot troops to many a carcass.

On approximately 2 September, St. Leger reached the St. Lawrence River. He did not stop at Carleton Island, as it would have been an embarrassment for him to face the major commanding there. Soon he reached Lachine, from where, in late June, his disastrous expedition had commenced.

Barry St. Leger, however, was not yet through. Still determined to assist Burgoyne, he began to raise another force.[26] Yet, little became of it. Governor-General Carleton's heart was no longer in raising another large contingent. In fact, he had already concluded weeks earlier that the entire British campaign of 1777 was lost and that Burgoyne was doomed to failure.

Why did St. Leger fail? Many factors may be cited. Among them are the late start and unnecessary arrival at Oswego; a lack of heavy weapons to reduce Fort Stanwix; poor security and control of the Indians; an effective Patriot spy system which ensured that the Northern Army always knew much more about St. Leger than he knew about the Patriots; unexpectedly stiff resistance at Fort Stanwix; the reluctant and unhappy Canadians, Indians and Loyalists; a long and difficult supply and communications line; a hostile populace; harsh weather conditions; Herkimer's resistance at Oriskany; and the lack of proper intelligence information, guidance, and support from the British Governor-General in Canada. Furthermore, despite years of service on the North American continent, St. Leger actually had very little wilderness knowledge and he had no experience working with Indians or indigenous forces.

St. Leger, along with the Butlers, Sir John and Guy Johnson, Joseph Brant, and Daniel Claus, viciously exploited the American and Canadian Indians in 1777. St. Leger's exploitation followed the typical British tactic of "divide and conquer." St. Leger never cared for any of the Indians, nor did he promote or encourage any fairness to them. Joseph Brant and Daniel Claus used a combination of lies, half-truths, false promises, coercion, and subtle threats to successfully raise and hold a number of the warriors together in a fighting force. As Mary Jemison said:

> The Senecas and, in general, the Indians were sent for to see the British whip the rebels. They were told that they were not wanted to fight, but merely to sit down, smoke their pipes, and look on. The Senecas went to a man; but, contrary to their expectations, instead of smoking and looking on they were obliged to fight for their lives; and in the end of the battle were completely beaten, with a great loss of killed and wounded.[27]

Joseph Brant also played a major role in committing the Indians into combat, such as at the Battle of Oriskany.[28]

In 1777, Brant also slaughtered a number of his own people. And prior to, during, and after 1777, he repeatedly frustrated the efforts of certain Iroquois leaders to establish a peaceful relationship with the Americans. What he and Claus did, in fact, to the Indians under their influence was a crime and they should have been held accountable. Ultimately, in the end, they, too, played a major role in harming and, to a large extent, in even destroying a great race of people with its rich heritage and culture.

Another major weakness was St. Leger's "intemperate consumption of alcohol,"[29] especially during stressful moments. Last but not least, the wilderness itself hampered St. Leger and his operations. He and his army quickly learned that amid the endless trees, there is no room for complacency or error.

As always in warfare, fascinating things occur. On the return to Canada, the heavy and bulky pay chest became a burden. One night, somewhere to the north of Oswego but south of the St. Lawrence River, St. Leger buried the chest in secrecy. As the starved and exhausted soldiers slept on the edge of the shoreline, St. Leger—accompanied by no more than two or three others—proceeded a short distance inland. Somewhere on the edge of the wilderness, they buried the chest. To this day the British military has never recovered it. Whether it still lies buried or has been recovered is not known. Regardless, through the years many treasure hunters have dug around the area in hopes of recovering the wealth.[30]

Tragically, there is another story to be told. It is the story that deals with the prisoners of war, both military and civilian, captured by St. Leger's forces. In his dispatches and messages, St. Leger made no reference as to what happened to his prisoners. In actuality, he never cared for his prisoners or made any strong effort to protect them. Whereas other British commanders, such as Burgoyne, displayed some concern for prisoners, St. Leger did not. Under modern circumstances, he would have been held accountable for "war crimes," and his list of offenses is extensive.

He tortured and killed innocents while en route to Fort Stanwix and allowed the same with prisoners in the immediate aftermath of Oriskany. He also failed to control the intoxicated mob which rampaged, looted, and murdered during the night of 22–23 August. When unable to capture Fort Stanwix, he threatened to unleash the Indians against the inhabitants of the Mohawk Valley under the guise that he would not be able to control them. St. Leger also offered a bounty of twenty dollars for scalps—regardless of where those scalps came from. Such actions mark a war criminal.

Following the Revolutionary War, Doctor Moses Younglove, who served in General Herkimer's militia and was captured at Oriskany, submitted a fairly lengthy report of the crimes committed by St. Leger's forces. Doctor Younglove himself had witnessed some of these crimes committed by St. Leger's Loyalists and Indians. Undoubtedly, Doctor Younglove himself was spared because doctors were needed. In due course, he made it to Montreal where British authorities released him.

Dr. Younglove was one of the fortunate exceptions. In his account he described the cruelties inflicted upon prisoners within the siege camps and upon the islands occupied by St. Leger's forces:

> . . . fellows were kept almost starved for provisions. . . were insulted, struck, etc. without mercy by the guards, without any provocation given. . . tortured prisoners for a long time. . . [Colonel] Isaac Paris, Esq., was kicked and abused by Tories; after which the savages thinking him for a notable offender, murdered him barbarously . . ."
>
> . . . prisoners were murdered in considerable numbers from day to day round the camp. Some of them so nigh that their shrieks were heard. . . tories were active as well as savages and

in particular one Davis, formerly known in Tryon County on the Mohawk river.[31]

In a letter dated 15 August 1777 from "Camp before Fort Stanwix" and written to Governor-General Carleton, Colonel John Butler acknowledged that prisoners had been tortured. He also added "any of the taken were, conformable to the Indian custom, afterwards killed."[32]

Doctor Younglove also documented how several of St. Leger's orderlies had informed him that, "General St. Leger, in his general orders, offered 20 dollars for every American scalp."[33] The doctor also witnessed how Captain Walter Butler encouraged the Indians to kill some of the captured and he also singled out Lieutenant Singleton, a Royal Greens officer, as another cruel individual. Dr. Younglove added:

> Lieutenant Singleton, of Sir John Johnson's regiment, being wounded, entreated the savages to kill the prisoners, which they accordingly did, as nigh as this deponent can judge, about six or seven.[34]

These words help to illuminate how the Wilderness War of 1777 reached an apex of viciousness on its western front, both in battle and during its aftermath. However, the Patriots' sacrifice was not in vain. Shorn of his secondary thrust that was intended to catch the Northern Army in a pincer, General Burgoyne's main British army was overwhelmed and forced to surrender during the following weeks, bringing what history calls the Saratoga Campaign to a close. And credit for America's first great strategic victory in the Revolution lies largely with the courageous Patriots who fought amongst the dark forests and trackless hills of the wilderness.

Notes

1   John Hyde Preston, *A Short History of the American Revolution* (New York: Pocket Books, Inc., 1952), 1st Ed., p. 192; *"St. Leger's Attack,"* p. 10, cites that Hon Yost and the Oneidas accompanying him spread a wave of terror; Stone, *Siege and Battle*, pp. 258–262, acknowledged that pro-American Indians assisted in this effort; and Eckert, *The Wilderness War*, pp. 152–153 says that Hon Yost succeeded in convincing the besiegers that the Americans

had much artillery, manpower, new weapons, and were not taking Indians and Loyalists as prisoners.

2   According to Robert Calhoon, *The Loyalists in Revolutionary War*, p. 428, "As St. Leger's troops retreated toward Oswego, some of the Indians who had served under the British plundered and assaulted British and Loyalist troops, turning the flight into a bloody nightmare." Lossing, Vol. I, p. 251, cites "the savages also gratified their passion for murder and plunder by killing many of their retreating allies on the borders of the lake, and stripping them of every article of value."

3   Johnson, *History of Oswego County*, p. 40. Many other authors and historical documents, along with St. Leger's testimony, acknowledge that a number of the Indians turned against the British force.

4   John Preston, p. 192; Stone, p. 261.

5   Stone, p. 261. Watt and Morrison, "The Operations of the St. Leger Expedition" in *The British Campaign of 1777*, p. 6, cite "They [the Indians] were already disgusted with the ineffectual siege and the lost opportunity to raid the [Mohawk] Valley below. St. Leger's Indians, emboldened by abandoned liquor, preyed upon the retreating soldiers, overtly looting and pillaging."

6   *"St. Leger's Attack,"* p. 11. Because Lieutenant Bird first arrived on 2 August and opened with the very first shots against the fort, 2 August may be rightfully cited as the opening day of the siege.

7   Colonel Gansevoort was unaware that just days before, General Schuyler had been replaced by General Horatio Gates.

8   *"St. Leger's Attack,"* p. 11. Colbrath did not specify how many prisoners were brought in, or who specifically they were.

9   Ibid.

10   Ibid.

11   Ibid.

12   Probably in the vicinity of Wood Creek/Oneida Lake.

13   *"St. Leger's Attack,"* p. 11. Of interest is the word "scattering" and its relation to "Tories." Clearly, in this context, "scattering" refers to an unorganized group of individuals. From such accounts it may be correctly surmised that panic, disorganization, and chaos, along with thievery, murder, and mayhem was rampant among those fleeing. The fact that no one in St. Leger's force even made an attempt to gather up the missing indicates that there was no firm control.

14   Ibid.

15   Ibid.

16   *"St. Leger's Attack,"* p. 11.

17   Eckert, p. 154, cites that 46 soldiers perished, 4 of whom were officers.

18   Benedict Arnold to Horatio Gates, Fort Schuyler (Stanwix) August 24, 1777. Cited from James Martin, *Benedict Arnold*, p. 513, fn. 54.

19   In the following days, Hon Yost was returned home, whereupon General Arnold released his younger brother as he had promised. Despite the tremen-

dous amount of damage he had caused not only to St. Leger but, indeed, to the entire British campaign of 1777, Hon Yost remained a loyal servant to the British Crown. Throughout the remaining years of the Revolutionary War, Hon continued to publicly denounce Generals Arnold, Gates, Schuyler, Washington, the Northern Army, and anyone or anything associated with the Patriots and the new American nation.

In the aftermath of the Wilderness War of 1777, Hon Yost was left alone by Mohawk Valley's authorities. But neither he, nor his mother or brother, found any peace. His mind, never strong, deteriorated further. Spiteful local citizens frequently taunted him, ridiculed the King in front of him, beat him up physically, poisoned the family well, and threatened both Hon Yost and his family with death. Even his mother was known to have been physically attacked and beaten. Since his mother and brother also suffered from mental health problems, it is clear that some type of mental illness plagued the entire family.

Hearing of the family's plight, former Northern Army General Philip Schuyler personally appealed to the community to leave the lad and his family alone. Local Mennonites, with Schuyler's urgings and a few other kind-hearted citizens, assisted him. Tragically, those who taunted and threatened the family never took into consideration the critical role Hon Yost had performed for the Patriots in 1777. In 1818, Hon Yost passed away. So hated was he that even his gravesite was desecrated.

20 This date is cited by Colonel Claus in a letter addressed to British Secretary Knox. See *"St. Leger's Attack,"* p. 11.

21 Numerous authors, historians, and military men cite that St. Leger's failure devastated the British campaign of 1777. According to the *Excelsior Studies in American History,* pp. 193–194, "Two events had occurred which deranged the plans of Burgoyne—St. Leger's Expedition/Battle of Oriskany [and the] Battle of Bennington."

22 *"St. Leger's Attack,"* pp. 10–11; Lossing, Vol. I, p. 252.

23 Upon his return to Montreal, Von Kreutzbourg completed his report. In turn, copies were submitted to various German commanders including Prince Carl, the German Regent in Germany who recruited many of the Germans for British service.

24 Johnson, p. 40.

25 See, Grinde, p. 88, Graymont, p. 105, cited "The full impact of British sovereignty would be felt by the Iroquois after the Revolutionary War when, to their surprise and anger, they found that England had ceded their lands to the United States. Fortunately for the British, the truth did not manifest until the war was at an end and the Iroquois no longer needed."

26 In early October St. Leger, accompanied by a small force, proceeded down the Richelieu River into Lake Champlain. In the vicinity of Crown Point, he encountered retreating stragglers who informed him that General Burgoyne was stuck at Saratoga and was systematically being destroyed. Accepting

this information as valid, St. Leger turned around and withdrew back to Canada. In actuality, had St. Leger continued and linked up with Burgoyne, he would have only met defeat and his force would have been annihilated.

27   Stone, *Siege and Battle*, p. 243.

28   As verified by David M. Ellis, "Joseph Brant, 1743–1807" in *New York State, Gateway to America. New York State, Revolutionary Cockpit, 1763–1789* (New York: Windsor Publications, 1988), p. 42, "He [Joseph Brant] organized the ambush of Herkimer's expedition at Oriskany."

29   Watt and Morrison, p.26, footnote 1.

30   Personally, the author feels that someone was in the brush watching the chest being buried. Afterwards, it was dug up.

31   Stone, *Siege and Battle*, Report No. IV in Appendix pp.xxxiii–xxxiv following p.264. See also footnote pp. 240–241.

32   See Bancroft, *The American Revolution*, Vol. III, p.380.

33   Stone, Report No. IV, pp. xxxiii and xxxiv. Doctor Younglove also cited that Captain Martin, who was captured on the bateaux near Fort Stanwix, was taken to Oswego. (Ibid., p. xxxiv.) And somewhere in that vicinity, he disappeared.

34   Ibid., pp. xxxiii and xxxiv.

Bibliography

John Adams, *Papers of John Adams* (Cambridge, M.A.: Harvard University Press, 1983). Edited by Robert J. Taylor.

John R. Alden, *A History of the American Revolution* (New York: Alfred A. Knopf, Inc., 1969).

Robert B. Asprey, *War in the Shadows* (New York: Doubleday & Company, Inc., 1975), Volume I.

Thomas A. Bailey, *The American Pageant. A History of the Republic* (Massachusetts: DC Heath and Company, 1975), 5th Edition, Volume I.

John Bakeless, *Turncoats, Traitors and Heroes* (NewYork: J. B. Lippincott Company, 1959).

George Bancroft, *History of the United States, From the Discovery of the American Continent* (Boston: Little, Brown and Company, 1875). (Volume IX, 5th edition).

_____, *The American Revolution* (Boston: Little, Brown, and Company, 1875). Volumes I–V.

Oscar Theodore Barck, Jr., *Colonial America* (New York: The MacMillan Company, 1958).

Oscar T. Barck, *New York City During the War For Independence* (New York: Columbia University Press, 1931). (Reprinted: New York: Ira J. Friedman, Inc., 1966).

James Phinney Baxter, *The British Invasion From the North. The Campaigns of Generals Carleton and Burgoyne From Canada, 1776–1777, With the Journal of Lieutenant. William Digby of the 53d, or Shropshire Regiment of Foot* (Albany, NY: Joel Munsell's Sons, 1887).

Charles A. Beard and Mary R. Beard, *A Basic History of the United States* (New York: Doubleday, Doran & Company, 1944).

Fred Anderson Berg, *Encyclopedia of Continental Army Units. Battalions, Regiments and Independent Corps* (New York: Stackpole Books, 1972).

Major Tharratt Gilbert Best, *A Soldier of Oriskany* (Boonville, NY: The Willard Press, 1935).

Biography of Colonel Peter Schuyler. (From: Documents Relative To the Colonial History of the State of New York) (Oswego, NY: Fort Ontario archives).

Jeremy Black, *War for America: The Fight for Independence, 1775–1783* (Great Britain: Sutton Publishing Company, 1998).

Paul E. Blackwood, *The How and Why Wonder Book of North American Indians* (New York: Wonder Books, 1965). (5th printing).

Bruce Bliven, *New York. A Bicentennial History* (W.W. Norton and Company, Inc., 1981).

Mark M. Boatner, *Landmarks of the American Revolution. People and Places Vital to the Quest for Independence* (Harrisburg, PA: Stackpole Books, 1992).

Benson Bobrick, *Angel In the Whirlwind: The Triumph of the American Revolution* (New York: Simon & Schuster, 1997).

Nikolai N. Bolkhovitinov, *The Beginnings of Russian–American Relation, 1775–1815*

(Massachusetts: Harvard University Press, 1975).

Captain Edward C. Boynton, *History of West Point: and Its Military Importance During the American Revolution; and the Origin and Progress of the United States Military Academy* (Freeport, NY: Book for Libraries Press, 1863). (Reprinted 1970).

John Brick, *The King's Rangers* (New York: Doubleday & Company, Inc., 1954).

Peter Brock, *Pacifism In the United States: From the Colonial Era to the First World War* (N.J.: Princeton University Press, 1968).

Richard Brookhiser, *Alexander Hamilton—American* (New York: The Free Press, 1999).

Wallace Brown, *Tories In the Revolution* (Oswego, NY: Fort Ontario Archives).

James W. Burbank, *Cushetunk, 1754–1784: The First White Settlement in the Upper Delaware River Valley* (New York: Sullivan County Democrat, 1975) (3rd Printing).

Bruce Burgoyne (ed.), *Enemy Views: The American Revolutionary War as Recorded by the Hessian Participants* (Maryland: Heritage Books, Inc., 1996).

General John Burgoyne, *A State of the Expedition from Canada as Laid Before the House of Commons* (New York: New York Times & Arno Press, 1969). (Reprinted).

H. C. Burleigh, *Captain MacKay and the Loyal Volunteers* (Ontario, Canada: Bayside Publishing Company, 1977).

Martha Byrd, *Saratoga: Turning Point In the American Revolution* (England: Auerbach Publishers, Inc., 1973).

A. L. Byron-Curtiss, *The Life and Adventures of Nat Foster, Trapper and Hunter of the Adirondacks* (Utica, NY: Thomas J. Griffiths Press, 1897) (Reprinted 1976 by Harbor Hill Books, Harrison, NY).

Robert M. Calhoon, *The Loyalists in Revolutionary America, 1760–1781* (New York: Harcourt Brace Jovanovich, Inc., 1973).

North Callahan, *Flight From the Republic: The Tories of the American Revolution* (New York: Boobs-Merrill Co., Inc., 1967).

Colin G. Calloway, *The American Revolution in Indian Country: Crisis and Diversity in Native American Communities* (M.A.: University of Cambridge, 1995).

Eugenia Campbell Lester and Allegra Branson, *Frontiers Aflame: Jane Cannon Campbell, Revolutionary War Heroine When America Only Had Heroes*

William W. Campbell and William L. Stone, *Siege Fort Stanwix [Schuyler] & Battle of Oriskany* (New York: J. & J. Harper, 1831) (Reprinted Rome, New York: Bropard Company, Inc., 1977).

Jill Canon, *Heroines of the American Revolution* (Santa Barbara, CA.: Bellerophon Books, 1998).

Henry B. Carrington, *Battles of the American Revolution, 1775–1781: Historical and Military Criticism, with Topographical Illustration* (New York: S. Barnes and Company, 1877).

Adrian G. Ten Cate, *Pictorial History of the Thousand Islands of the St. Lawrence River* (Canada: Besancourt Publishers, 1982).

Donald Barr Chidsey, *The Loyalists: The Story of Those Americans Who Fought Against Independence* (New York: Crown Publishers, Inc., 1973).

George T. Clark, *Oswego: An Historical Address* (Oswego, NY: Fort Ontario Archives).

George Clinton, *The Public Papers of George Clinton* (New York: Albany, 1904. Published by New York State, Volumes 1–10).

Patricia Edwards Clyne, *Patriots In Petticoats* (New York: Dodd, Mead and company, 1976).

William Colbrath, *Days of Siege: A Journal of the Siege of Fort Stanwix in 1777* (New York: Publishing Center for Cultural Resources, 1983).

Hubbard Cobb, *American Battlefields: A Complete Guide to the Historic Conflicts in Words, Maps, and Photos* (New York: Simon & Schuster Macmillan Company, 1995).

William Colbrath, *Days of Siege: A Journal of the Siege of Fort Stanwix in 1777* (New York: Publishing Center for Cultural Resources, 1983).

William T. Couch (ed.), *Collier's Encyclopedia* (New York: P.F. Collier and Son Corporation, 1955).

William P. Cumming and Hugh Rankin, *The Fate of a Nation: The American Revolution Through Contemporary Eyes* (London, England: Phaidon Press, Limited, 1975).

Edward E. Curtis, *The Organization of the British Army in the American Revolution* (New York: Ams Press, 1969). (Reprinted from 1926 edition).

Anthony D. Darling, *Red Coat and Brown Bess* (Canada: Museum Restoration Service, 1970).

Jay David and Elaine Crane, *The Black Soldier: From the American Revolution to Vietnam* (New York: William Morrow and Co., Inc., 1971).

Philip Davies, *The History Atlas of North America: From First Footfall To New World Order* (New York: Simon & Schuster Macmillan Company, 1998).

Burke Davis, *George Washington and the American Revolution* (New York: Random House, 1975).

Linda Grant DePauw, *Four Traditions: Women of New York During the American Revolution* (Albany, NY: New York State American Revolution Bicentennial Commission, 1974).

Description of the Country Between Oswego and Albany–1757. (Paris Doc. XIII). (Oswego, NY: Fort Ontario Archives).

Lieutenant William Digby (ed. by James Phinney Baxter), *The British Invasion From the North: Digby's Journal of the Campaigns of Generals Carleton and Burgoyne From Canada, 1776–1777* (Albany, 1887).

Richard M. Dorison (ed.), *Patriots of the American Revolution: True Accounts of Great Americans from Ethan Allen to George Rogers Clark* (New York: Gramercy Books, 1998).

Lieutenant Colonel Fairfax Downey, *Indian Wars of the U.S. Army, 1776–1865* (New York: Doubleday and Company, 1962).

Ann Bailey Dunn, "Raven Majesty and Myth" in The Conservationist (New York: Latham Publishing Co., April, 1999).

R. Ernest Dupuy and Colonel Trevor N. Dupuy, *The Encyclopedia of Military History From 3500 B.C. to the Present* (New York: Harper and Row, Publishers, 1977) (Revised Edition).

Trevor N. Dupuy, Curt Johnson, and David L. Bongard, *The Harper Encyclopedia of Military Biography. An Invaluable Compilation and Assessment of the 3,000 Most Important Worldwide Military Figures From Earliest Times to the Present* (New York: Castle Books, 1995).

"Echoes of War. Central New York's Connection to the Struggle for Independence," *Herald-American* (Syracuse, NY:, Sunday, July 2, 2000).

Allan W. Eckert, *The Wilderness Empire* (Boston: Little, Brown and Company, 1969).

Allen N. Eckert, *The Wilderness War: A Narrative* (Boston: Little, Brown & Co., 1978).

Edward K. Eckert, *In War and Peace: An American Military History Anthology* (C.A.: Wadsworth Publishing, Co., 1990).

Elizabeth F. Ellet, *The Women of the American Revolution* (New York: Baker and Scribner, 1849). (Reprinted Massachusetts: Corner House Publishers, 1980) (Volumes I–II)

David M. Ellis, *New York State: Gateway to America.* (New York: Windsor Publications, 1988).

Paul Engle, *Women in the American Revolution* (Illinois: Follett Publishing Company, 1976).

Colonel Vincent J. Esposito (ed.), *The West Point Atlas of the Civil War [Adapted From the West Point Atlas of American Wars]* (New York: Praeger Publishers, 1962).

Excelsior Studies in American History (New York: William H. Sadlier, 1921).

Cyril Falls (ed.), *Great Military Battles* (London, England: The Hamlyn Publishing Group Limited, 1969).

John C. Fitzpatrick (ed.), *Writings of George Washington from the Original Manuscript Sources, 1745–1799* (Washington, DC: Government Printing Office, 1931–1944), 39 volumes.

Thomas Fleming, *Liberty!: The American Revolution* (New York: Viking Publishers, 1997).

Sylvia R. Frey, "Between Slavry and Freedom: Virginia Blacks in the American Revolution" in *Journal of Southern History* (History Journal 49, 1983).

Rear Admiral Rea Furlong, Commodore Byron McCandles, Harold D. Langley, *So Proudly We Hail: The History of the United States Flag* (Washington, DC: Smithsonian Institution Press, 1981).

Robert Furneaux, *The Battle of Saratoga* (New York: Stein and Day, 1971).

Rupert Furneaux, *The Pictorial History of the American Revolution* (Chicago: J. G. Ferguson Publishing Co., 1973).

Charles Gehring, *Agriculture and the Revolution in the Mohawk Valley* (New York: Fort Klock).

Don R. Gerlach, *Philip Schuyler and the American Revolution in New York, 1733–1777* (Nebraska: University of Nebraska Press, 1964).

Major Tharratt Gilbert, *A Soldier of Oriskany* (Boonville, NY: The Willard Press, 1935).

Henry F. Graff, *America: The Glorious Republic* (Boston: Houghton Mifflin, Co., 1990).

R. G. Grant, *Commanders, History's Greatest Military Leaders* (New York: DK Publishing, 2010.

Barbara Graymont, *The Iroquois in the American Revolution* (Syracuse, NY: Syracuse University Press, 1972).

Donald A. Grinde, Jr., *The Iroquois and the Founding of the American Nation* (New York: Indian Historian Press, 1977).

Edward A. Hagan, *War In Schohary, 1773–1783* (The Middleburgh News Press, 1980).

Robert E. Hager, *Mohawk River Boats and Navigation Before 1820* (Syracuse, NY: Canal Society of New York State, 1987).

Reginald Hargreaves, *The Bloodybacks: The British Serviceman in*

North America and the Caribbean, 1655–1783 (New York: Walker and Company, 1968).

David J. Harkness, *Northeastern Heroines of the American Revolution* (Tennessee: University of Tennessee, 1977).

Henry Harrison, *Battles of the Republic, By Sea and Land* (Philadelphia, P.A.: Porter and Coates, 1858).

Hugh Hastings and J.A. Holden (eds.), *The Public Papers of George Clinton, First Governor of New York, 1777–1795, 1801–1804* (New York: AMS Press) (Volumes I–10).

Carlton J. H. Hayes, *A Political and Social History of Modern Europe* (New York: Macmillan Company, 1916), Volume I.

"Herkimer Home" in *State Historic Site, Little Falls, New York, Central Region* (New York: Office of Parks, Recreation and Historic Preservation).

History of Civil Affairs (Fort Bragg, N.C.: U. S. Army John F. Kennedy Special Warfare Center and School, October 1992).

Ronald Hoffman and Peter J. Albert, eds., *Women In the Age of the American Revolution* (Virginia: University Press of Virginia, 1989).

James A. Huston, *The Sinews of War: Army Logistics, 1775–1953* (Washington, DC: U.S. Government Printing Office, 1966).

Islands. A Description. (Oswego, NY: Fort Ontario Archives).

Mary Jemison, *The Life of Mary Jemison* (New York: James D. Bemis, Publishers, 1823).

Crisfield Johnson, *History of Oswego County, New York, 1739–1877* (New York: 1878).

Lieutenant Colonel James M. Johnson, "Staff Rides and the Flawed Works of Fort Constitution" in *Engineer. The Professional Bulletin for Army Engineers* (October 1990).

Crisfield Johnson, *History of Oswego County, New York* (New York: 1878).

David E. Jones, *Women Warriors: A History* (Washington, DC: Brassey's, 2000).

Thomas Jones, *History of New York During the Revolutionary War* (New York: 1879), Volumes I–II.

Philip R. Katcher, *The American Provincial Corps, 1775–1784* (New York: Osprey Publishing, Ltd., 1973).

Philip Katcher, *The Encyclopedia of British, Provincial, and German Army Units, 1775–1783* (Pennsylvania: Stackpole Books, 1973).

John Keegan, *Warpaths: Fields of Battle in Canada and America* (Canada: Vintage Books, 1996).

Alan Kemp, *The British Army In the American Revolution* (Great Britain: Almark Publishing Co., Ltd., 1973).

Richard M. Ketchum, *Saratoga: Turning Point of America's Revolutionary War* (New York: Henry Holt and Company, 1997).

Richard M. Ketchum, *The Winter Soldier: The Battles For Trenton and Princeton* (New York: Henry Holt and Company, 1973).

Irving S. Kull, Nell M. Kull, Stanley H. Friedelbaum, *A Chronological Encyclopedia of American History* (New York: Popular Library Press, 1952).

Mark V. Kwasny, *Washington's Partisan War, 1775–1783* (Ohio: Kent State University Press, 1996).

Richard B. LaCrosse, Jr., *The Frontier Rifleman. His Arms, Clothing and Equipment During the Era of the American Revolution* (Union City, T.N.: Pioneer Press, 1989).

Richard B. La Crosse, *Revolutionary Rangers: Daniel Morgan's Riflemen and Their Role on the Northern Frontier, 1778–1783* (Bowie, Maryland: Heritage Books, Inc., 2002).

_____, *Daniel Morgan's Riflemen on America's Northern Frontier, 1778–1783* (Unpublished text. Oswego, NY: Fort Ontario Archives).

Roger Lamb, *An Original and Authentic Journal of Occurrences During the late American War* (New York: New York Times & Arno Press, 1968).

Bruce Lancaster and J. H. Plumb, *The American Heritage Book of the Revolution* (New York: Dell Publishing Co., Inc., 1981).

Harry F. Landon, *History of the North Country: A History of Embracing Jefferson, St. Lawrence, Oswego, Lewis and Franklin Counties* (Indiana: Historical Publishing Company, 1932), Volumes I–III.

A. J. Langguth, *Patriots: The Men Who Started the American Revolution* (New York: Simon and Schuster, Inc., 1989).

Harold D. Langley, *So Proudly We Hail: The History of the United States Flag* (Washington, DC: Smithsonian Institution Press, 1981).

Robert Leckie, *The Wars of America (Updated Edition)* (New York: HarperCollins Publishers, 1992).

Eugenia Campbell Lester and Allegra Branson, *Frontiers Aflame!: Jane Cannon Campbell. Revolutionary War Heroine When America*

Had Only Heroes (New York: Heart of the Lakes Publishing, 1987).

Phillip Lord, Jr., *War Over Walloomscoick: Land Use and Settlement Pattern on the Bennington Battlefield—1777* (Albany, NY: State University of New York, 1989).

Benson J. Lossing, *The Empire State: A Compendious History of the Commonwealth of New York* (Hartford, C.T.: American Publishing Co., 1888).

_____, *The Empire State. New York: Settlement Through 1875* (C.T.: American Publishing Co., 1888).

Benson Lossing, *The Pictorial Field-Book of the [American] Revolution* (New York: Harper & Brothers, Publishers, 1860), Volumes I–II.

Christine Lunardini, *What Every American Should Know About Women's History. 200 Events that Shaped Our Destiny* (M.A.: Bob Adams, Inc., 1994).

John Luzader, *The Saratoga Campaign of 1777* (Washington, DC: National Park Service Publications, 1975).

John Luzader, Louis Torres, Orville W. Carroll, *Fort Stanwix: Construction and Military History, Historic Furnishing Study, Historic Structure Report* (Washington, DC: U.S. Government Printing Office, 1976).

Mary C. Lynn (ed.), *The Sprecht Journal. A Military Journal of the Burgoyne Campaign* (Contributions in Military Studies, Number 158, 1995)

Piers Mackesy, *The War for America, 1775–1783* (Nebraska: University of Nebraska, 1993).

John K. Mahon and Romana Danysh, *Army Lineage Series: Infantry Part I: Regular Army* (Washington, DC: 1972).

James Kirby Martin, *Benedict Arnold, Revolutionary Hero. An American Reconsidered* (New York: New York University Press, 1997).

Joseph Plumb Martin, *Private Yankee Doodle: Being a Narrative of Some of the Adventures, Dangers and Sufferings of a Revolutionary Soldier* (Boston: Little, Brown and Company, 1962).

David McCullough, *John Adams* (New York: Simon & Schuster, 2001).

Ann McGovern, *The Secret Soldier: The Story of Deborah Sampson* (New York: Scholastic Press, Inc., 1975).

Edgar J. McManus, *A History of Negro Slavery in New York* (New York: Syracuse University Press, 1966).

Mary McNeer, *The Hudson, River of History* (Illinois: Garrard Publishing Co., 1962).

Roy Meredith, *The American Wars: A Pictorial History from Quebec to Korea 1755–1953* (New York: The World Publishing Co., p. 1955).

Charles E. Miller, Jr., Donald V. Lockey, Joseph Visconti, Jr., *Highland Fortress: The Fortification of West Point During the American Revolution, 1775–1783* (West Point: Unpublished text at the United States Military Academy Library).

Lieutenant Colonel Joseph B. Mitchell and Sir Edward Creasy, *Twenty Decisive Battles of the World* (New York: The MacMillan Company, 1964).

Lynn Montross, *The Reluctant Rebels: The Story of the Continental Congress, 1774–1789* (New York: Harper & Brothers Publishers, 1950).

Frank Moore, *The Diary of the American Revolution* (New York: Washington Square Press, Inc., 1968).

Samuel Eliot Morison and Henry Steele Commager, *The Growth of the American Republic* (New York: Oxford University Press, 1952). (3rd printing).

Richard B. Morris and James Woodress (eds.), *Voices From America's Past Vol One The Colonies and the New Nation* (New York: E. P. Dutton and Company, Inc., 1961).

Jim Murphy, *A Young Patriot: The American Revolution as Experienced by One Boy* (New York: Clarion Books, 1996).

David Saville Muzzey, *An American History* (Boston: Ginn and Company, 1911).

Lee N. Newcomer, *The Embattled Farmer: A Massachusetts Countryside in the American Revolution* (New York: 1953).

New York State Preservationist (Fall/Winter), Volume II/Number 2, 1998.

James F. O'Neil, *Their Bearing is Noble and Proud: A Collection of narratives regarding the appearance of Native Americans from 1740–1815* (Dayton, OH: J. T. G. S. Publishing, 1995).

LTC William L. Otten, Jr., *Colonel J. F. Hamtramck: His Life and Times Volume One (1756–1783) Captain of the Revolution* (Port Aransas, T.X., 1997).

William L. Otten, *Colonel J. F. Hamtramck, His Life and Times Volume*

Two (1783–1791) Frontier Major (Port Aransas, T.X., 2003).

General Dave Palmer, *The River and the Rock: The History of Fortress West Point, 1775–1783* (New York: Greenwood Publishing Co., 1969).

Rod Paschall, "George Washington, the Father of U.S. Intelligence" in *Spies and Secret Missions. A History of American Espionage* (Newtown, P.A.: 2002).

Michael Pearson, *Those Damned Rebels: The American Revolution As Seen Through British Eyes* (New York: G. P. Putnam's Sons, 1972).

Lucille Recht Penner, *The Liberty Tree: The Beginning of the American Nation* (New York: Random House, 1998).

Deborah Pessin, *History of the Jews in America* (New York: The United Synagogue Press of America, 1957).

Walter Pilkington, *The Journal of Samuel Kirkland: 18th Century Missionary to the Iroquois, Government Agent, Father of Hamilton College* (Clinton, New York: Hamilton College Publishing, 1980).

Joseph Plumb Martin, *Private Yankee Doodle: Being a Narrative of Some of the Adventures, Dangers and Sufferings of a Revolutionary Soldier* (Boston: Little, Brown and Company, 1962).

John A. Pope, Jr. (ed.), *Strange Stories, Amazing Facts of America's Past* (Pleasantville, New York: Reader's Digest Press, Inc., 1989).

Arthur Pound, *Lake Ontario: The American Lakes Series* (New York: The Bobbs-Merrill Company Publishers, 1945).

John Hyde Preston, *A Short History of the American Revolution* (New York: Pocket Books, Cardinal edition, 1952).

Benjamin Quarles, *The Negro in the American Revolution* (N.C.: University of North Carolina Press, 1961).

Emily Raabe, *Ethan Allen: The Green Mountain Boys and Vermont's Path to Statehood* (New York: Rosen publishing Group, Inc., 2002).

Willard Sterne Randall, *George Washington: A Life* (New York: Henry Holt and Company, 1997).

Hugh F. Rankin, *The Fate of a Nation: The American Revolution Through Contemporary Eyes* (London, England: Phaidon Press limited, 1975).

George Reed, *Fort Ontario* (Unpublished Text). (Oswego, NY: Fort Ontario Archives).

"Revolutionary Vet's Grave Found in Montezuma" in *The Post-*

Standard (Syracuse, NY: Wednesday, June 24, 1998).

Revolutionary War Dates Relating To Oswego (Unpublished text) (Oswego, NY: Fort Ontario Archives).

Revolutionary War Diaries Relating to Oswego (Unpublished text) (Oswego: NY: Fort Ontario Archives).

George W. Roach, *Colonial Highways in the Upper Hudson Valley* (New York: New York State Historical Association, April, 1959).

Lemuel Roberts, *Memoirs of Captain Lemuel Roberts* (New York: New York Times & Arno Press, 1969). (Reprinted).

Clinton Rossiter, *The Federalist Papers* (New York: The New American Library, Inc., 1961).

Barnet Schecter, *The Battle for New York: The City at the Heart of the Revolution* (New York: Walker Publishing Company, Inc., 2002).

George F. Scheer and Hugh F. Rankin, *Rebels and Redcoats* (New York: The New American Library, Inc., 1957).

Elizabeth Eggleston Seelye, *Hudson, Mohawk, Schoharie. History From America's Most Famous Valleys and the Border Wars* (New York: Dodd, Mead and Company, Publishers, 1879).

William Seymour, "Turning Point at Saratoga," *Military History* (December 1999).

Victoria Sherrow, *The Iroquois Indians* (New York: Chelsea House Publishers, Inc., 1992).

Jeanne Meader Schwarz and Minerva J. Goldberg, *New York State in Story* (New York: Frank E. Richards, 1962), Books I–II.

Jeptha R. Simms, *History of Schoharie County and Border Wars of New York* (Albany: Musell and Tanner, 1845).

Jeptha R. Simms, *The Frontiersmen of New York* (Albany, NY: George C. Riggs, 1882).

Ted Smart, *Colonial Virginia: A Picture Book To Remember Her* (New York: Crescent Books, 1979).

Linda Spizzirri (ed.), *Northeast Indians* (South Dakota: Spizzirri Publishing, Inc., 1982).

"St. Leger's Attack on Ft. Stanwix in 1777 Proved Fiasco" in *Oswego Palladium-Times* (Tuesday, November 20, 1945).

Stephen G. Strach, *Some Sources For the Study of the Loyalist and Canadian Participation In the Military Campaign of Lieutenant-General John Burgoyne 1777* (Eastern National Park and Monument Association, 1983).

William L. Stone, *Life of Joseph Brant—Thayendanegea: Including the*

Border Wars of the American Revolution, and Sketches of the Indian Campaigns of Generals Armar, St. Clair, and Wayne (New York: George Dearborn and Co., 1838), Volume I.

William L. Stone, *Life of Joseph Brant—Thayendanegea Including the Indian Wars of the American Revolution* (New York: H. & E. Phinney, 1845).

William L. Stone, *The Campaign of Lieut.Gen. John Burgoyne and the Expedition of Lieut.Col. Barry St. Leger* (New York: Da Capo Press, 1970) (Reprinted).

James Sullivan, *The Papers of Sir William Johnson* (Albany, NY: University of New York State, 1922).

Hallie DeMass Sweeting, *Pioneers of Sterling, NY (Cayuga County).* (Red Creek: Wayuga Press, 1998).

Howard Swiggert, *War Out of Niagara* (Port Washington, NY: Friedman Publishers, 1963).

"The Battle of Oriskany" in *The Herald-American (Sunday, July 4, 1999.)*

The Campaign of 1777 (Unpublished text). (Oswego, NY: Fort Ontario Archives).

The Encyclopedia Americana. International Edition (Danbury, C.T.: Grolier Inc., Publishers, 1982).

The Encyclopedia Americana. International Edition. U.S. Constitution Bicentennial Commemorative Edition (Connecticut: Grolier Incorporated, 1988), Volume 21.

The Forts of Oswego (Unpublished text) (Oswego, NY: Fort Ontario Archives).

The Loyalist Papers (New York: New York Public Library). (Oswego, NY: Fort Ontario Archives).

The Papers of Sir William Johnson (New York: Albany University, 1922).

The Military Journals of Two Private Soldiers, 1758–1775, with Numerous Illustrative Notes (Poughkeepsie, NY: 1845).

Adrian G. Ten Cate, *Pictorial History of the Thousand Islands* (Canada: Besancourt Publishers, 1982).

Lowell Thomas and Berton Bradley, *Stand Fast for Freedom* (Philadelphia, P.A.: The John C. Winston Company, 1940).

Barbara W. Tuchman, *The First Salute* (London, England: Penguin Group Publishers, 1989).

Colonel Stanley M. Ulanoff (ed.), *American Wars and Heroes: Revo-*

lutionary Through Vietnam (New York: Arco Publishing, Inc., 1985).

Highland Commanders (Unpublished text at West Point Archives).

Carl Van Doren, *Secret History of the American Revolution* (New York: Viking Press, 1941).

Dale Van Every, *A Company of Heroes: The American Frontier, 1775–1783* (New York: William Morrow and Company, 1962).

Baron Friedrich Adolph Von Riedesel, *Letters and Journals Relating to the War of the American Revolution* (Albany, NY: Joel Munsell, 1867). (Translated by William L. Stone). (Reprinted, NY: New York Times & Arno Press, 1968).

John G. Waite and Paul R. Huey, *Herkimer House: An Historic Structure Report* (New York: 1972).

Christopher Ward, *The War of the Revolution* (New York: The Macmillan Co., 1952) Volumes I–II.

George Washington, *Papers of George Washington* (Virginia: University of Virginia Press, 1983). Edited by W. W. Abbot.

William H. Watkins, "Slavery in Herkimer County. African Americans Were Here in the Valley From the Beginning" in *Legacy. Annals of Herkimer County* (New York: Herkimer County Historical Society, 1990). (Issue Number 3), p. 6.

Gavin K. Watt and James F. Morrison, *The British Campaign in 1777. Volume One, The St. Leger Expedition, the forces of the Crown and Congress* (Canada: Global Heritage Press, 2003).

Gavin K. Watt, *The Flockey, 13 August 1777, The Defeat of the Tory Uprising in the Schoharie Valley* (Canada: Global Heritage Press, 2011).

Richard Wheeler, *Voices of 1776* (New York: Thomas Y. Crowell, Co., 1972).

David C. Whitney, *The People of the Revolution: The Colonial Spirit of '76* (1974).

William B. Willcox, *Portrait of a General: Sir Henry Clinton in the War of Independence* (New York: Alfred A. Knopf, 1962).

William M. Willett, *A Narrative of The Military Actions of Colonel Marinus Willett, Taken Chiefly From His Own Manuscript* (New York: G. & C. & H. Carvill, 1831).

T. Harry Williams, *The History of American Wars. From Colonial Times to World War I* (New York: Alfred A. Knopf, Inc., 1981).

John E. Wilmot (ed.), *Journals of the Provincial Congress of New York* (Albany, 1842), Vol. 1.

Thomas G. Wnuck, "The Last Offensive of the American Revolution" in *The Dispatch* (Summer '80) (Oswego, NY: Fort Ontario Archives).

James Albert Woodburn and Thomas Francis Moran, *American History and Government. A Text-Book on the History and Civil Government of the United States* (New York: Longmans, Green, and Co., 1907).

Wallace F. Workmaster, *The Forts of Oswego: A Study in the Art of Defense* (Oswego, NY: Fort Ontario Archives).

Esmond Wright (ed.), *The Fire of Liberty: The American War of Independence seen through the eyes of the men and women, the statesmen and soldiers who fought it.* (New York: St. Martin's Press, 1983).

George M. Wrong, *Canada and the American Revolution. The Disruption of the First British Empire* (New York: Cooper Square Publishers, Inc., 1968).

Karen Zeinert, *Those Remarkable Women of the American Revolution* (Connecticut: The Millbrook Press, 1996).

Index